Glencoe Health

Reading Tutor

New York, New York   Columbus, Ohio   Chicago, Illinois   Peoria, Illinois   Woodland Hills, California

The McGraw-Hill Companies

Printed in the United States of America.

Send all inquiries to:
Glencoe/McGraw-Hill
21600 Oxnard Street, Suite 500
Woodland Hills, CA 91367

ISBN 0-07-861868-1

2 3 4 5 6 7 8 9 079 09 08 07 06 05 04

Table of Contents

Table of Contents (cont.)

Table of Contents (cont.)

To the Teacher

The *Glencoe Health Reading Tutor* is designed to help students use and recognize reading strategies to improve their reading-for-information skills. For each lesson given in the Student Edition, the students are alerted to vocabulary terms, asked to draw from prior knowledge, organize their thoughts or notes with a graphic organizer, and then follow a process to read and understand the text. The brief Read to Learn summaries provide a condensed version of the important information in each lesson and contain and define all vocabulary words that appear in the Student Edition. Each summary ends with a question for students to answer. The *Reading Tutor* can be used as a prereading activity for reluctant readers or students in need of additional reading skills support, or as quick review of chapter content for all students.

Living a Healthy Life: Your Health and Wellness

Vocabulary

health	The combination of physical, mental/emotional, and social well being *(page 4)*
wellness	An overall state of well-being, or total health *(page 5)*
prevention	Practicing health and safety habits to remain free of disease and injury *(page 6)*
health education	The providing of accurate health information to help people make healthy choices *(page 7)*
Healthy People 2010	A nationwide health promotion and disease prevention plan designed to serve as a guide for improving the health of all people in the United States *(page 7)*
health literacy	A person's capacity to learn about and understand basic health information and services and use these resources to promote his or her health and wellness *(page 8)*

Drawing from Experience

Are you a healthy person? Do you have healthy habits? How much sleep do you get? Do you eat a healthy breakfast? How do you deal with stress? Do you help others make healthy choices? Are you in charge of your own wellness? Think about these things as you read Lesson 1.

In this lesson, you will learn about wellness and the importance of good health.

Reading Tutor, Lesson 1 *(continued)*

USE WITH CHAPTER 1, PAGES 4–9.

Organizing Your Thoughts

Use the chart below to help you take notes as you read the summaries that follow. In the first box, list some of the healthy lifestyle factors. In the other box, list some of the ways to reach the goals of *Healthy People 2010*.

Healthy Lifestyle Factors	Ways to Meet *Healthy People 2010* Goals

Read to Learn

Read each passage carefully. Write in complete sentences to answer the following questions.

The Importance of Good Health *(pages 4–5)*

Health is your *physical, mental/emotional, and social well-being*. Being healthy does not mean that you are never sick. You can think about your health as a point on a continuum. A continuum is a sliding scale with many degrees of health and wellness.

Wellness is *an overall state of well-being, or total health*. It takes hard work to keep well. Being well helps you reach your goals.

1. Why is it important to keep well?

____

____

____

____

Promoting Your Health *(pages 6–9)*

Your habits can affect your health. Habits are lifestyle factors. These are behaviors that relate to the way you live. Smoking is a lifestyle factor that can lead to lung cancer. Here are some lifestyle factors that can lead to good health.

- Get 8 to 10 hours of sleep each night.
- Start each day with a healthy breakfast.
- Eat a variety of nutritious foods each day.
- Be physically active at least 20 minutes a day. Do this three or more times a week.
- Keep a healthy weight.
- Avoid tobacco. Avoid alcohol and other drugs.
- Abstain from sexual activity before marriage.
- Deal with stress.
- Keep positive friendships.
- Practice safe behavior to avoid getting hurt.

Reading Tutor, Lesson 1 *(continued)*

USE WITH CHAPTER 1, PAGES 4–9.

Prevention is *practicing health and safety habits to remain free of disease and injury.* Wear a seat belt. Use sunscreen. Avoid places that are not safe.

Health education is *providing accurate health information to help people make healthy choices.* It gives people the tools they need to stay healthy.

Healthy People 2010 is *a nationwide health promotion and disease prevention plan. It serves as a guide for improving the health of all people in the United States.* There are two goals:

- Help Americans live longer and healthier lives.
- Take away health differences that come from factors such as gender, race, and education.

Here are some ways people can help meet the goals of *Healthy People 2010.*

- **Individuals** can take an active role in their own health. You can learn to make healthy decisions. You can learn where to get health information. You can learn to help others.
- **Families** play an important role. Parents and guardians teach their children how to maintain good health.
- **Communities** can offer health classes. They can teach people how to quit smoking. They can provide health services. They can make sure the environment is safe.

Health literacy is *a person's capacity to learn about and understand basic health information and services.* The person is able to use these resources to promote his or her health and wellness. Here are some ways to be health literate.

- Be a critical thinker and problem solver. Know how to make healthy choices.
- Be a responsible and productive citizen. Choose safe and legal behaviors.
- Be a self-directed learner. Be able to find out if information is reliable and accurate.
- Be a good communicator. Be able to express your health knowledge.

2. What are some of the ways that a person can be health literate?

____

____

____

____

Name Class Date

Lesson 2

USE WITH CHAPTER 1, PAGES 10–16.

Living a Healthy Life: Promoting a Healthy Lifestyle

Vocabulary

heredity	All the traits that are biologically passed from parents to their children *(page 12)*
environment	The sum of your surroundings *(page 13)*
peers	People of similar age who share similar interests *(page 13)*
culture	The collective beliefs, customs, and behaviors of a group *(page 14)*
media	The various methods of communicating information *(page 15)*

Drawing from Experience

Why should you care about your health? Are you physically active? Do you express your feelings in a positive way? Do you get along with others? What factors have an influence on your health? Think about these things as you read Lesson 2.

In the last lesson, you learned about your health and wellness. In this lesson, you will learn about your health triangle and influences on your health.

Reading Tutor, Lesson 2 *(continued)*

USE WITH CHAPTER 1, PAGES 10–16.

Organizing Your Thoughts

Use the chart below to help you take notes as you read the summaries that follow. In the top triangle, list the things you can do to stay physically healthy. In the left lower triangle, list the things you can do to keep your mental and emotional health strong. In the last triangle, list the things you can do to keep your social health in balance. In the center space, list some of the influences on your health.

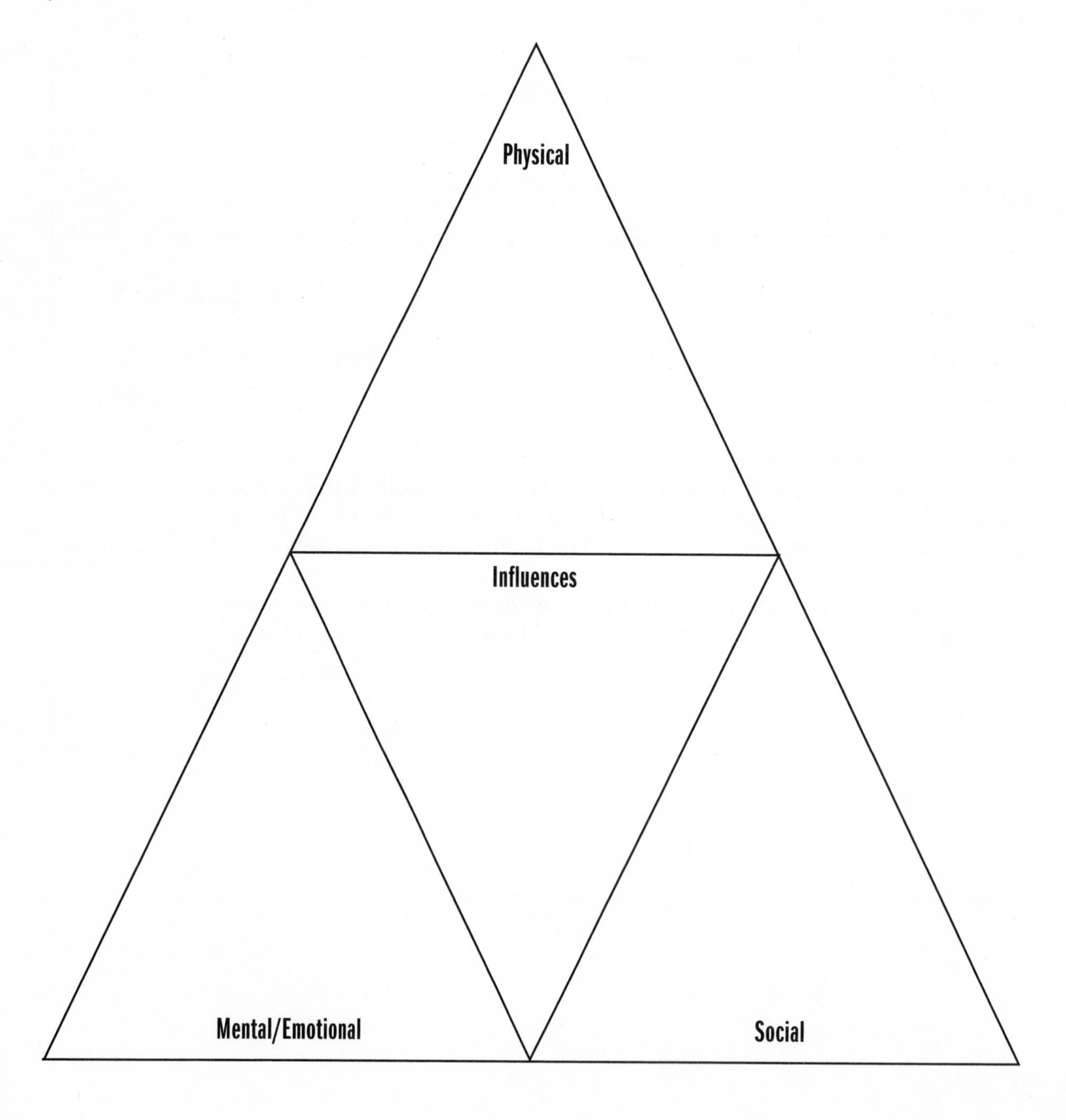

Reading Tutor, Lesson 2 *(continued)*

USE WITH CHAPTER 1, PAGES 10–16.

Read to Learn

Read each passage carefully. Write in complete sentences to answer the following questions.

Your Health Triangle *(pages 10–12)*

The three elements of health are physical, mental/emotional, and social. Think of them as the angles of a triangle. Here are some of the ways to keep your health triangle in balance.

- **Physical health.** Get enough sleep. Eat nutritious meals. Drink lots of water. Be active on a regular basis. Keep yourself clean. Get regular medical and dental checkups. Avoid tobacco and alcohol. Avoid other drugs.
- **Mental/emotional health.** Learn new things. See mistakes as a chance to grow. Accept responsibility for your actions. Express your feelings in proper ways. Deal with anger and stress. Have a positive attitude.
- **Social health.** Do your best to get along with others. Make friends. Work and play in a cooperative way. Give support when others need it. Communicate well. Show respect and care for others.

1. What are the three parts of the health triangle? How can you keep them in balance?

____

____

____

____

____

Influences on Your Health *(pages 12–16)*

What factors can affect your health? What people can affect your health? Here are some of the major influences on your health.

Heredity is *all the traits that are biologically passed from parents to their children.* Your eye color, your hair color, and your height are traits you get from your parents. You may also inherit genes that put you at risk for some illnesses.

Reading Tutor, Lesson 2 *(continued)*

USE WITH CHAPTER 1, PAGES 10–16.

Environment is *the sum of your surroundings.* It includes all of the places you go to and live in. It includes all of the people in your life.

- Physical environment factors affect all parts of your health. These include a safe neighborhood, air pollution, and secondhand smoke.
- Social environment includes your family and other people in your life. Family members can provide support and model positive values. **Peers** are *people of the same age who share similar interests.* Peers can give you positive support. Some peers can also pressure you to take part in unhealthy behaviors such as smoking and taking drugs.
- **Culture** is *the collective beliefs, customs, and behaviors of a group.* Language, food, tradition, and religion are all parts of your culture that can affect your well-being.

Attitude is the way you look at situations. It affects the choices you make. People who have a positive attitude are more likely to have better health than people who have a negative outlook.

Behavior affects all parts of your health triangle. This is a factor that you can control. You can develop good health habits. You can choose healthy foods. You can choose to be active. You can choose to learn new skills. You can choose to resolve conflict in a peaceful way.

Media is *the various methods of communicating information.* It includes radio, television, film, newspapers, magazines, books, and the Internet. You need to find sources of information you can rely on. Some ads make false claims about products. Government agencies and health organizations like the American Heart Association are reliable sources of health information.

Technology can also affect your health. Medical tests and treatment help many people to live longer lives. Some technology helps keep our air, water, and land clean. Other technology has made our work easier. We ride in cars and play games on the computer rather than walk or play outside. It is important to live an active and healthy life.

2. What are some of the influences on your health?

____

____

____

____

____

Name Class Date

Lesson 3 — Reading Tutor

USE WITH CHAPTER 1, PAGES 17–21.

Living a Healthy Life: Your Behavior and Reducing Health Risks

Vocabulary

risk behaviors	Actions that can potentially threaten your health or the health of others *(page 17)*
cumulative risks	Related risks that increase in effect with each added risk *(page 19)*
abstinence	A deliberate decision to avoid harmful behaviors, including sexual activity before marriage and the use of tobacco, alcohol, and other drugs *(page 20)*

Drawing from Experience

Do you wear a helmet when you ride your bike? Do you avoid tobacco? Do you avoid alcohol and drugs? Are you physically active? How can you lower your health risks? Think about these things as you read Lesson 3.

In the last lesson, you learned about your health triangle and influences on your health. In this lesson, you will learn about health risks and abstaining from risk behaviors.

Reading Tutor, Lesson 3 *(continued)*

USE WITH CHAPTER 1, PAGES 17–21.

Organizing Your Thoughts

Use the chart below to help you take notes as you read the summaries that follow. In the first box, list some of the types of risk behaviors. In the other box, list some of the reasons to abstain from risk behaviors.

Types of Risk Behaviors	Reasons to Abstain from Risk Behaviors

Reading Tutor, Lesson 3 *(continued)*

USE WITH CHAPTER 1, PAGES 17–21.

Read to learn

Read each passage carefully. Write in complete sentences to answer the following questions.

Understanding Health Risks *(pages 17–19)*

Risk behaviors are *actions that can threaten your health or the health of others.* Here are six types of risk factors.

- Behavior that adds to the risk of injury
- Tobacco use
- Alcohol and other drug use
- Sexual behavior that adds to the risk of pregnancy and sexually transmitted diseases (STDs)
- Poor eating habits
- Lack of physical activity

Cumulative risks are *related risks that increase in effect with each added risk.* Driving fast is a risk. Not wearing a safety belt is a second risk. Driving in the rain is a third risk. The chance of harm grows with each added risk.

1. What are some of the types of risk behaviors that can harm your health?

____

____

____

____

Abstaining from Risk Behaviors (pages 20–21)

Abstinence is *avoiding harmful behavior. It is avoiding the use of tobacco, alcohol and other drugs. It is not having sexual activity before marriage.*

The use of tobacco, alcohol, and other drugs can affect all parts of your health. It can cause addiction and serious harm to the body. It can even cause death. It may also upset your family and friends. It is not legal for people under 21 to buy or use alcohol. It is not legal to buy or use other drugs. Your health will benefit when you abstain from the use of tobacco, alcohol, and other drugs.

Reading Tutor, Lesson 3 *(continued)*

USE WITH CHAPTER 1, PAGES 17–21.

Abstinence from sexual activity before marriage protects you from a number of consequences.

- You will not have to worry about pregnancy.
- You will not have to make hard decisions about being parents.
- You will not have to care for a child.
- You do not have to worry about getting an STI or HIV.
- You are free from guilt and regret.
- You are making a choice that is always legal.

When you choose to abstain from sexual activity, you can set goals and follow your dreams.

2. What are some of the reasons teens should abstain from risk behaviors?

____

____

____

____

____

Building Health Skills and Character: Building Health Skills

Vocabulary

health skills	Specific tools and strategies that help you maintain, protect, and improve all aspects of your health *(page 28)*
interpersonal communication	The exchange of thoughts, feelings, and beliefs between two or more people *(page 28)*
refusal skills	Communication strategies that can help you say no when you are urged to take part in behaviors that are unsafe, unhealthful, or that go against your values *(page 30)*
conflict resolution	The process of ending a conflict through cooperation and problem solving *(page 30)*
stress management	Ways to deal with or overcome the negative effects of stress *(page 31)*
advocacy	Taking action to influence others to address a health-related concern or to support a health-related belief *(page 32)*

Drawing from Experience

Are you a good listener? Do you know how to say no? What do you do when there is a conflict? How do you deal with stress? What affects your health choices? What kinds of skills do you need to be a healthy person? Think about these things as you read Lesson 1.

In the last chapter, you learned about living a healthy life. In this lesson, you will learn about building your health skills.

Reading Tutor, Lesson 1 *(continued)*

USE WITH CHAPTER 2, PAGES 28–32.

Organizing Your Thoughts

Use the chart below to help you take notes as you read the summaries that follow. List some of the factors of each health skill in the spaces below.

Communication Skills
Refusal Skills
Conflict Resolution Skills
Practicing Healthful Behaviors
Managing Stress
Analyzing Influences
Accessing Information
Advocacy

Reading Tutor, Lesson 1 *(continued)*

USE WITH CHAPTER 2, PAGES 28–32.

Read to Learn

Read each passage carefully. Write in complete sentences to answer the following questions.

Interpersonal Skills *(pages 28–30)*

Health skills are life skills. They are *tools and strategies that help you maintain, protect, and improve all parts of your health.* **Interpersonal communication** is *the exchange of thoughts, feelings, and beliefs between two or more people.* It includes communication skills, refusal skills, and conflict resolution skills.

Communication skills include these strategies.

- Be clear. Say what you mean. Use "I" messages.
- Pay attention to *how* you say something. Speak in a calm and clear voice. Be respectful.
- Be a good listener. Do not interrupt. Nod and make eye contact. Ask questions.

Refusal skills are *communication strategies that can help you say no when people urge you to take part in behaviors that are unsafe or unhealthful, or that go against your values.* Here are some refusal strategies.

- Say no in a firm voice.
- Explain why you feel this way.
- Suggest other things you could do instead.
- Use the right body language.
- Leave if you have to. Just walk away.

Conflict resolution is *the process of ending a conflict through cooperation and problem solving.* Here are some steps to deal with conflict.

- Take time to calm down. Think about the situation.
- Speak calmly. Listen carefully. Ask a few questions.
- Be polite. Think of solutions for both sides. Find a peaceful way to end the conflict.

1. What are the three kinds of skills that are a part of interpersonal communication?

___

___

___

___

Reading Tutor, Lesson 1 *(continued)*

USE WITH CHAPTER 2, PAGES 28–32.

Self-Management Skills *(page 31)*

Self-management skills include practicing healthful behaviors and managing stress.

Practicing healthful behaviors means that you eat nutritious foods. It means that you wear safety gear. It means that you get regular checkups. You stay away from tobacco, alcohol, and other drugs. You express your feelings in healthy ways. You have healthy friendships.

Stress management is *ways to deal with or overcome the negative effects of stress.* Some ways to deal with stress are engaging in physical activity, listening to soft music, using your time wisely, and laughing.

2. What are some of the ways that you can practice healthful behaviors and manage stress?

____

____

____

____

Analyzing Influences *(page 31)*

Many factors affect your health. **Internal influences** are what you know, your likes and dislikes, your values, and your desires. You have control over these. **External influences** come from outside sources like your family, your peers, where you live, your culture, laws, and the media. You can make better health choices when you know what influences you.

3. What are the two main types of influences that can affect your health?

____

____

____

____

Accessing Information *(page 32)*

How can you find out more about health issues? Here are some of the reliable sources of health information.

- Parents and guardians and other trusted adults
- The library; books on nutrition and fitness

Reading Tutor, Lesson 1 *(continued)*

- Internet sites such as government sites
- Newspaper and magazine articles by health experts
- Government agencies, health care providers, and health care organizations

4. What are some of the reliable sources of health information?

____

____

____

____

Advocacy *(page 32)*

Advocacy is *taking action to influence others to address a health concern or to support a health related belief.* This skill can help you affect the health of others. You can tell others about health issues. You can help your family and your friends practice healthy behavior.

5. What does advocacy mean?

____

____

____

____

Lesson 2 — Reading Tutor

USE WITH CHAPTER 2, PAGES 33–36.

Building Health Skills and Character: Making Responsible Decisions and Setting Goals

Vocabulary

decision-making skills	Steps that enable you to make a healthful decision *(page 33)*
values	The ideas, beliefs, and attitudes about what is important that help guide the way you live *(page 34)*
goal	Something you aim for that takes planning and work *(page 34)*
short-term goal	A goal that you can reach in a short length of time *(page 35)*
long-term goal	A goal that you plan to reach over an extended period of time *(page 35)*
action plan	A multistep strategy to identify and achieve your goals *(page 36)*

Drawing from Experience

Have you ever had a big decision to make? What did you do? What steps did you take to make your choice? What are your goals? How do you form your goals? Think about these things as you read Lesson 2.

In the last lesson, you learned about health skills. In this lesson, you will learn about making decisions and setting goals.

Reading Tutor, Lesson 2 *(continued)*

USE WITH CHAPTER 2, PAGES 33–36.

Organizing Your Thoughts

Use the chart below to help you take notes as you read the summaries that follow. In one box, list the steps of the decision-making process. In the other box, list the steps to reach your goals.

The Decision-Making Process	Steps to Reach Your Goals

Reading Tutor, Lesson 2 *(continued)*

USE WITH CHAPTER 2, PAGES 33–36.

Read to Learn

Read each passage carefully. Write in complete sentences to answer the following questions.

The Decision-Making Process *(pages 33–34)*

Decision-making skills are *steps that enable you to make a healthful decision.* Here are the steps of the decision-making process.

Step 1: **State the situation.** Think about the facts.

Step 2: **List the options.** What are your choices?

Step 3: **Weigh the possible outcomes.** Use the H.E.L.P. method.

- **H**ealthful. Is this choice a health risk?
- **E**thical. Do you believe this is the right thing to do?
- **L**egal. Is it against the law?
- **P**arent approval. Would your parents approve?

Step 4: **Consider values. Values** are *the ideas, beliefs, and attitudes about what is important. They help guide the way you live.*

Step 5: **Make a decision and act on it.**

Step 6: **Evaluate the decision.** What was the outcome? How did it affect your health?

1. What are the six steps of the decision-making process?

____

____

____

____

Reading Tutor, Lesson 2 *(continued)*

USE WITH CHAPTER 2, PAGES 33–36.

Setting Personal Health Goals *(pages 34–36)*

A **goal** is *something you aim for that takes planning and work.* A **short-term goal** is *a goal that you can reach in a short period of time.* A **long-term goal** is *a goal that you plan to reach over an extended period of time.*

An **action plan** is *a multistep strategy to identify and achieve your goals.* Here are the steps in an action plan.

- **Set a goal and write it down.** Be specific. Be realistic.
- **List the steps you will take to meet your goal.** Break your goal into smaller goals.
- **Identify sources of help.** List the names of people who can help and support you.
- **Set a time frame to reach your goal.** Be reasonable. Write it down.
- **Evaluate your progress.** Check how you are doing. Adjust your goals if you need to.
- **Reward yourself when you reach your goal.**

2. What are the steps of an action plan that can help you to reach your goals?

Name Class Date

Lesson 3

Reading Tutor

USE WITH CHAPTER 2, PAGES 37–41.

Building Health Skills and Character: Building Character

Vocabulary

character	Those distinctive qualities that describe how a person thinks, feels, and behaves *(page 37)*
role model	Someone whose success or behavior serves as an example for others *(page 40)*

Drawing from Experience

Do you tell the truth? Do you play by the rules? How do you show respect for yourself and others? What are values? What do you think it means to have good character? Is there someone you know who you look up to? Think about these things as you read Lesson 3.

In the last lesson, you learned about making decisions and goal setting. In this lesson, you will learn about good character.

Reading Tutor, Lesson 3 *(continued)*

USE WITH CHAPTER 2, PAGES 37–41.

Organizing Your Thoughts

Use the chart below to help you take notes as you read the summaries that follow. In the first box, list some of the traits of good character. In the other box, list some of the ways to develop and demonstrate your character.

Traits of Good Character	Ways to Develop and Show Character

Reading Tutor, Lesson 3 *(continued)*

USE WITH CHAPTER 2, PAGES 37–41.

Read to Learn

Read each passage carefully. Write in complete sentences to answer the following questions.

What Is Good Character? *(page 37)*

Character is *those qualities that describe how a person thinks, feels, and behaves.* A person with good character has core ethical values. Some of these values are responsibility, honesty, integrity, and respect. These values help you to know right from wrong. They are important to all cultures and age groups.

1. What is character?

___

___

___

Character and Health *(page 38)*

Your character affects all sides of your health triangle. You will take care of your body if you respect yourself. Your mental/emotional and social health will improve when you feel good about yourself.

Here are the six primary traits of good character.

- **Trustworthiness** means you are honest, loyal, and reliable. It means you do what you say you will do. You do not cheat or steal.
- **Respect** means you are considerate of others. You tolerate differences in others. You use good manners. You treat people and property with care.
- **Responsibility** means you have self-control. You think before you act. You do not blame others for your actions. You always do your best.
- **Fairness** means you play by the rules. You take turns and share. You listen to others. You do not take advantage of or blame others.
- **Caring** means you are kind to others. You are grateful for things. You forgive others. You help people who are in need.
- **Citizenship** means you obey laws and rules. You respect authority. You are a good neighbor. You try to make your school a safe and healthy place.

2. What are the six primary traits of good character?

___

___

___

___

Developing Your Character *(pages 39–40)*

Here are some of the ways that you can develop good character.

- Stand up for your beliefs.
- Learn from others who have good character traits.
- Be a volunteer at your school or in your community. Make friends with people who have core ethical values.

A **role model** is *someone whose success or behavior serves as an example for others.* Family members can be good role models. They can teach you basic values such as working hard, planning ahead, and being honest. Other role models might be teachers or coaches.

3. What are some of the ways that you can develop good character?

____

____

____

____

Demonstrating Character *(page 41)*

Here are some of the ways you can demonstrate or show good character.

- **Make a difference at home.** You demonstrate that you are trustworthy and reliable at home when you are responsible and do your chores.
- **Make a difference at school.** You show you have respect for teachers and fellow students when you follow school rules.
- **Make a difference in your community.** You show you are a good citizen when you obey the laws and respect other people. You show you have good character when you have a positive effect on others.

4. What are some of the ways that you can show good character?

____

____

____

____

Name Class Date

Being a Health-Literate Consumer: Making Consumer Choices

Vocabulary

health consumer	Anyone who purchases or uses health products or services *(page 48)*
media	The various methods of communicating information *(page 49)*
advertising	A written or spoken message designed to interest consumers in purchasing a product or service *(page 49)*
comparison shopping	A method of judging the benefits of different products by comparing several factors, such as quality, features, and cost *(page 50)*
warranty	A company's or a store's written agreement to repair a product or refund your money should the product not function properly *(page 50)*
online shopping	Using the Internet to buy products and services *(page 52)*

Drawing from Experience

Are you a consumer? Do you ever buy shampoo or sunscreen? Have you ever bought safety gear? Did anything influence your choices? Did you compare prices? What rights do you have as a consumer? Think about these things as you read Lesson 1.

In the last chapter, you learned about building health skills and character. In this lesson, you will learn about making consumer choices.

Reading Tutor, Lesson 1 *(continued)*

USE WITH CHAPTER 3, PAGES 48–53.

Organizing Your Thoughts

Use the chart below to help you take notes as you read the summaries that follow. In the first box, list some of the things that influence your consumer choices. In the other box, list some of the rights you have as a consumer.

Things That Influence Your Choices	Your Rights As a Consumer

Reading Tutor, Lesson 1 *(continued)*

USE WITH CHAPTER 3, PAGES 48–53.

Read to Learn

Read each passage carefully. Write in complete sentences to answer the following questions.

Being an Informed Health Consumer *(page 48)*

A **health consumer** is *anyone who purchases or uses health products or services.* Your parents make many decisions about health services. You can make your own choices about things like shampoo and soap. You need to learn how to choose reliable and effective products.

1. What is a health consumer?

____

____

____

Influences on Your Decisions *(pages 49–51)*

Your own likes and dislikes can influence your decision to buy certain products. External influences can also affect you. The **media** is *the various methods of communicating information*. It includes TV, radio, newspapers, and the Internet.

Advertising is *a written or spoken media message designed to interest consumers in buying a product or service.* Here are some of the ways that ads try to get you to buy a product.

- The **bandwagon** method tells you that everyone is using the product and you should too.
- The **rich and famous** method says you will feel rich if you use this product.
- **Free gifts** make you feel that the deal is too good to pass up.
- The **great outdoors** method says that an item that has to do with nature must be healthy.
- The **good times** method shows people smiling and laughing when they use the product.
- **Testimonial** methods say that the product will work for you if it worked for others.

Reading Tutor, Lesson 1 *(continued)*

USE WITH CHAPTER 3, PAGES 48–53.

Comparison shopping is *a way of judging the benefits of products by comparing factors, such as quality, features, and cost.* Here are some of the factors you can look at and compare.

- **Cost.** Check the cost of the same brand at other stores. Check the cost of similar brands.
- **Features.** Decide what you want. Do not pay for lots of features you do not want.
- **Quality.** A cheap product is not a better deal if it falls apart.
- **A product's warranty.** *A company's or a store's written agreement to repair a product or refund your money if the product does not work properly.*
- **Safety.** This is very important when you are choosing sports or home safety products.
  - **The Underwriters Laboratory (UL)** is a safety testing company. The UL logo on electrical appliances shows that the product has been safety tested.
  - **Snell** and the **American National Standards Institute (ANSI)** check safety standards for helmets and other safety gear.
- **Recommendations.** Ask your parents and friends what products they buy.

You can get a lot of information by reading product labels. Here is some of the information you can find on a product label.

- Product name and its intended use
- Directions for use
- Warnings
- Amount in the container
- Ingredients
- Manufacturer's address or phone number

2. What are some of the factors to look at when you are comparison shopping?

____

____

____

____

Reading Tutor, Lesson 1 *(continued)*

USE WITH CHAPTER 3, PAGES 48–53.

Your Rights as a Consumer *(page 52)*

Here are some of the rights you have when you buy a product or a service.

- The right to safety
- The right to choose. You can pick from many products.
- The right to be informed. You need to get truthful information.
- The right to be heard. You can have input on laws about buying and selling.
- The right to have problems corrected
- The right to consumer education. Learn more about consumer skills.

3. What are some of the rights you have when you buy a product or a service?

____

____

____

____

____

Today's Consumer Choices *(pages 52–53)*

Online shopping is *using the Internet to buy products and services.* Here are some things to think about when you shop online.

- **Price.** Some prices are lower online. Shipping costs may add more to the price.
- **Convenience.** Items you order come right to your home. You may have to repack the item and send it back if there is a problem.
- **Product information.** The item may not look like it did in a picture. Clothes may not fit.

4. What are some of the things to think about when you shop online?

____

____

____

Name Class Date

Lesson 2 **Reading Tutor**

USE WITH CHAPTER 3, PAGES 54–59.

Being a Health-Literate Consumer: Managing Consumer Problems

Vocabulary

health care system	All the medical care available to a nation's people, the way they receive care, and the method of payment *(page 54)*
primary care physician	A medical doctor who provides physical checkups and general care *(page 54)*
specialist	A medical doctor trained to handle particular kinds of patients or medical conditions *(page 54)*
preventive care	Actions that prevent the onset of disease or injury *(page 55)*
health insurance	A plan in which private companies or government programs pay for part or all of a person's medical costs *(page 57)*
medical history	Complete and comprehensive information about your immunizations and any health problems you have had to date *(page 58)*

Drawing from Experience

Do you have a family doctor? Where do you go to get health care? How do your parents pay for health care? Do you have health insurance? Think about these things as you read Lesson 2.

In the last lesson, you learned about making consumer choices. In this lesson, you will learn about types of health services and health care.

Reading Tutor, Lesson 2 *(continued)*

USE WITH CHAPTER 3, PAGES 54–59.

Organizing Your Thoughts

Use the chart below to help you take notes as you read the summaries that follow. In the first box, list some of the types of health care. In the next box, list some of the facilities for health care. In the last box, list some of the ways to pay for health care.

Types of Health Care	Facilities for Health Care	Ways to Pay for Health Care

Reading Tutor, Lesson 2 *(continued)*

USE WITH CHAPTER 3, PAGES 54–59.

Read to Learn

Read each passage carefully. Write in complete sentences to answer the following questions.

Types of Health Services *(pages 54–55)*

A **health care system** is *all the medical care available to a nation's people. It is the way they receive care and the method of payment.* A **primary care physician** is *a doctor who provides physical checkups and general care.*

A **specialist** is *a doctor trained to help certain kinds of patients or medical conditions.* Here are some types of health care specialists.

- Allergist – treats allergies.
- Dermatologist – treats skin diseases.
- Gynecologist – treats problems of the female reproductive system.
- Oncologist – treats cancer.

Preventive care involves *actions that prevent the onset of disease or injury.* Going to the doctor or dentist for a checkup is this type of care.

1. What are some of the types of health care services?

____

____

____

____

Facilities for Health Care Services *(pages 55–56)*

Inpatient care is when a person must stay overnight at a care facility. It is for people with serious illness or injury. **Outpatient care** is when a person gets treated and then goes home. Here are some types of health care facilities.

- **Private practices.** These are doctors who see patients in their office.
- **Clinics.** This is a place in the community where doctors can give outpatient care.
- **Group practices.** These are a group of doctors who share office space and staff.
- **Hospitals.** These are places that provide inpatient and outpatient care.
- **Emergency rooms.** These are places that provide care for serious injury or illness.
- **Urgent care centers.** These are places to treat emergencies that are not as serious.

Reading Tutor, Lesson 2 *(continued)*

USE WITH CHAPTER 3, PAGES 54–59.

2. What are some of the types of health care facilities?

____

____

____

____

How People Pay for Health Services *(page 57)*

Health insurance is *a plan in which private companies or government programs pay for part or all of a person's medical costs.* The person pays a monthly fee or premium. A deductible is an amount the person pays out of his or her own pocket before the plan starts to pay.

Some insurance plans are managed care plans. Here are some types of these plans.

- **Health Maintenance Organization (HMO).** You pay a monthly fee and a co-pay for office visits. You can only see doctors in the plan.
- **Preferred Provider Organization (PPO).** You pay a monthly fee and a co-pay for office visits. You can see doctors outside the plan. You pay more out-of-pocket expenses than people who have an HMO plan do.
- **Point of Service (POS) plans.** You choose doctors inside or outside of the plan. You pay higher fees for doctors outside the plan.

3. What are the three major types of managed care plans?

____

____

____

____

Trends in Health Care *(page 58)*

Here are some other types of health care.

- **Birthing centers** are homelike places where women can have their babies.
- **Drug treatment centers** help people who have drug and alcohol problems.
- **Continuing care and assisted living facilities** give care for people who do not need to be in the hospital but who need help with everyday tasks.

Reading Tutor, Lesson 2 *(continued)*

- **Hospices** care for people who will die soon. They also help the person's family.
- **Telemedicine** is using phones or video to practice medicine over a long distance.

4. What are some other types of health care?

____

____

____

____

You and Your Health Care *(pages 58–59)*

Your **medical history** is *complete information about your immunizations and any health problems that you have had to date.* A doctor may ask you to fill out a medical history on your first visit. Here are some things to do before, during, and after a visit to the doctor.

- Write down your reasons for seeing the doctor before you go.
- Ask questions about anything that you do not understand.
- Tell the nurse about any allergies you have or any medicine you are taking.
- Ask the pharmacist about any type of medicine that the doctor may order for you.

5. What are some of the things that you can do when you go to see the doctor?

____

____

____

____

USE WITH CHAPTER 3, PAGES 60–63.

Being a Health-Literate Consumer: Managing Consumer Problems

Vocabulary

fraud	Deliberate deceit or trickery *(page 61)*
health fraud	Sale of worthless products or services claimed to prevent diseases or cure other health problems *(page 61)*
malpractice	Failure by a health professional to meet accepted standards *(page 61)*
consumer advocates	People or groups whose sole purpose is to take on regional, national, and even international consumer issues *(page 63)*

Drawing from Experience

Have you ever bought an item that did not work? What did you do? Did you take the item back to the store? Where can you go to get help with a health fraud problem? Think about these things as you read Lesson 3.

In the last lesson, you learned about types of health services. In this lesson, you will learn about consumer problems.

Reading Tutor, Lesson 3 *(continued)*

USE WITH CHAPTER 3, PAGES 60–63.

Organizing Your Thoughts

Use the chart below to help you take notes as you read the summaries that follow. In the first box, list some of the types of health fraud. In the other box, list some of the groups that can help with consumer problems.

Types of Health Fraud	Groups That Can Help Consumers

Reading Tutor, Lesson 3 *(continued)*

USE WITH CHAPTER 3, PAGES 60–63.

Read to Learn

Read each passage carefully. Write in complete sentences to answer the following questions.

Problems with Products *(page 60)*

Sometimes you buy a product that does not work. Here are some of the steps you can take.

- You can take some items back to the store where you bought them.
- You must send some items back to the company that made the item.
- Read the directions to be sure you are using the item correctly.
- Decide if you want to get a new item or get your money back.
- Write down your reason for returning the item. Keep a copy.
- Get a receipt if you mail the item.

1. What are some of the steps you can take if you buy an item that does not work?

____

____

____

____

Health Fraud *(pages 61–63)*

Fraud is *deliberate deceit or trickery*. **Health fraud** is the *sale of worthless products or services. They claim to prevent diseases or cure other health problems.*

Here are some of the types of products and treatments that may have health fraud problems.

- **Weight-loss products.** Some ads for diet pills and exercise gear say that people can lose weight almost overnight. You can only keep a healthy weight if you stay active and eat healthy foods.
- **Beauty and anti-aging products.** Tooth whiteners and wrinkle creams may work for a short time. They will not last. Some products can even harm you.
- **Cures for arthritis or other ailments.** Some treatments promise miracle cures. Most do not work and some may harm you. Check with a doctor.

Reading Tutor, Lesson 3 *(continued)*

USE WITH CHAPTER 3, PAGES 60–63.

Malpractice is *failure by a health professional to meet accepted standards.* Get a second opinion from another doctor. You can get help from the American Medical Association if you have a serious problem.

Here are some groups that can help you if you have a problem with health products.

- **Business organizations** such as the Better Business Bureau can help you issue a complaint.
- **Consumer advocates** are *people or groups whose sole purpose is to take on regional, national, and even international consumer issues.* Some groups test products and tell the public what they find.
- **Local, state, and federal government agencies** protect the rights of consumers.
  - The Federal Trade Commission works to prevent false ads.
  - The Food and Drug Administration makes sure medicines are safe.
  - The Consumer Product Safety Commission makes sure products are safe.
  - Small-claims courts make decisions when a buyer and a seller cannot agree.

2. What are some of the products and treatments that have health fraud problems?

____

____

____

____

Name Class Date

Lesson 4

Reading Tutor

USE WITH CHAPTER 3, PAGES 64–67.

Being a Health-Literate Consumer: Understanding Public Health Services

Vocabulary

public health	A community-wide effort to monitor and promote the welfare of the population *(page 64)*
epidemiology	The scientific study of patterns of disease in a population *(page 65)*

Drawing from Experience

What do you know about the American Red Cross or the National Cancer Institute? Why do you think we have groups like these? What do they do? Think about these things as you read Lesson 4.

In the last lesson, you learned how to deal with consumer issues. In this lesson, you will learn about public health agencies.

Reading Tutor, Lesson 4 *(continued)*

USE WITH CHAPTER 3, PAGES 64–67.

Organizing Your Thoughts

Use the chart below to help you take notes as you read the summaries that follow. In the first box, list some of the public health agencies. In the other box, list some of the ways that teens can advocate for public health.

Public Health Agencies	Ways Teens Can Advocate

USE WITH CHAPTER 3, PAGES 64–67.

Read to Learn

Read each passage carefully. Write in complete sentences to answer the following questions.

Public Health Agencies *(pages 64–66)*

Public health is *a community-wide effort to monitor and promote the welfare of the population.*

Here are some of the jobs of state, county, and local health departments.

- Work to prevent disease.
- Take care of the water and the sewer systems.
- Take care of waste disposal.
- Inspect restaurants to make sure they are clean.

Here are the names of some nonprofit groups. They give help and data on certain diseases.

- American Cancer Society
- March of Dimes
- American Red Cross

Here are some of the federal agencies that work to protect our health.

- The **National Cancer Institute (NCI).** This is the main agency for cancer research.
- The **Environmental Protection Agency (EPA).** It takes care of our water, air, and land.
- The **Occupational Safety and Health Administration (OSHA).** It helps prevent injuries to workers.
- The **U.S. Department of Agriculture (USDA).** It runs food stamp, school lunch, and school breakfast programs.
  - **Food Safety and Inspection Service (FSIS).** It makes sure meat, poultry, and eggs are safe for us to eat.
- The **Department of Health and Human Services (DHHS)** has 13 agencies.
  - The **Centers for Medicare and Medicaid Services (CMS).** They provide health insurance for elderly and low-income people.
  - The **Food and Drug Administration (FDA).** It makes sure food, drugs, and makeup are safe.
  - The **National Institutes of Health (NIH).** It does medical research.
  - The **Substance Abuse and Mental Health Services Administration (SAMHSA).** It has programs for drug users and people with mental health problems.

Reading Tutor, Lesson 4 *(continued)*

USE WITH CHAPTER 3, PAGES 64–67.

- The **Centers for Disease Control and Prevention (CDC).** They gather data for research to help stop disease. **Epidemiology** is *the study of patterns of disease in a population.*
- The **Federal Trade Commission (FTC).** It enforces trade laws and consumer laws.

Here are some groups that provide help around the world.

- The **World Health Organization** is a part of the United Nations. It works to stop disease and pollution.
- The **International Committee of the Red Cross**. It gives aid to victims of war, disease, or natural disasters.

1. What are the names of some of the agencies that work to protect our health?

____

____

____

____

Advocacy—Taking Action for Public Health *(page 67)*

Here are some of the ways that teens can advocate for public health.

- Follow all health safety laws. Get the shots you need to prevent diseases.
- Practice healthful behaviors. Wear safety gear.
- Stay away from risky actions. Do not drive in a reckless way.
- Be a part of health events such as 10K runs.
- Support groups that deal with public health.
- Report things you see that may harm public health.

2. What are some of the ways that teens can advocate for public health?

____

____

____

____

USE WITH CHAPTER 4, PAGES 74–79.

Physical Activity for Life: Physical Activity and Your Health

Vocabulary

physical activity	Any form of movement that causes your body to use energy *(page 74)*
physical fitness	The ability to carry out daily tasks easily and have enough reserve energy to respond to unexpected demands *(page 74)*
sedentary lifestyle	A way of life that involves little physical activity *(page 77)*
osteoporosis	A condition characterized by a decrease in bone density producing porous and fragile bones *(page 78)*
metabolism	The process by which the body breaks down substances and gets energy from food *(page 78)*

Drawing from Experience

Do you like to play sports? Do you like to ride your bike? Do you dance? What are some of the types of physical activity that you like to do? What can happen if you are not physically active? Think about these things as you read Lesson 1.

In the last chapter, you learned about being a health consumer. In this lesson, you will learn about physical activity and your health.

Reading Tutor, Lesson 1 *(continued)*

USE WITH CHAPTER 4, PAGES 74–79.

Organizing Your Thoughts

Use the chart below to help you take notes as you read the summaries that follow. In the first box, list some of the benefits of physical activity. In the other box, list some of the risks of not being physically active.

Benefits of Physical Activity	Risks of Physical Inactivity

Reading Tutor, Lesson 1 *(continued)*

USE WITH CHAPTER 4, PAGES 74–79.

Read to Learn

Read each passage carefully. Write in complete sentences to answer the following questions.

What Is Physical Activity? *(page 74)*

Physical activity is *any form of movement that causes your body to use energy*. It can be walking or moving as a part of your normal day. It can be playing sports or doing exercise.

Physical fitness is *the ability to carry out daily tasks easily. It means that you have energy left over to respond to unexpected demands*. A high level of fitness adds to your total well being.

1. What is physical fitness?

____

____

____

____

What Are the Benefits of Physical Activity? *(pages 75–77)*

Physical health. Physical activity makes your muscles and bones strong. It gives you energy. It improves your posture. Here are some of the ways it affects the body systems.

- Cardiovascular system—Your heart muscle gets stronger. It pumps more blood.
- Respiratory system—You breathe deeper. You can do more without running out of breath.
- Nervous system—You respond faster. Your reaction time improves.

Mental and emotional health. Physical activity helps reduce stress. It helps you sleep better. It helps you deal with anger. It can improve your mood. Here are some other ways it can help.

- You look and feel better. It gives you self-confidence. You feel you can try new things.
- You feel proud of yourself. It improves your self-concept.
- It lowers your mental fatigue. You can think more clearly.

Social health. Being on a sports team, hiking in the hills, or swimming at a local pool can help you meet new people. Here are other ways physical activity can affect your social health.

- It builds your self-confidence. It makes it easier for you to meet new people.

- It gives you the chance to work or interact with others.
- It helps you deal with stress. This can help your relationships with others.

2. What are some of the benefits of physical activity?

____

____

____

____

Risks of Physical Inactivity *(pages 77–78)*

The *CDC Fact Book* has some facts about physical activity and high school students.

- One out of three teens does not do physical activity at least 20 minutes three times a week.
- Seventy-three percent of ninth graders are physically active. Only sixty-one percent of twelfth graders are active.
- Twenty-nine percent of teens have a daily physical education class. It was forty-two percent in 1991.

A **sedentary lifestyle** is *a way of life that involves little physical activity*. Here are some risks of not being active.

- You may gain too much weight. This can lead to heart disease, diabetes, and cancer. **Diabetes** is a serious disorder that prevents the body from converting food into energy.
- You may be more likely to get **osteoporosis.** This is *a decrease in bone density that produces porous and fragile bones*.
- You may have a lower ability to deal with stress.
- You may have fewer chances to meet new friends who have active lifestyles.

Here are some ways to include more physical activity in your life.

- Take the stairs instead of taking an elevator.
- Play soccer or basketball instead of playing a video game.
- Walk or ride your bike instead of getting a ride in the car.
- Mow the lawn instead of watching TV or taking a nap.

Reading Tutor, Lesson 1 *(continued)*

USE WITH CHAPTER 4, PAGES 74–79.

3. What are some of the risks of not being active?

Physical Activity and Weight Control *(pages 78–79)*

More than one-half of adults and 14 percent of teens are overweight. A sedentary lifestyle and overeating may be the cause. It is important to eat right and to stay active.

Metabolism is *the process by which your body gets energy from food.* We measure food in units of heat called calories. Your metabolic rate goes up and you burn more calories when you are physically active. This helps you keep a healthy weight.

4. How does physical activity help you keep a healthy weight?

Fitting Physical Activity into Your Life *(page 79)*

Teens should get 60 minutes of physical activity every day. Any activity that gets you to move can count toward your total. Walk or ride your bike to school. Go for a hike or a swim on the weekend. Have a basketball game with friends. Ride your bike, golf, or bowl. Find things that you can do to stay active for life.

5. What are some of the ways that you can be active for life?

Lesson 2 **Reading Tutor**

USE WITH CHAPTER 4, PAGES 80–86.

Physical Activity for Life: Fitness and You

Vocabulary

cardiorespiratory endurance	The ability of the heart, lungs, and blood vessels to use and send fuel and oxygen to the body's tissues during long periods of moderate-to-vigorous activity *(page 80)*
muscular strength	The amount of force a muscle can exert *(page 80)*
muscular endurance	The ability of the muscles to perform physical tasks over a period of time without becoming fatigued *(page 80)*
flexibility	The ability to move a body part through a full range of motion *(page 81)*
body composition	The ratio of body fat to lean body tissue, including muscle, bone, water, and connective tissue such as ligaments, cartilage, and tendons *(page 81)*
exercise	Purposeful physical activity that is planned, structured, and repetitive and that improves or maintains personal fitness *(page 81)*
aerobic exercise	Any activity that uses large muscle groups, is rhythmic in nature, and can be maintained continuously for at least 10 minutes three times a day or for 20 to 30 minutes at one time *(page 83)*
anaerobic exercise	Intense short bursts of activity in which the muscles work so hard that they produce energy without using oxygen *(page 84)*

Drawing from Experience

How many sit-ups can you do? How far can you run? Can you bend and touch your toes? What does it mean to be physically fit? Think about these things as you read Lesson 2.

In the last lesson, you learned about physical activity and your health. In this lesson, you will learn how to improve your fitness.

Reading Tutor, Lesson 2 *(continued)*

USE WITH CHAPTER 4, PAGES 80–86.

Organizing Your Thoughts

Use the chart below to help you take notes as you read the summaries that follow. In the first box, list the elements of fitness. In the other box, list some of the ways to improve your fitness.

Elements of Fitness	Ways to Improve Your Fitness

Reading Tutor, Lesson 2 *(continued)*

USE WITH CHAPTER 4, PAGES 80–86.

Read to Learn

Read each passage carefully. Write in complete sentences to answer the following questions.

Elements of Fitness ***(pages 80–83)***

Here are the five elements of fitness. You can test each area of fitness and improve it with exercise. **Exercise** is *physical activity that you plan and structure. It is repetitive. It improves or maintains your fitness.*

Cardiorespiratory endurance is *the ability of the heart, lungs, and blood vessels to use and send fuel and oxygen to the body's tissues during long periods of moderate-to-vigorous activity.* A strong heart and lungs can lower your risk of heart disease.

- **Step test**—This test lets you find your heart rate after an activity.
  1. Use a sturdy 12-inch-high bench. Step up with your right foot and then with your left. Step down with your right foot and then with your left.
  2. Repeat at the rate of 24 steps per minute for three minutes.
  3. Find a pulse point on your wrist using the first two fingers of your other hand. Count the number of beats for one minute.

Muscular strength is *the amount of force a muscle exerts.* It is needed to lift, push, or jump.

- **Curl-ups**—You can use these to test your abdominal strength.
  1. Lie on your back with your knees up and your feet a little apart.
  2. Keep your feet flat on the floor. Curl forward and move your arms toward your feet as you rise.
  3. Slowly lie back down. Do one curl-up every three seconds until you cannot do any more.

Muscular endurance is the ability of the muscles to do physical tasks over a period of time without getting tired.

- **Arm hang**—This test measures your upper body strength and endurance.
  1. Grasp a horizontal bar with your palms facing away from you.
  2. Raise your body so that your chin is above the bar.
  3. Hold the position for as long as you can. Have a friend time you with a stopwatch.

Reading Tutor, Lesson 2 *(continued)*

USE WITH CHAPTER 4, PAGES 80–86.

Flexibility is *the ability to move a body part through a full range of motion*. It lowers your risk of muscle strains and lower back problems.

- **Sit and reach**—This tests the flexibility of your lower back and the back of your thighs.
  1. Tape a yardstick to the top of a 12-inch box. Put the box against a wall.
  2. Sit on the floor. Put the sole of your bare foot flat against the side of the box. Bend your other knee so your foot is flat on the floor.
  3. Put the palm of one hand over the other hand. Reach forward as far as you can.
  4. Hold the position of your fourth reach for at least one second. Record your score.
  5. Switch the position of your legs and repeat the test.

Body composition is *the ratio of body fat to lean body tissue. It includes muscle, bone, water, and connective tissue such as ligaments, cartilage, and tendons.*

- **Pinch test**—This tests the amount of fat in your body.
  1. Use a skin-fold caliper tool. This measures the thickness of fat under a fold of skin.
  2. Measure a fold of skin on your shoulder, back of your arm, abdomen, hip, and thigh.
  3. Figure out the average of the numbers to estimate your total body fat.

1. What are the five elements of fitness?

___

___

___

___

Improving Your Fitness *(pages 83–86)*

Aerobic exercise is *any activity that uses large muscle groups, is rhythmic, and that you can do nonstop for at least 10 minutes three times a day or for 20 to 30 minutes at one time*. You can run, cycle, swim, or dance.

Anaerobic exercise is *intense short bursts of activity. The muscles work so hard that they produce energy without using oxygen*. You can lift weights or run sprints.

Reading Tutor, Lesson 2 *(continued)*

USE WITH CHAPTER 4, PAGES 80–86.

You can improve your cardiorespiratory endurance with aerobic exercise. It makes your heart strong. It increases the amount of air your lungs hold. Be sure to stop if you feel exhausted.

You can improve your muscular strength and endurance with anaerobic exercise. This helps keep your blood sugar and cholesterol levels normal. Here are some types of resistance exercise.

- **Isometric exercise** is an activity that uses muscle tension with little movement. One way to do this is to push against a wall.
- **Isotonic exercise** is an activity that contracts muscles and repeats movements. Some types are calisthenics, push-ups, sit-ups, and rowing.
- **Isokinetic exercise** is an activity in which resistance moves at a controlled rate of speed. Some types are using a stationary bike or a treadmill.

You can improve your flexibility with stretching exercises. Move slowly and gently. One stretch is to clasp your hands and extend your arms behind your back. Raise your arms and hold.

You can improve your bone strength by getting enough calcium. You also need resistance exercises and weight-bearing aerobic exercise. Walk and climb stairs. It is important to build your bone mass during your teen years.

2. What are some of the ways that you can improve your fitness?

___

___

___

___

USE WITH CHAPTER 4, PAGES 87–92.

Physical Activity for Life: Planning a Personal Activity Program

Vocabulary

overload	Working the body harder than it is normally worked *(page 90)*
progression	The gradual increase in overload necessary to achieve higher levels of fitness *(page 90)*
specificity	Particular exercises and activities that improve particular areas of health-related fitness *(page 90)*
warm-up	An activity that prepares the muscles for work *(page 90)*
workout	The part of an exercise program when the activity is performed at its highest peak *(page 90)*
F.I.T.T.	Frequency, intensity, time/duration, and type of activity *(page 90)*
cool-down	An activity that prepares the muscles to return to a resting state *(page 91)*
resting heart rate	The number of times your heart beats in one minute when you are not active *(page 92)*

Drawing from Experience

Do you have any fitness goals? What kinds of activities do you like to do? Do you warm-up before you work out? Have you ever made a fitness plan? Think about these things as you read Lesson 3.

In the last lesson, you learned about fitness. In this lesson, you will learn how to plan your own activity program.

Reading Tutor, Lesson 3 *(continued)*

USE WITH CHAPTER 4, PAGES 87–92.

Organizing Your Thoughts

Use the chart below to help you take notes as you read the summaries that follow. In the first box, list some of the factors that affect your activity choices. In the other box, list some of the parts of a fitness plan.

Choosing Activities	Parts of a Fitness Plan

Reading Tutor, Lesson 3 *(continued)*

USE WITH CHAPTER 4, PAGES 87–92.

Read to Learn

Read each passage carefully. Write in complete sentences to answer the following questions.

Setting Physical Activity Goals *(pages 87–88)*

Teens should get 60 minutes of physical activity every day. This may be sports or exercise. It may be mowing the lawn or cleaning your room. Here are some ways you can be active.

- Do moderate-intensity activities for about 30 minutes per day. You can walk, climb stairs, do yard work, walk a dog, or clean the house.
- Do aerobic activities three to five days per week for 20 to 60 minutes per session. You can cycle, walk fast, run, dance, skate, play basketball, or ski.
- Do anaerobic activities two to three days per week. You can do curls, push-ups, or bench presses.
- Do flexibility activities 2 or more days per week. You can do lunges, stretches, and yoga.
- Do not do sedentary activities very often. These include watching TV, talking on the phone, and playing computer games.

1. What are some of the ways a teen can be active every day?

____

____

____

____

Choosing Activities *(pages 88–90)*

Here are some of the factors that may affect your choice of activities.

- **Cost.** You need to buy expensive gear for some activities. Keep in mind that you may lose interest in an activity after a time.
- **Where you live.** You will want to pick activities that are close to where you live. Think about the climate in your area. Think about what activities you can do in your area.
- **Your level of health.** Know what you are able to do. Some types of activity can be a risk if you have a condition such as asthma.
- **Time and place.** Plan your program wisely. Do not plan an activity at 6:00 A.M. if you do not like to wake up early.
- **Personal safety.** Stay away from unsafe areas. Do not run after it gets dark.

- **Comprehensive planning.** Choose activities from all the areas of fitness.
- **Cross training.** Choose a variety of activities to work out many muscle groups.

2. What are some of the factors that may affect your choice of activities?

____

____

____

____

____

Basics of a Physical Activity Program *(pages 90–92)*

Here are some elements that all fitness programs should have.

- **Overload** is *working the body harder than you normally work it.* You increase the number of times you do an exercise.
- **Progression** is *the gradual increase in overload needed to meet higher levels of fitness.* An exercise gets easier as time goes by. You must add more or do it for a longer time.
- **Specificity** means that these are *certain exercises and activities that improve certain areas of fitness.* Aerobic activity will improve your heart and lung endurance.

Here are the three basic stages you need for each activity.

1. The **warm-up** is *an activity that gets the muscles ready for work.* Start with a fast walk. Then slowly stretch your large muscles. Begin your activity at a slow pace. Go faster after 5 minutes.
2. The **workout** is *the part of an exercise program when the activity is performed at its highest peak.* The workout **F.I.T.T.** formula is *frequency, intensity, time/ duration, and type of activity.*
   - **Frequency** is how often you will work out. You need to work out *more* than 3 times a week to *get* in shape. You need to work out *at least* 3 times a week to *stay* in shape.
   - **Intensity** is how hard you must work to reach overload. Start slowly. Work a little harder each time until you reach your goal.
   - **Time/duration** is the time you spend doing your activity. The goal is to work in your target heart range for 20 to 30 minutes.
   - **Type** means which activities you choose. Be sure to choose aerobic activities for 80 percent of your time. Choose anaerobic for the rest. Choose activities you like to do.

Reading Tutor, Lesson 3 *(continued)*

3. The **cool-down** is *an activity that gets the muscles ready to return to a resting state.* Start to slow down at the end of an activity. Go slower for about five minutes. Then stretch for about five minutes.

3. What are the three basic stages for each activity?

Monitoring Your Progress *(page 92)*

Keep a fitness journal to make sure you meet your goals. Write down the frequency, intensity, time, and type of each activity you do. Check your goals at the end of 12 weeks.

Resting heart rate is *the number of times your heart beats in one minute when you are not active.* A resting heart rate that is lower than 72 is good. It shows you have a good fitness level.

4. What is a resting heart rate?

USE WITH CHAPTER 4, PAGES 93–97.

Physical Activity for Life: Training and Safety for Physical Activities

Vocabulary

training program	A program of formalized physical preparation for involvement in a sport or another physical activity *(page 93)*
hydration	Taking in fluids so that the body functions properly *(page 94)*
anabolic steroids	Synthetic substances similar to the male hormone testosterone *(page 94)*
health screening	A search or check for diseases or disorders that an individual would otherwise not have knowledge of or seek help for *(page 95)*

Drawing from Experience

What type of physical activity do you like to do? What kind of safety gear do you need to wear or use? Do you need to prepare or train for your activity before you begin? Think about these things as you read Lesson 4.

In the last lesson, you learned about planning an activity program. In this lesson, you will learn about safety during physical activities.

Reading Tutor, Lesson 4 *(continued)*

USE WITH CHAPTER 4, PAGES 93–97.

Organizing Your Thoughts

Use the chart below to help you take notes as you read the summaries that follow. In the first box, list some of the ways to prepare and train for physical activity. In the other box, list some of the ways to lower your risk of injury.

Ways to Train	Safety Tips

Reading Tutor, Lesson 4 *(continued)*

USE WITH CHAPTER 4, PAGES 93–97.

Read to Learn

Read each passage carefully. Write in complete sentences to answer the following questions.

Training and Peak Performance *(pages 93–95)*

A **training program** is *formal physical preparation for a sport or physical activity.* Ask a teacher or coach to help you with your training goals. Here are some of the ways to prepare.

- Eat nutritious foods to build your energy. Stay hydrated. **Hydration** is *taking in fluids so that the body works properly.* Drink lots of water before, during, and after your activity.
- Get lots of sleep. Teens need 8–10 hours of sleep each night. You react more slowly and you have trouble paying attention when you do not get enough sleep.
- Avoid substances that can harm you. Stay away from tobacco, alcohol, and other drugs.
- Abstain from the use of **anabolic steroids.** These are *man-made substances that are like the male hormone testosterone.* They can cause cancer, heart disease, sterility, acne, violent behavior, and more. Some athletes take steroids to gain muscle and strength. It is not legal to use steroids in this way.
- Use nutrition supplements with care. The best way to get nutrients is in food. Take the right dose of vitamins. High doses or megadoses may harm you.

1. What are some of the ways to prepare or train for physical activity?

____

____

____

____

Safety First! *(pages 95–97)*

Here are some of the ways to lower your risk of injury while you are being active.

- Get a **health screening.** This is *a check for diseases or disorders that a person would otherwise not know of or seek help for.* It lets you know that you are fit and can begin your activity.
- Use the right safety gear.
- Be aware of who and what is near you.

Reading Tutor, Lesson 4 *(continued)*

USE WITH CHAPTER 4, PAGES 93–97.

- Play at your skill level. Know your limits.
- Warm up and cool down.
- Stay in the right area. Stay on a bike path if you are riding your bike.
- Obey all rules.
- Be a good sport.
- Tell an adult if you feel sick or get hurt.

Here are some of the ways to lower risk to your personal safety during your activity.

- Choose the right time and place.
- Be aware if you are alone.
- Use the park during the day.
- Wear reflective clothes at night.
- Wear a whistle. Use it if you need help.
- Be aware of the weather.

Here are some tips to help you use the right gear.

- Check your gear. Make sure it fits. Make sure it is in good condition.
- Wear a helmet when you bike. Wear a helmet, knee and elbow pads, gloves, and wrist guards when you skate or skateboard.
- Avoid riding at night. Use a headlight if you must ride at night. Use reflective tape. Wear light-colored clothes. Wear reflective patches.
- Males in contact sports should wear athletic cups. Females should wear sports bras.
- Wear comfortable clothes. Shoes should fit right and have arch support. Dress lightly when it is hot out. Wear layers when it is cold.

2. What are some of the ways to lower your risk of injury when you are being active?

____

____

____

____

____

Name Class Date

Lesson 5

Reading Tutor

USE WITH CHAPTER 4, PAGES 98–103.

Physical Activity for Life: Physical Activity Injuries

Vocabulary

overexertion	Overworking the body *(page 99)*
heat cramps	Muscle spasms that result from a loss of large amounts of salt and water through perspiration *(page 99)*
heatstroke	A condition in which the body loses the ability to rid itself of excessive heat through perspiration *(page 99)*
frostbite	A condition that results when body tissues become frozen *(page 100)*
hypothermia	A condition in which body temperature becomes dangerously low *(page 101)*
muscle cramp	A spasm or sudden tightening of a muscle *(page 102)*
strain	A condition resulting from damaging a muscle or tendon *(page 102)*
sprain	An injury to the ligament surrounding a joint *(page 102)*

Drawing from Experience

Have you ever felt sick when you were playing sports? Do you know what to do if you feel overheated? Do you wear sunscreen when you are outside? Have you ever had a muscle cramp? Do you know how to treat a sprain? Think about these things as you read Lesson 5.

In the last lesson, you learned about training and safety. In this lesson, you will learn about physical activity injuries and risks.

Reading Tutor, Lesson 5 *(continued)*

USE WITH CHAPTER 4, PAGES 98–103.

Organizing Your Thoughts

Use the chart below to help you take notes as you read the summaries that follow. In the first box, list some of the weather-related risks of outdoor activities. In the other box, list some of the minor and major types of sport- and physical- activity–related injuries.

Weather Related Risks	Types of Sport/Activity Injuries

Reading Tutor, Lesson 5 *(continued)*

USE WITH CHAPTER 4, PAGES 98–103.

Read to Learn

Read each passage carefully. Write in complete sentences to answer the following questions.

Weather-Related Risks *(pages 98–101)*

Be sure to drink water before, during, and after physical activity. Avoid outdoor activity when there is a smog alert. Here are some of the other types of hot weather health risks.

- **Overexertion** is *overworking the body*. Heat exhaustion is when overexertion causes the body to overheat. It may cause cold, clammy skin, dizziness, and nausea.
- **Heat cramps** are *muscle spasms that result from a loss of large amounts of salt and water by sweating*. Move to a cool place, lie down, and sip water.
- **Heatstroke** is *when the body loses the ability to get rid of excessive heat by perspiration*. This can cause hyperthermia. This is a sudden rise in body heat. Call for medical help right away. Move the person to a cool place. Sponge him or her with cool water.

Be sure to dress in three layers when it is cold. Wear a hat. Drink water. Warm up slowly. Here are some of the types of cold weather health risks.

- **Frostbite** occurs *when body tissues become frozen*. Your skin gets white and you lose feeling. You must seek medical help right away. Avoid this by dressing warmly and keeping ears, face, feet, and fingers covered. Get indoors. Warm the area with warm water.
- **Hypothermia** is *when body temperature becomes dangerously low*. The body cannot warm itself. The brain and body begin to shut down. Get medical help right away.

Be sure to protect your skin from the sun and wind. Sunburn is when the sun's UV rays burn the outer layers of the skin. It makes the skin red and it can cause blisters. This may lead to skin cancer. Here are some of the ways to protect your skin.

- Cover your body with clothes. Wear a hat with a brim.
- Use sunscreen and lip balm with a sun protection factor (SPF) of at least 15.
- Put on sunscreen 30 minutes before you go outside. Apply it again every two hours.
- Wear sunglasses. A cataract is a cloudy lens over the eye that sunlight may cause.

Reading Tutor, Lesson 5 *(continued)*

USE WITH CHAPTER 4, PAGES 98–103.

1. What are some of the health risks related to the weather?

____

____

____

____

____

Minor Injuries *(page 102)*

Warming up, cooling down, and stretching can help prevent muscle soreness. Here are some other types of minor injuries.

- A **muscle cramp** is *a spasm or sudden tightening of a muscle.* A drink of water may help.
- A **strain** is *a condition that results from hurting a muscle or tendon.*
- A **sprain** is *an injury to the ligament around a joint.* There may be pain and swelling. You may need medical help.

Treatment for minor strains and sprains may include the R.I.C.E. method.

- **R**est. Do not use the muscle or joint for a few days.
- **I**ce. Ice reduces pain and swelling. Ice for 20 minutes. Remove for 20 minutes. Ice again for 20 minutes. Repeat every three hours while you are awake. Do this for three days.
- **C**ompression. Use an elastic bandage to reduce swelling. Wrap lightly and loosen at night.
- **E**levation. Raise the area above the heart.

2. What are the parts of the R.I.C.E. method of treatment?

____

____

____

____

____

Reading Tutor, Lesson 5 *(continued)*

USE WITH CHAPTER 4, PAGES 98–103.

Major Injuries *(pages 102–103)*

Here are some of the more serious or major types of injuries.

- **Fractures and dislocations.** A fracture is a break in a bone. A dislocation is when a bone moves out of its normal place at a joint. You need to get medical help in both cases.
- **Tendonitis.** This is when tendons stretch or tear. A tendon is a band of fiber that connects muscles to bones. You must rest. You may need medicine or therapy from a doctor.
- **Concussions.** This is the result of a blow to the head. The brain swells. The person may be unconscious. This may lead to death. Other signs may be headache and dizziness. Get medical help right away.

3. What are some of the major types of sports injuries?

____

____

____

____

____

Nutrition and Your Health: Nutrition During the Teen Years

Vocabulary

nutrition	The process by which the body takes in and uses food *(page 110)*
calories	Units of heat that measure the energy used by the body and the energy that foods supply to the body *(page 110)*
nutrients	Substances in food that your body needs to grow, to repair itself, and to supply you with energy *(page 110)*
hunger	A natural physical drive that protects you from starvation *(page 111)*
appetite	A desire, rather than a need, to eat *(page 111)*

Drawing from Experience

What are some of the foods you eat most often? Do you choose healthy foods? What affects your food choices? Who influences what you eat? Think about these things as you read Lesson 1.

In the last chapter, you learned about having physical activity in your life. In this lesson, you will learn about good nutrition during your teen years.

Reading Tutor, Lesson 1 *(continued)*

USE WITH CHAPTER 5, PAGES 110–113.

Organizing Your Thoughts

Use the chart below to help you take notes as you read the summaries that follow. In the first box, list the things that good nutrition provides. In the other box, list some of the things that influence your food choices.

What Good Nutrition Provides	What Affects Your Food Choices

Reading Tutor, Lesson 1 *(continued)*

USE WITH CHAPTER 5, PAGES 110–113.

Read to Learn

Read each passage carefully. Write in complete sentences to answer the following questions.

The Importance of Good Nutrition *(page 110)*

Nutrition is *the process by which the body takes in and uses food*. Good nutrition provides your body with what it needs to be well and have energy. It provides calories and nutrients.

Calories are the *units of heat that measure the energy used by the body and the energy that foods supply to the body*. This energy provides fuel for all of your activities.

Nutrients are the *substances in food that your body needs to grow, to repair itself, and to supply you with energy*. You must make healthy food choices to get all the nutrients you need.

1. What does good nutrition provide for the body?

____

____

____

____

____

What Influences Your Food Choices? *(pages 111–112)*

Hunger is *a natural physical drive that protects you from starvation*. The nerves in your stomach send a signal to your brain that your body needs food. The nerves stop sending signals when you eat. **Appetite** is *a desire, rather than a need, to eat*.

Emotional needs may affect your eating habits. You may eat more when you feel stress or when you are bored. You may eat food as a reward. You might eat less when you are upset. You may not get all the nutrients you need.

Here are some of the ways that your environment can affect your food choices.

- **Family, friends, and peers.** You may eat some foods that your family likes to eat. You may try new foods that your friends like to eat.
- **Cultural and ethnic background.** You may like to eat some foods that are part of your ethnic background.

- **Ease and cost.** You may want to choose food that is easy to make. You may want to choose food that does not cost too much.
- **Advertising.** Ads may influence what kinds of food you buy. Be aware of any hidden messages in the ads. Make careful food choices.

2. What are some of the things that can influence your food choices?

____

____

____

____

____

Nutrition Throughout the Life Span *(page 113)*

It is important to eat well while you are a teen. Your teen years are a time of rapid growth. Healthy food will give you the nutrients that you need to grow. It will give you energy for sports and keep your mind alert. You will also look and feel your best.

A healthy and balanced diet will also keep you at a healthy weight. You can avoid obesity and type 2 diabetes. You also lower your risk for heart disease, stroke, some cancers, and osteoporosis.

3. What are some of the long-term benefits of having healthy eating habits when you are a teen?

____

____

____

____

____

USE WITH CHAPTER 5, PAGES 114–121.

Nutrition and Your Health: Nutrients

Vocabulary

carbohydrates	The starches and sugars present in foods *(page 114)*
fiber	An indigestible complex carbohydrate *(page 115)*
proteins	Nutrients that help build and maintain body cells and tissues *(page 116)*
lipid	A fatty substance that does not dissolve in water *(page 117)*
vitamins	Compounds that help regulate many vital body processes, including the digestion, absorption, and metabolism of other nutrients *(page 119)*
minerals	Substances that the body cannot manufacture but that are needed for forming healthy bones and teeth and for regulating many vital body processes *(page 120)*

Drawing from Experience

Do you take a daily vitamin? Do you drink lots of water? What kinds of food do you eat? What kind of meal do you think is a healthy meal? Think about these things as you read Lesson 2.

In the last lesson, you learned about the factors that can affect your food choices while you are a teen. In this lesson, you will learn about nutrients.

Name Class Date

Reading Tutor, Lesson 2 *(continued)*

USE WITH CHAPTER 5, PAGES 114–121.

Organizing Your Thoughts

Use the chart below to help you take notes as you read the summaries that follow. In each of the following boxes, list factors about the six types of nutrients.

Carbohydrates	**Proteins**
Fats	**Vitamins**
Minerals	**Water**

Reading Tutor, Lesson 2 *(continued)*

USE WITH CHAPTER 5, PAGES 114–121.

Read to Learn

Read each passage carefully. Write in complete sentences to answer the following questions.

Carbohydrates *(pages 114–115)*

Carbohydrates are *the starches and sugars in foods.* They give your body energy. They give your body four calories per gram. They should make up 55 to 60 percent of your daily calories.

Simple carbohydrates are sugars. Fructose is in fruit. It is in sugar cane and sugar beets. We make it into table sugar and add it to many foods. Lactose is in milk.

Complex carbohydrates are starches. They are in whole grains, seeds, and nuts. They are in peas, beans, and potatoes. The body turns them into simple carbohydrates to use as energy.

Your body turns carbohydrates into **glucose**. Your body stores glucose in your liver as **glycogen**. Your body will turn glucose into body fat when you have too much glycogen.

Fiber is *an indigestible complex carbohydrate.* It is in vegetables, fruits, and whole grains. It helps move waste in your digestive system. It may lower your risk of heart disease and diabetes.

1. What are simple and complex carbohydrates?

____

____

____

____

Proteins *(page 116)*

Proteins are *nutrients that help build and maintain body cells and tissues.* They are made of amino acids. There are 9 essential amino acids that you must get from the food you eat.

Complete proteins have all nine essential amino acids. Some good sources are fish, meat, and poultry. Others are eggs, milk, cheese, yogurt, and soybeans.

Incomplete proteins do not have all nine essential amino acids. Some sources are beans, peas, nuts, and whole grains. You can combine some of these to make a complete protein.

Proteins build new cells during major growth times like the teen years. Your body replaces old cells by making new ones from protein. Protein also makes enzymes, hormones, and antibodies. There are four calories of energy per gram. Extra protein turns into body fat.

2. What are complete and incomplete proteins?

____

____

____

____

Fats *(pages 117–118)*

Fats are a type of lipid. A **lipid** is *a fatty substance that does not dissolve in water*. There are nine calories of energy per fat gram. Fats are made of fatty acids. Essential fatty acids are fatty acids that the body cannot make.

A **saturated fatty acid** is solid at room temperature. Some sources are palm oil, coconut oil, beef, pork, egg yolks, and dairy foods. Too many of these fats can raise the risk of heart disease.

An **unsaturated fatty acid** is liquid at room temperature. Some sources are olive, canola, soybean, and corn oils. They may lower the risk of heart disease.

We need fats to move vitamins in the blood. Fats are a source of linoleic acid. This is an essential fatty acid that we need to grow and have healthy skin. Fats are high in calories. They can lead to obesity. They should only make up 20 to 30 percent of your daily calories.

Cholesterol is a waxy substance in the blood. It makes hormones and bile. Too much cholesterol builds up in your arteries. Limit your intake of egg yolks, meat, and dairy foods.

3. What are saturated and unsaturated fatty acids?

____

____

____

____

Vitamins *(pages 119–120)*

Vitamins are *compounds that help regulate many body processes. These include the digestion, absorption, and metabolism of other nutrients.*

Water-soluble vitamins dissolve in water and pass into the blood. The body does not store these vitamins. Some of these are vitamins C, B_1, B_2, niacin, B_6, folic acid, and B_{12}.

- **Vitamin C** protects against infection. It is in citrus fruits, cantaloupe, and broccoli.

- **Vitamin B1** turns glucose into energy or fat. It is in whole grains, liver, and nuts.
- **Vitamin B2** helps keep skin healthy. It is in milk, cheese, spinach, eggs, and liver.
- **Niacin** helps maintain all body systems. It is in milk, eggs, poultry, and beef.
- **Vitamin B6** helps with amino acid metabolism. It is in wheat bran, liver, and meat.
- **Folic acid** builds red blood cells. It is in nuts, orange juice, and green vegetables.
- **Vitamin B12** builds red blood cells and aids growth. It is in meat, fish, and dairy.

Fat-soluble vitamins are absorbed in fat. Your body stores them in your liver and kidneys. Too much of these can be toxic. Some of theses are vitamins A, D, E, and K.

- **Vitamin A** helps skin, teeth, bones, and eyes. It is in milk and other dairy foods, and green vegetables.
- **Vitamin D** helps develop bones and teeth. It is in fortified milk, eggs, cereal, and more.
- **Vitamin E** slows the effects of aging and aids red blood cells. It is in oils, fruit, and nuts.
- **Vitamin K** helps blood clot. It is in spinach, broccoli, eggs, liver, cabbage, and tomatoes.

4. What are water-soluble and fat-soluble vitamins?

____

____

____

____

____

Minerals *(page 120)*

Minerals are *substances that the body cannot make. Your body needs them for healthy bones and teeth and for many vital body processes*. Here are some of the types of minerals.

- **Calcium** builds bones and teeth. It is in dairy foods, leafy vegetables, and canned fish.

- **Phosphorous** helps with bones, teeth, and metabolism. It is in milk, dairy foods, fish, and more.
- **Magnesium** aids in bone growth and metabolism. It is in grains and dark leafy vegetables.
- **Iron** helps build red blood cells. It is in meat, shellfish, poultry, legumes, liver, and more.

5. What are some of the important types of minerals?

___

___

___

___

___

Water *(pages 120–121)*

Water is vital to your entire body. It moves other nutrients. It carries waste out of your body. It helps you digest food. It helps maintain your body heat. Drink at least eight cups of water or fluid every day. Avoid too much caffeine in coffee or soda.

6. How does water benefit your entire body?

___

___

___

___

___

USE WITH CHAPTER 5, PAGES 122–129.

Nutrition and Your Health: Guidelines for Healthful Eating

Vocabulary

Dietary Guidelines for Americans	A set of recommendations for healthful eating and active living *(page 122)*
Food Guide Pyramid	A guide for making healthful daily food choices *(page 123)*

Drawing from Experience

What is healthy eating? What do you know about the five food groups? Do you eat breakfast every day? Do you choose healthy snacks? Think about these things as you read Lesson 3.

In the last lesson, you learned about nutrients. In this lesson, you will learn about guidelines for healthy eating.

Reading Tutor, Lesson 3 *(continued)*

USE WITH CHAPTER 5, PAGES 122–129.

Organizing Your Thoughts

Use the chart below to help you take notes as you read the summaries that follow. In the first box, list ways you can aim for fitness. In the next box, list the guidelines that can help you build a healthy base. In the last box, list some of the sensible food choices.

Aim for Fitness	Build a Healthy Base	Choose Sensibly

Reading Tutor, Lesson 3 *(continued)*

USE WITH CHAPTER 5, PAGES 122–129.

Read to Learn

Read each passage carefully. Write in complete sentences to answer the following questions.

Dietary Guidelines for Americans *(page 122)*

The ***Dietary Guidelines for Americans*** is *a set of recommendations for healthful eating and active living*. It divides wellness into three areas. These are the ABCs of good health. The ABCs can help you stay fit and make balanced food choices.

1. What are the *Dietary Guidelines for Americans*?

A: Aim for Fitness *(page 123)*

Here are the guidelines to improve or maintain your fitness.

- **Aim for a healthy weight.** Ask your doctor to help you find the right weight for your height and age. Find out how to achieve and keep that weight.
- **Be physically active every day.** Do at least 60 minutes of physical activity every day.

2. What are the two guidelines to help you keep fit?

B: Build a Healthy Base *(pages 123–125)*

The **Food Guide Pyramid** is *a guide for making healthful daily food choices*. The following guidelines can help you build a healthy base or eating plan.

- **Make your food choices with care.** Eat the right number of daily servings.

Reading Tutor, Lesson 3 *(continued)*

USE WITH CHAPTER 5, PAGES 122–129.

- **Choose a variety of grains and whole grains.** Try whole-wheat bread, oatmeal, or brown rice.
- **Choose a variety of fruits and vegetables daily.** They give you vitamins and minerals.
- **Keep food safe to eat.** Cook food well. Use clean utensils. Wash your hands.
- **Use the Food Guide Pyramid to make your daily food choices.**
    - **Bread, Cereal, Rice, and Pasta Group (Grains Group).** Eat 6 to 11 servings.
    - **Vegetable Group.** Eat 3 to 5 servings.
    - **Fruit Group.** Eat 2 to 4 servings.
    - **Milk, Yogurt, and Cheese Group (Milk Group).** Eat 3 to 4 servings (teens); 2–3 servings (adults).
    - **Meat, Poultry, Fish, Dry Beans, Eggs, and Nuts Group (Meat and Beans Group).** Eat 2 to 3 servings.
    - **Fats, Oils, and Sweets.** Use very little.
- **Understand serving sizes.** A portion is how much of a food you eat in one meal.
    - **Grains Group.** 1 slice of bread. 1 tortilla. 1 cup cereal. 1/2 cup rice or pasta.
    - **Vegetable Group.** 1 cup raw leafy vegetables. 1/2 cup cooked or raw vegetables. 3/4 cup juice.
    - **Fruit Group.** 1 medium apple, orange, pear, or banana. 1/2 cup chopped, cooked, or canned fruit. 3/4 cup juice.
    - **Milk Group.** 1 cup milk or yogurt. 1.5 oz. natural cheese. 2 oz. processed cheese.
    - **Meat and Beans Group.** 2 to 3 oz. cooked lean meat, fish, or poultry. To equal 1 oz. of meat: 1/2 cup cooked beans or tofu. 1 egg. 2 tbsp. peanut butter. 1/3 cup nuts.

3. What are the six parts of the Food Guide Pyramid?

____

____

____

____

____

Reading Tutor, Lesson 3 *(continued)*

USE WITH CHAPTER 5, PAGES 122–129.

C: Choose Sensibly *(pages 125–127)*

Here are some guidelines to help you make healthy food choices.

- **Choose a diet that is low in fat and low in cholesterol.** You need some fat in your diet to stay healthy. Limit your fat to no more than 30 percent of daily calories.
- **Choose drinks and foods with less sugar.** Here are some ways to lower sugar intake.
  - Find hidden sugars on food labels. Some of these are corn syrup, honey, and sucrose.
  - Choose some foods with added sugar and some foods with less sugar.
  - Choose 100 percent fruit juice or water instead of regular soda.
  - Choose fresh fruit or canned fruit that is packed in water or juice.
- **Choose foods with less salt.** You need some sodium to be healthy. Here are some tips.
  - Read food labels to find out how much sodium is in food.
  - Use herbs and spices instead of salt. Do not add very much salt to your food.
  - Ask for foods that do not have salt when you eat in a restaurant.
  - Choose fruits and vegetables. They have very little salt.

4. What are some of the ways to make healthy food choices?

____

____

____

____

____

Healthful Eating Patterns *(pages 127–129)*

Variety, moderation, and balance are the basis of a healthy eating plan. Here are some tips.

- **Eat breakfast.** Your body needs energy when you wake up. You do better in school or at work when you eat a good breakfast. It helps you keep a healthy weight. Try these ideas.
  - Eat cereal or eggs. Try pizza or peanut butter on toast.
  - Drink citrus, fruit, or tomato juice. Have a serving of milk, yogurt, or cheese.

Reading Tutor, Lesson 3 *(continued)*

USE WITH CHAPTER 5, PAGES 122–129.

- **Eat healthy snacks.** Many snacks are full of fat, sugar, or salt. Here are some healthy ones.
  - 3 cups air-popped popcorn or 1 medium apple or 1/2 small bagel.
  - A frozen juice bar or 1 cup skim milk or 50 small pretzel sticks or 3 graham crackers.
- **Eat right when you eat out.** Use the Food Guide Pyramid when you eat out.
  - Order grilled, baked, or broiled foods. Ask for sauces on the side. Watch portion size.

5. What are some of the tips you can use to make a healthy eating plan?

___

___

___

___

___

USE WITH CHAPTER 5, PAGES 130–137.

Nutrition and Your Health: Food and Healthy Living

Vocabulary

food additives	Substances intentionally added to food to produce a desired effect *(page 131)*
food allergy	A condition in which the body's immune system reacts to substances in some foods *(page 133)*
food intolerance	A negative reaction to food or a part of food caused by a metabolic problem, such as the inability to digest parts of certain foods or food components *(page 134)*
foodborne illness	Food poisoning *(page 134)*
pasteurization	The process of treating a substance with heat to destroy or slow the growth of pathogens *(page 135)*
cross-contamination	The spreading of bacteria or other pathogens from one food to another *(page 136)*

Drawing from Experience

Have you ever read a food label? Do you know anyone who has a food allergy? Have you ever had a case of food poisoning? How can you prevent food illness? Think about these things as you read Lesson 4.

In the last lesson, you learned about guidelines for healthy eating. In this lesson, you will learn about food labels, food illness, and healthy living.

Reading Tutor, Lesson 4 *(continued)*

USE WITH CHAPTER 5, PAGES 130–137.

Organizing Your Thoughts

Use the chart below to help you take notes as you read the summaries that follow. In the first box, list some of the facts about nutrition and product labels. In the other box, list some of the facts about food allergies, food intolerances, and foodborne illness.

Nutrition and Product Labels	Food Sensitivities and Illness

Reading Tutor, Lesson 4 *(continued)*

USE WITH CHAPTER 5, PAGES 130–137.

Read to Learn

Read each passage carefully. Write in complete sentences to answer the following questions.

Nutrition Labeling *(pages 130–132)*

A Nutrition Facts panel lets you find out information about a food product. Here are some of the facts you will see on a label.

- Serving size and servings per container
- Calories and calories from fat
- Names and amounts of nutrients
- Percent Daily Value. This is how much of a nutrient in one serving adds to your total daily eating plan.

Food labels also list the ingredients that are in the food item. The label lists those with the most weight first. Some sugars may be separate on the list. Here are other facts about ingredients.

- **Food additives** are *substances that we add to food to make a desired effect.* They may add flavor or color. They may let the food last longer.
- **Aspartame** is a sweetener that does not have calories. It is often in diet drinks. **Olestra** is a fat replacer. It is often in potato chips to give them fewer calories from fat.

1. What are some of the facts that you may find on a product label?

____

____

____

____

____

Product Labeling *(pages 132–133)*

Here are some of the terms that might be on a product label.

- **Light or Lite.** This means there are one-third less calories or 50 percent less fat or sodium.
- **Less.** This means the food has 25 percent less of a nutrient or calories.
- **Free.** This means there is no amount of fat, cholesterol, sodium, sugar, or calories.
- **More.** This means the food has 10 percent more of the Daily Value for a vitamin, mineral, protein, or fiber.

Reading Tutor, Lesson 4 *(continued)*

- **High, Rich In,** or **Excellent Source Of.** This means the food has 20 percent more of the Daily Value for a vitamin, mineral, protein, or fiber.
- **Lean.** This refers to meat, poultry, fish, or shellfish that has less than 10 grams of total fat, less than 4 grams of saturated fat, and less than 95 mg of cholesterol per 3-ounce serving.

Open dates are on milk, canned goods, and meat labels. Here are some facts about open dates.

- **Expiration date.** This is the last day you should use the product.
- **Freshness date.** This is the last day a food is fresh.
- **Pack date.** This is the date the store packaged the food.
- **Sell-by date (or pull date).** This is the last day the store can sell the product. You can still use the product after the sell-by date.

2. What are some of the terms that you may find on a product label?

____

____

____

____

____

Food Sensitivities *(pages 133–134)*

A **food allergy** is *when the body's immune system reacts to substances in some foods.* The substances that cause allergies are called allergens. The body reacts to allergens as if they are germs. Some common food allergens are peanuts, eggs, wheat, soy, fish, and shellfish.

People with food allergies have reactions. These may be a rash, hives, itchy skin, vomiting, diarrhea, or stomach pain. They may include itchy eyes or sneezing. Call for medical help if someone has a serious reaction.

A food intolerance is *a negative reaction to a food caused by a metabolic problem, such as the inability to digest parts of certain foods.* It may be tied to certain foods like milk or wheat. It may be hereditary.

3. What are two types of food sensitivity?

____

____

____

____

____

Reading Tutor, Lesson 4 *(continued)*

USE WITH CHAPTER 5, PAGES 130–137.

Foodborne Illness *(pages 134–137)*

Foodborne illness is *food poisoning. Campylobacter, Salmonella,* and *E. coli* are some of the bacteria that contaminate food. Here are some of the ways that foods get germs.

- Food may pick up pathogens from a person who is sick.
- Animals may have disease in their tissues. Meat or milk that comes from a sick animal may make a person ill. **Pasteurization** *is the process of treating a substance with heat to destroy or slow the growth of pathogens.*

Some of the symptoms of foodborne illness are nausea, vomiting, diarrhea, and fever. Most people get well in one or two days. Older adults and young children may get very ill. Get medical help if someone is very ill or dehydrated.

Most foodborne illness occurs at home. Here are some of the ways to keep food safe.

- **Clean.** Wash your hands in hot soapy water before and after you handle food. Wash cutting boards, utensils, plates, and countertops to prevent cross-contamination. **Cross-contamination** is *the spreading of bacteria from one food to another.*
- **Separate.** Separate raw meat, seafood, and poultry from other foods. Use a separate cutting board. Wash countertops and your hands with hot soapy water after coming in contact with raw meats.
- **Cook.** Cook foods well. Use a meat thermometer to be sure you cook meats completely. Do not eat meat that is raw or still pink. Avoid eating raw eggs. Boil soups and gravy.
- **Chill.** Refrigerate or freeze food as soon as you get home from the store. Refrigerate or freeze leftover food within two hours after a meal.

4. What are some of the ways you can keep food safe?

Managing Weight and Body Composition: Maintaining a Healthy Weight

Vocabulary

body image	The way you see your body *(page 144)*
body mass index (BMI)	A ratio that allows you to assess your body size in relation to your height and weight *(page 145)*
overweight	A condition in which a person is heavier than the standard weight range for his or her height *(page 146)*
obesity	Having an excess amount of body fat *(page 146)*
underweight	A condition in which a person is less than the standard weight range for his or her height *(page 147)*
nutrient-dense foods	Foods that are high in nutrients as compared with their calorie content *(page 148)*

Drawing from Experience

How do you feel about the way you look? Do you know how much you weigh? How do you know if you are the right weight? Have you ever set goals to gain or lose weight? Think about these questions as you read Lesson 1.

In the last chapter, you learned about nutrition. In this lesson, you will learn about healthy ways to manage your weight.

Reading Tutor, Lesson 1 *(continued)*

USE WITH CHAPTER 6, PAGES 144–150.

Organizing Your Thoughts

Use the chart below to help you take notes as you read the summaries that follow. In the first box, list some of the factors about diet, body composition, and weight-related health risks. In the other box, list some of the healthy ways to manage your weight.

Factors About Weight and Health	Ways to Manage Your Weight

Reading Tutor, Lesson 1 *(continued)*

USE WITH CHAPTER 6, PAGES 144–150.

Read to Learn

Read each passage carefully. Write in complete sentences to answer the following questions.

The Weight-Calorie Connection *(pages 144–145)*

Your **body image** is *the way you see your body*. The media and your family and friends can affect your body image. Your feeling about your weight can also affect your body image.

You must burn the same number of calories that you eat to maintain a healthy weight. Carbohydrates and proteins have four calories per gram. Fats have nine calories per gram.

One pound of body fat equals about 3,500 calories. You will gain weight if you eat more calories than your body needs. You will lose weight if you eat fewer calories than your body needs. You may also lose weight if you burn more calories doing physical activity.

1. What is body image? How can you maintain a healthy weight?

___

___

___

___

Determining Your Appropriate Weight Range *(pages 145–146)*

Your age, height, gender, body frame, growth rate, and level of activity all affect your weight. **Body mass index (BMI)** is *a ratio that allows you to assess your body size in relation to your height and weight*. See the BMI charts on page 146 of your textbook.

Many ratios of height to weight can be healthy. Teens grow at different rates. There is no one size or shape that is normal for everyone.

2. What is the body mass index (BMI)?

___

___

___

___

Reading Tutor, Lesson 1 *(continued)*

USE WITH CHAPTER 6, PAGES 144–150.

Body Composition *(page 146)*

Body composition is the ratio of body fat to lean body tissue. A high-calorie diet can add to the amount of body fat. Weight lifting can add to the lean body tissue or muscle mass.

Overweight is *when a person is heavier than the standard weight range for his or her height*. **Obesity** is *having an excess amount of body fat*. Some athletes may be overweight because of their muscle mass. Being overweight or obese is usually a health risk.

3. What is obesity?

____

____

____

____

Weight-Related Health Risks *(pages 146–147)*

It is a risk to be overweight. Extra body fat strains the heart and the skeletal system. It can lead to high blood pressure and type 2 diabetes. Here are some ways to keep a healthy weight.

- **Aim for Fitness.** Get 60 minutes of physical activity every day.
- **Build a Healthy Base.** Follow the guidelines for daily servings from the Food Guide Pyramid.
- **Choose Sensibly.** Eat a balanced diet. Eat low-fat and low-sugar foods.

Underweight is *when a person is less than the standard weight range for his or her height*. Some teens are very thin while they are growing. Other persons may not be eating enough. Being too thin may lead to weakness and illness. Check with a doctor if you think you may be too thin.

4. What are the risks of being overweight or underweight?

____

____

____

____

Healthful Ways to Manage Weight *(pages 148–150)*

Here are some healthful ways to manage weight.

- **Figure out your appropriate weight.** Ask your doctor to help you.
- **Set realistic goals.** Gaining or losing one pound a week is a safe goal.

- **Personalize your plan.** Think about your likes and dislikes while you make your plan.
- **Put your goal and plan in writing.** Keep a list of what you eat.
- **Evaluate your progress.** Weigh yourself once a week at the same time of day.

The best weight-loss plan is to eat fewer calories and burn more calories. Here are some tips.

- **Eat 1,700 to 1,800 calories daily.** Eat the minimum servings from the Food Guide Pyramid.
- **Include your favorite foods.** Eat smaller portions. Eat them less often.
- **Eat low-calorie and nutrient-dense foods. Nutrient-dense foods** are *foods that are high in nutrients as compared with their calorie content.* Some are whole grains, vegetables, and fruits.
- **Drink lots of water.** Drink eight glasses a day.

Here are some ways to gain weight in a healthy way.

- **Increase your calorie intake.** Eat complex carbohydrates like bread, pasta, and potatoes.
- **Eat often. Take seconds.** Eat more than the minimum servings from the Food Guide Pyramid.
- **Eat nutritious snacks.** Snack two or three hours before meals.
- **Build muscle.** Gain weight by adding to your muscle mass.

Regular physical activity should be a part of your plan. Here are some benefits of being active.

- It burns calories and helps you lose fat. It adds muscle mass and gives you a lean body.
- It helps you deal with stress. It gives you a normal appetite.
- It builds your self-esteem and helps you stay on your plan.

5. What are some of the ways that you can manage your weight?

____

____

____

____

____

Name Class Date

Lesson 2 — Reading Tutor

USE WITH CHAPTER 6, PAGES 151–156.

Managing Weight and Body Composition: Fad Diets and Eating Disorders

Vocabulary

fad diets	Weight-loss plans that are popular for only a short time *(page 151)*
weight cycling	The repeated pattern of loss and regain of body weight *(page 152)*
eating disorder	An extreme, harmful eating behavior that can cause serious illness or even death *(page 153)*
anorexia nervosa	A disorder in which the irrational fear of becoming obese results in severe weight loss from self-imposed starvation *(page 154)*
bulimia nervosa	A disorder in which some form of purging or clearing of the digestive tract follows cycles of overeating *(page 154)*
binge eating disorder	A disorder characterized by compulsive overeating *(page 155)*

Drawing from Experience

What do you think when you hear the word diet? Do you know anyone who has an eating disorder? Where can you go to get help for a friend? Think about these questions as you read Lesson 2.

In the last lesson, you learned how to maintain a healthy weight. In this lesson, you will learn about fad diets and eating disorders.

Reading Tutor, Lesson 2 *(continued)*

Organizing Your Thoughts

Use the chart below to help you take notes as you read the summaries that follow. In the first box, list some of the risky kinds of weight-loss plans. In the other box, list some of the risks of eating disorders.

Risky Weight-Loss Plans	Risks of Eating Disorders

Reading Tutor, Lesson 2 *(continued)*

USE WITH CHAPTER 6, PAGES 151–156.

Read to Learn

Read each passage carefully. Write in complete sentences to answer the following questions.

Risky Weight-Loss Strategies *(pages 151–152)*

Fad diets are *weight-loss plans that are popular for only a short time.* They limit the variety of food you can eat. They are hard to stay on. Some cost a lot of money. A dieter who loses weight on a fad diet usually gains it back.

Liquid diets replace food with a liquid formula. They are very-low-calorie diets. They do not give the body enough energy. These diets can lead to serious health problems.

Fasting means to abstain from eating. Your body does not get the nutrients or energy it needs. Your body may become dehydrated. Fasting for religious reasons is for a short period and is usually not dangerous. Check with your doctor if you are not sure.

Diet pills take away your appetite. They may cause serious side effects such as a racing heart or dehydration. They may also be addictive.

1. What are some of the types of risky weight-loss plans?

____

____

____

____

Weight Cycling *(pages 152–153)*

Weight cycling is *the repeated pattern of loss and regain of body weight.* People who follow fad diets often lose weight and gain it back. Slow and steady weight loss is the best way to have results that last.

2. What is weight cycling?

____

____

____

____

The Risks of Eating Disorders *(pages 153–156)*

An **eating disorder** is *an extreme, harmful eating behavior that can cause serious illness or even death.* Teen girls and young women are most at risk. People with eating disorders need medical help.

Reading Tutor, Lesson 2 *(continued)*

USE WITH CHAPTER 6, PAGES 151–156.

Anorexia nervosa is *a disorder in which a person has a fear of being obese. It results in severe weight loss from starving oneself.* It relates to a person's self-concept. A person with anorexia eats very little food and exercises all the time. The person may deny he or she has an eating problem.

- Anorexia may cause a female to stop having her period. It may lead to loss of bone density, small body organs, heart trouble, and sudden death.

Bulimia nervosa is *a disorder in which some form of purging or clearing of the digestive tract follows cycles of overeating*. The person may diet and then binge or eat large amounts of food. The person vomits or takes a laxative after eating. The person diets again after the binge.

- Binge eating, purging, and fasting can cause serious health problems. It can lead to dehydration, kidney problems, tooth decay, harm to the esophagus, and more.

Binge eating disorder is *compulsive overeating*. The person eats huge amounts of food but does not try to purge. It may be a sign of using food to cope with problems.

- Binge eating disorder can cause weight gain, type 2 diabetes, heart disease, and stroke. It can lead to gallbladder problems and high blood pressure.

People with eating disorders need medical help and psychological counseling. Tell a trusted adult if you think a friend has an eating disorder. Be supportive. Urge your friend to get help.

3. What are some of the types of eating disorders?

____

____

____

____

____

Name Class Date

Lesson 3 Reading Tutor

USE WITH CHAPTER 6, PAGES 157–163.

Managing Weight and Body Composition: Nutrition for Individual Needs

Vocabulary

electrolytes	Minerals that help maintain the body's fluid balance *(page 158)*
rehydration	Restoring lost body fluids *(page 158)*
vegetarian	A person who eats mostly or only foods that come from plant sources *(page 159)*
vegan	A vegetarian who eats only foods of plant origin *(page 160)*
dietary supplement	A nonfood form of one or more nutrients *(page 161)*
megadose	A very large amount of a dietary supplement *(page 161)*
herbal supplement	A chemical substance from plants that may be sold as a dietary supplement *(page 161)*

Drawing from Experience

Do you play sports or do aerobics? What type of nutrition plan do you need? Do you know anyone who is a vegetarian? What do they eat? What kind of nutrition plan do older people need? Think about these questions as you read Lesson 3.

In the last lesson, you learned about eating disorders. In this lesson, you will learn about special kinds of nutrition needs.

Reading Tutor, Lesson 3 *(continued)*

USE WITH CHAPTER 6, PAGES 157–163.

Organizing Your Thoughts

Use the chart below to help you take notes as you read the summaries that follow. In the first box, list some of the tips for sports nutrition. In the next box, list some of the facts about nutrition for vegetarians. In the last box, list some of the pros and cons of using dietary supplements.

Sports Nutrition	Vegetarian Nutrition	Pros/Cons of Dietary Supplements

Reading Tutor, Lesson 3 *(continued)*

USE WITH CHAPTER 6, PAGES 157–163.

Read to Learn

Read each passage carefully. Write in complete sentences to answer the following questions.

Performance Nutrition *(pages 157–159)*

Training diets for athletes must have a balance of nutrients. Your body needs protein, vitamins, and minerals. Athletes burn lots of calories. Athletes use large amounts of fluid.

- Eat more nutrient-dense foods. Eat more calories to maintain weight and build energy.
- Drink lots of water before, during, and after a workout. **Electrolytes** are *minerals that help keep the body's fluids in balance*. An imbalance of fluids can lead to dehydration and heatstroke. **Rehydration** means *restoring lost body fluids*.

Athletes must be a certain weight to wrestle or box. Be sure to compete at the right weight.

- Follow a sensible plan if you need to lose weight. Fasting or dieting before a weigh-in can cause dehydration and harm your health.
- Follow a balanced plan of nutrition and exercise to gain weight. Using steroids is not a healthy way to gain weight. It is not legal to use them for this purpose.
- Eat three to four hours before you compete. Choose carbohydrates such as pasta, rice, vegetables, bread, and fruit. Drink lots of water before, during, and after a workout.

1. What are some of the tips to follow for good sports nutrition?

____

____

____

Vegetarianism *(pages 159–161)*

A **vegetarian** is *a person who eats mostly or only plant foods*. People make this choice for various reasons. Here are some vegetarian eating plans.

- A **lacto-ovo** vegetarian eats dairy foods, eggs, and foods from plant sources.
- A **lacto** vegetarian eats dairy foods and foods from plant sources.
- An **ovo** vegetarian eats eggs and foods from plant sources. Soy milk and soy cheese substitute for dairy foods.
- A **vegan** eats foods from plant sources only. Soy milk and soy cheese substitute for dairy.

Vegetarians need to eat more than one incomplete protein to get complete proteins each day. They must get enough of the nutrients that other people get from animal products. They can eat fruits, vegetables, leafy greens, whole grains, nuts, seeds, dairy foods, and eggs to get these nutrients.

- **Vegans** are *vegetarians who eat only plant foods.* They do not eat meat or dairy foods. They must get vitamin D, B_{12}, and calcium from other sources.

2. What are the four types of vegetarian eating plans?

____

____

____

____

Dietary Supplements *(page 161)*

A **dietary supplement** is a *nonfood form of one or more nutrients.* It may be vitamins, minerals, fiber, protein, or herbs. Eating healthy meals from the Food Guide Pyramid will give you all the nutrients you need. You may need to take some vitamins if there are foods that you cannot eat. A doctor may suggest other supplements such as calcium for a vegan.

A **megadose** is *a very large amount of a dietary supplement.* It can be dangerous. An **herbal supplement** is *a chemical from plants that stores may sell as a dietary supplement.* Some of these supplements may also be dangerous. Check with your doctor before you take them.

3. What is a dietary supplement?

____

____

____

____

Nutrition Throughout the Life Span *(pages 162–163)*

Most people can get all the calories and nutrients they need by following the *Dietary Guidelines for Americans* and the Food Guide Pyramid. People may have other needs at some stages of life.

Here are some nutrients a pregnant female may need to take.

- **Folate.** A fetus needs folate or folic acid to avoid spinal defects. It is a B vitamin that is in fruits, dark green leafy vegetables, and grains.

Reading Tutor, Lesson 3 *(continued)*

USE WITH CHAPTER 6, PAGES 157–163.

- **Iron.** This is in meat, poultry, fish, green vegetables, and grains. It helps build blood cells.
- **Calcium.** This helps build the bones and teeth of the fetus. It is in dairy foods, dark green leafy vegetables, canned fish, and juices.

Here are some facts about nutrients a baby or child may need.

- Breast milk is the best food for a baby. Formula will also give the nutrients a baby needs.
- Add cereal grains, vegetables, fruits, and then meats to the baby's diet in the first year.
- A child can begin to drink whole milk instead of formula or breast milk after the first year.
- A child can drink low-fat or nonfat milk after the second year.

Here are some facts about nutrients that older adults may need.

- Most older adults get all the nutrients they need by following the Food Guide Pyramid.
- Some older adults may need a special diet if they have a health problem.
- A doctor may suggest that an older adult take a supplement if he or she cannot eat some foods.

4. What are some of the nutrients a pregnant female may need to take?

____

____

____

____

Name Class Date

CHAPTER 7
Lesson 1

Reading Tutor

USE WITH CHAPTER 7, PAGES 170–177.

Achieving Good Mental Health: Your Mental and Emotional Health

Vocabulary

mental/ emotional health	The ability to accept yourself and others, adapt to and manage emotions, and deal with the demands and challenges you meet in life *(page 170)*
hierarchy of needs	A ranked list of needs essential to human growth and development, presented in ascending order starting with basic needs and building toward the need for reaching your highest potential *(page 172)*
self-actualization	The striving to become the best you can be *(page 174)*
personality	A complex set of characteristics that makes you unique *(page 175)*
modeling	Observing and learning from behaviors of those around you *(page 175)*

Drawing from Experience

Are you a happy person? Do you have a good attitude? What are some of the things you need in life? What are some of the things that make you different from others? Think about these questions as you read Lesson 1.

In the last chapter, you learned how to manage your weight. In this lesson, you will learn about your mental and emotional health.

Reading Tutor, Lesson 1 *(continued)*

USE WITH CHAPTER 7, PAGES 170–177.

Organizing Your Thoughts

Use the chart below to help you take notes as you read the summaries that follow. In the first box, list some of the traits of good mental health. In the next box, list some of the types of human needs. In the last box, list some of the things that affect your personality.

Good Mental Health Traits	Types of Needs	What Affects Your Personality

Reading Tutor, Lesson 1 *(continued)*

USE WITH CHAPTER 7, PAGES 170–177.

Read to Learn

Read each passage carefully. Write in complete sentences to answer the following questions.

The Characteristics of Good Mental/Emotional Health *(pages 170–171)*

Mental/emotional health is *the ability to accept yourself and others, adapt to and manage emotions, and deal with the demands and challenges you meet in life.* Here are some of the traits of good mental/emotional health.

- **Positive self-esteem.** This helps you accept new challenges and take failure in stride.
- **Sense of belonging.** Being close to family and friends gives comfort and stability.
- **Sense of purpose.** This helps you set and meet your goals.
- **Positive outlook.** This lessens your stress. It gives you more energy.
- **Autonomy.** Your ability to make good decisions lets you take care of yourself.

Here are some signs of good mental/emotional health in teens.

- They know their strengths and weaknesses.
- They are responsible for their own actions.
- They avoid the use of tobacco, alcohol, and other drugs.
- They are fair and can see both sides of an issue.
- They respect their own needs and the needs of others.

1. What are some of the traits of good mental/emotional health?

____

____

____

____

A Pyramid of Needs *(pages 172–174)*

The **hierarchy of needs** is *a list of needs for human growth and development, in order, starting with basic needs and building up to the need for reaching your highest potential.*

- **Level 1–Physical needs.** This is the need to satisfy hunger, thirst, sleep, and shelter.
- **Level 2–Safety needs.** This is the need to be and feel secure from danger.

Reading Tutor, Lesson 1 *(continued)*

USE WITH CHAPTER 7, PAGES 170–177.

- **Level 3–The need to love and belong.** This is the need to love and to have others love you. It is the need to belong to a family or a group of friends.
- **Level 4–The need to be valued and recognized.** This is the need to feel appreciated by family, friends, and peers.
- **Level 5–The need to reach your potential.** This is **self-actualization**, or *striving to become the best you can be*. It means making changes in your life to reach your goals.

2. What are the five levels of needs?

____

____

____

____

____

Meeting Your Needs *(page 174)*

The way you choose to meet your needs affects your mental and emotional health. Having respectful friendships will help meet your need for love. Here are some risky actions to avoid.

- Some teens may join a gang to meet the need to belong. This can lead to physical harm and trouble with the law.
- Some teens may engage in sexual activity to meet the need to feel love. This can lead to unplanned pregnancy, sexually transmitted diseases, and loss of self-respect.

Practice abstinence. Find healthy ways to meet your emotional needs. This will help you have good mental health.

3. How might the ways you choose to meet your needs affect your mental and emotional health?

____

____

____

____

____

Understanding Your Personality *(pages 175–177)*

Your **personality** is *a set of traits that makes you unique*. It makes you different from others. It affects the way you choose to meet your needs. It is your attitude, thoughts, and behaviors. Here are some of the factors that influence your personality.

- **Heredity.** You inherit some of your traits from your parents. Heredity may affect how smart you are or the way you react to events. It may affect athletic or artistic talent.
- **Environment.** This is everything that is around you in your life. It is family and friends and where you live. **Modeling** is *observing and learning from the actions of those around you*. You learn values from your role models and they help shape the person you are.
- **Behavior.** You have control over the way you act. You have control over how smart you become or what you do. Your choices will affect your mental and emotional health.

4. What are some of the factors that have an influence on your personality?

___

___

___

___

Promoting Mental/Emotional Health *(page 177)*

Choose actions that will promote good mental and emotional health. Meet your needs in healthy ways. Avoid gangs and sexual activity to protect your physical health. Deal with your emotions and cope with stress. Good mental and emotional health can make all three sides of your health triangle strong.

5. What are some of the ways that you can promote good mental and emotional health?

___

___

___

___

Name Class Date

Lesson 2 — Reading Tutor

USE WITH CHAPTER 7, PAGES 178–183.

Achieving Good Mental Health: Developing a Positive Identity

Vocabulary

personal identity	Your sense of yourself as a unique individual *(page 178)*
developmental assets	Building blocks of development that help young people grow up as healthy, caring, and responsible individuals *(page 179)*
constructive criticism	Nonhostile comments that point out problems and encourage improvement *(page 183)*

Drawing from Experience

What are some of the things you like to do? How do you use your talents? What are some of the assets you have that help you make healthy decisions? Do you have good self-esteem? Think about these questions as you read Lesson 2.

In the last lesson, you learned about your mental and emotional health. In this lesson, you will learn about having a positive identity.

Reading Tutor, Lesson 2 *(continued)*

USE WITH CHAPTER 7, PAGES 178–183.

Organizing Your Thoughts

Use the chart below to help you take notes as you read the summaries that follow. In the first box, list some of the kinds of developmental assets. In the other box, list some of the ways to work toward a healthy identity and self-esteem.

Developmental Assets	Ways to Achieve a Healthy Identity

Reading Tutor, Lesson 2 *(continued)*

USE WITH CHAPTER 7, PAGES 178–183.

Read to Learn

Read each passage carefully. Write in complete sentences to answer the following questions.

Your Personal Identity *(page 178)*

Your **personal identity** is *your sense of yourself as a unique person*. Here are some of the parts of your own identity.

- Your name and age
- Your role as a son or daughter or brother or sister or student
- Your interests
- Your likes and dislikes
- Your talents and abilities
- Your values and beliefs
- Your goals

1. What are some of the elements that make up your personal identity?

___

___

___

___

___

Your Developmental Assets *(pages 179–180)*

Developmental assets are *the building blocks of development that help young people grow up as healthy, caring, and responsible persons*. Here are some of these assets.

- **Support.** Family support. Positive family communication. Relations with other adults. A caring neighborhood. A caring school climate. Parent involvement in school.
- **Empowerment.** Be valued by adults. Serve a role in the community. Feel safe at home, at school, and in the neighborhood.
- **Boundaries and expectations.** Family rules and consequences. School rules. Neighborhood rules. Adult role models. Positive peer influences. High standards.
- **Good use of time.** Creative activities. Youth programs. Time at home. Sports.
- **Commitment to learning.** Be motivated to do well. Be involved at school. Do homework. Read for pleasure.

Reading Tutor, Lesson 2 *(continued)*

USE WITH CHAPTER 7, PAGES 178–183.

- **Positive values.** Compassion. Equality and social justice. Integrity. Honesty. Responsibility. Self-control.
- **Social skills.** Planning and decision making. Communication skills. Tolerance of other cultures. Refusal skills. Conflict-resolution skills.
- **Positive identity.** Personal power. Self-esteem. Sense of purpose. Positive view of the future.

2. What are some of the assets that can help you grow up to be a healthy person?

____

____

____

____

____

Working Toward a Healthy Identity *(pages 180–182)*

Here are some ways to strengthen your assets and build a healthy identity.

- **Know your strengths and weaknesses.** Feel proud of your talents and the things you do well. Set goals to improve the things you need to work on.
- **Show positive values.** Show honesty by not cheating on tests. Show caring by comforting a sad friend. Make sure that your behavior reflects your values.
- **Have a purpose in your life.** Set goals. Work to meet your goals.
- **Form healthy relationships.** Family and friends share feelings and good times with you. They give you a support system. They give you a sense of belonging.
- **Give to your community.** Giving is a part of being a good citizen. You might help a neighbor. You might help clean up the area. It helps others and makes you feel good.
- **Avoid unhealthy risk behaviors.** Healthy risk-taking can build you up. This might be participating in sports, traveling, or meeting someone new. Unhealthy risk-taking is dangerous. It is using tobacco, alcohol, or other drugs. It is reckless driving or being in a gang. Refuse to act this way.

Reading Tutor, Lesson 2 *(continued)*

USE WITH CHAPTER 7, PAGES 178–183.

3. What are some of the ways that you can build a healthy identity?

____

____

____

____

____

Self-Esteem and Positive Outlook *(pages 182–183)*

Self-esteem comes from knowing that you have value. People with a positive outlook live longer. They are mentally and physically healthier. Here are some tips for you to follow.

- Look at events realistically. A bad grade does not mean that you will always fail. It means you were not ready for the test. You will study hard and do better next time.
- **Constructive criticism** is *helpful comments that point out problems and urge you to do better*. It can help you look at things from a different point of view.
- Listen to your self-talk. Tell yourself that all people make mistakes. Learn from yours and move on. Tell yourself, "Good job!"

4. What are some of the tips you can use to build your self-esteem and positive outlook?

____

____

____

____

____

Name Class Date

Lesson 3

USE WITH CHAPTER 7, PAGES 184–187.

Achieving Good Mental Health: Understanding Emotions

Vocabulary

emotions	Signals that tell your mind and body how to react *(page 184)*
hormone	A chemical substance that is produced in glands and helps regulate many of your body's functions *(page 185)*
empathy	The ability to imagine and understand how someone else feels *(page 186)*
hostility	The intentional use of unfriendly or offensive behavior *(page 187)*

Drawing from Experience

What does it mean when people smile at you? Are they happy? Are they sad? Do you ever feel fear or anger? Which emotions do you feel most often? What can you do if a friend is feeling really sad? Think about these questions as you read Lesson 3.

In the last lesson, you learned about having a positive identity. In this lesson, you will learn about your emotions.

Reading Tutor, Lesson 3 *(continued)*

USE WITH CHAPTER 7, PAGES 184–187.

Organizing Your Thoughts

Use the chart below to help you take notes as you read the summaries that follow. In the first box, list some ways to understand your emotions. In the other box, list some of the ways to identify your emotions.

Understand Your Emotions	Ways to Identify Your Emotions

Reading Tutor, Lesson 3 *(continued)*

USE WITH CHAPTER 7, PAGES 184–187.

Read to Learn

Read each passage carefully. Write in complete sentences to answer the following questions.

Understanding Your Emotions *(pages 184–185)*

Emotions are *signals that tell your mind and body how to react.* You may show emotions or feelings with words, actions, or facial expressions. Emotions can affect all sides of your health triangle.

- Joy can make you have a sense of well-being. It is good for your mental/emotional health. Joy also makes you fun to be with. It is good for your social health.
- Fear can affect your physical health. It can trigger the "fight-or-flight" response. This makes your heart beat faster and your muscles get tight.
- Anger may cause physical and mental reactions. It can make your heart rate go up. You may lash out at others. It can cause you and others to feel distress.

1. What are emotions?

____

____

____

____

Identifying Your Emotions *(pages 185–187)*

Sometimes you do not know why you feel a certain way. Puberty and hormones cause some emotions. A **hormone** is *a chemical from your glands that regulates the activities of different body cells.* They may cause mood swings and mixed emotions. Here are some facts to help you identify your emotions.

- **Happiness.** You feel pleased, good, or positive. You may also feel energy or creativity.
- **Sadness.** You feel disappointed or you feel a loss. The feeling may be mild or it may last a long time. You may feel discouraged and have no energy.
- **Love.** You feel affection, concern, and respect. You can use words, actions, or good deeds to show your love.
- **Empathy. Empathy** is *the ability to imagine and understand how someone else feels.* You listen to others and show that you care. It makes your friendships strong.

Reading Tutor, Lesson 3 *(continued)*

USE WITH CHAPTER 7, PAGES 184–187.

- **Fear.** You feel startled or on alert. A phobia is an exaggerated fear. It can keep a person from leading a normal life. A doctor may be able to help.
- **Guilt.** You may feel guilt when you have acted against your values. It can help you make positive changes in your life. Some teens feel guilty for things they have no control over. Be able to figure out what you have control over and what is not your fault.
- **Anger.** You feel this reaction when you are emotionally or physically hurt. **Hostility** is *the use of unfriendly or offensive behavior.* Violence is not good for you or others. Know what causes your anger and learn to deal with it in a positive way.

2. What are some of the facts to help you identify your emotions?

____

____

____

____

USE WITH CHAPTER 7, PAGES 188–191.

Achieving Good Mental Health: Managing Emotions

Vocabulary

defense mechanisms	Mental processes that protect individuals from strong or stressful emotions and situations *(page 189)*
suppression	Holding back or restraining *(page 189)*

Drawing from Experience

What are some of the ways you deal with your feelings? How do you handle fear? Are you able to manage your anger? Do you ever hold your feelings inside? Think about these questions as you read Lesson 4.

In the last lesson, you learned about your emotions. In this lesson, you will learn how to manage your emotions.

Reading Tutor, Lesson 4 *(continued)*

USE WITH CHAPTER 7, PAGES 188–191.

Organizing Your Thoughts

Use the chart below to help you take notes as you read the summaries that follow. In the first box, list some of the positive ways to deal with your emotions. In the other box, list some of the ways to manage difficult emotions.

Positive Ways to Deal with Emotions	Ways to Manage Difficult Emotions

Read to Learn

Read each passage carefully. Write in complete sentences to answer the following questions.

Dealing with Emotions in Positive Ways *(pages 188–189)*

Feelings are not good or bad. How you deal with them is what can affect your health. Some people talk about and share their emotions. Others keep their feelings private. Here are some ways to respond to your emotions.

- Think about your emotion. Ask yourself what it is that you are reacting to. Ask yourself if your emotion is appropriate for the situation.
- Think about the situation. Is it something that will still matter next week?
- Do not take action until you think about all the consequences of your action.
- Get rid of your negative feelings by doing physical activity or talking to a friend.
- Seek help from a parent or adult if your feeling does not go away.

1. What are some of the ways that you can deal with your emotions in a positive way?

____

____

____

____

____

Managing Difficult Emotions *(pages 189–191)*

You can learn to manage strong emotions. Take slow, deep breaths. Relax. Walk away from the situation. Write your feelings in a journal. Talk to family or friends. Here are some other ways to deal with your emotions.

- **Defense mechanisms.** These are *mental processes that protect individuals from strong or stressful emotions and situations*. Here are some of the common types.
  - **Repression.** This is pushing bad feelings out of your mind. You don't know you're doing it.
  - **Suppression** means *holding back or restraining*. This is intentionally pushing bad feelings out of your mind.
  - **Rationalization.** This is making excuses rather than taking responsibility for your actions.

Reading Tutor, Lesson 4 *(continued)*

USE WITH CHAPTER 7, PAGES 188–191.

- **Regression.** This is acting like you did when you were younger rather than acting in a mature way.
- **Denial.** This is when you do not want to believe something that is obvious to others.
- **Compensation.** This is making up for something by gift-giving, hard work, or effort.
- **Projection.** This is believing that other people or groups feel the same way you do.
- **Idealization.** This is seeing someone else as perfect, ideal, or more worthy than you are.

- **Handling fear.** You must identify your fear to overcome your fear. Think about what causes the fear. Talk to someone else about your fear. Some fear is normal. Fear is a problem when there is no basis for it.
- **Dealing with guilt.** Try to figure out why you feel guilty. Make up with someone you may have hurt. Learn from your mistake and be more careful. Talk to family or friends to help you feel better. Some things are not your fault. You should not feel guilty for them.
- **Managing anger.** Anger can be a very hard emotion to deal with. You need to figure out what made you angry. Here are some ways to manage anger.
- Do something to relax.
- Direct your energy to something else.
- Talk to someone you trust.
- Get some physical activity.

2. What are some of the ways that you can deal with difficult emotions?

___

___

___

___

___

Name Class Date

CHAPTER 8
Lesson 1

Reading Tutor

USE WITH CHAPTER 8, PAGES 198–204.

Managing Stress and Anxiety: Effects of Stress

Vocabulary

stress	The reaction of the body and mind to everyday challenges and demands *(page 198)*
perception	The act of becoming aware through the senses *(page 198)*
stressor	Anything that causes stress *(page 199)*
psychosomatic response	A physical reaction that results from stress rather than from an injury or illness *(page 202)*
chronic stress	Stress associated with long-term problems that are beyond a person's control *(page 204)*

Drawing from Experience

Have you ever felt "stressed out"? What made you feel that way? What did you do to feel better? Could you have done something to prevent the stress? Think about these questions as you read Lesson 1.

In the last chapter, you learned how to achieve good mental health. In this lesson, you will learn about the causes and effects of stress.

Reading Tutor, Lesson 1 *(continued)*

USE WITH CHAPTER 8, PAGES 198–204.

Organizing Your Thoughts

Use the chart below to help you take notes as you read the summaries that follow. In the first box, list some of the causes of stress. In the next box, list the three stages of the body's response to stress. In the last box, list the effects of stress on all the parts of your health triangle.

Causes of Stress	The Body's Response	Effects of Stress

Reading Tutor, Lesson 1 *(continued)*

USE WITH CHAPTER 8, PAGES 198–204.

Read to Learn

Read each passage carefully. Write in complete sentences to answer the following questions.

Stress in Your Life *(page 198)*

Stress is *the reaction of the body and mind to everyday challenges and demands.* You may feel stress when you are running late or taking a test. You may feel stress when you are playing in a key game or arguing with a friend. It is important to deal with stress in a healthy way.

Perception is *the act of becoming aware through the senses.* One way to deal with stress is to change how you perceive what causes your stress. Try not to make something worse than it is.

1. What is stress?

____

____

____

____

Reacting to Stress *(page 199)*

Stress is not good or bad. It can have a positive effect. It can motivate you to do well. It can give you extra energy to reach your goals. You may play better when you are in a stressful game. Stress can also have a negative effect. You may lose sleep after you argue with a friend. You may be so worried about a test that you do not do well.

2. What are some of the ways that we react to stress?

____

____

____

____

What Causes Stress? *(page 199)*

A **stressor** is *anything that causes stress.* There are five general areas of stress.

- **Biological stressors.** These may be illness, disability, or injury.
- **Environmental stressors.** These may be poverty, pollution, crowds, noise, or disasters.

Reading Tutor, Lesson 1 *(continued)*

USE WITH CHAPTER 8, PAGES 198–204.

- **Thinking stressors.** These may be the way you perceive a situation or how it affects you.
- **Personal behavior stressors.** These may be using from tobacco, alcohol, or other drugs.
- **Life situation stressors.** These may be the death of a pet, the divorce of parents, or trouble with your peers.

3. What are some of the causes of stress?

____

____

____

____

The Body's Stress Response *(pages 200–201)*

The nervous system and the endocrine system are active in the body's response to stress. This is automatic. Here are the three stages of response.

Alarm is the first stage. Here are the stages of the "fight-or-flight" response.

1. The brain receives danger signals. The hypothalamus acts on the pituitary gland.
2. The pituitary gland sends out a hormone that acts on the adrenal glands.
3. The adrenal glands make adrenaline. This hormone prepares the body to respond to a stressor.
   - Your pupils dilate. You begin to sweat.
   - Your heart rate and pulse are faster. Your blood pressure rises.
   - You breathe faster. Less blood flows to internal organs and skin.
   - More blood flows to muscles and the brain. Muscle tension increases.
   - Blood sugar, fats, and cholesterol are released in the body.

Resistance is the next stage. Here is what happens during this stage.

- Your body can perform at a higher level of endurance for a short while.
- Your ability to fight or attack is greater.
- You can run faster and farther than usual.

Fatigue is the third stage. Here is what happens when the stress occurs over time.

- **Physical fatigue** is when the muscles work hard for long periods.
- **Psychological fatigue** comes from worry, overwork, depression, or feeling overwhelmed.
- **Pathological fatigue** is tiredness from overworking the body's disease defenses.

Reading Tutor, Lesson 1 *(continued)*

USE WITH CHAPTER 8, PAGES 198–204.

4. What are the three stages of the body's stress response?

____

____

____

____

____

Stress and Your Health *(pages 202–203)*

Stress can affect all of the parts of your health triangle.

1. **Physical effects. A psychosomatic response** is *a physical reaction that results from stress rather than from an injury or illness*. Here are some stress-related health problems.
   - **Headache.** Many headaches relate to tension. Muscles in the head and neck get tight. Stress may also trigger migraine headaches.
   - **Asthma.** Stress can trigger an asthma attack. The bronchioles constrict. The person may cough and wheeze or fight to get air.
   - **High blood pressure.** Stress can increase cholesterol levels. It can block arteries.
   - **Weak immune system.** You may be prone to more colds or flu.
2. **Mental/emotional and social effects.** Stress can affect daily activity and relationships with others. Here are some effects.
   - **Difficulty paying attention.** It is hard to focus. You may feel that you will fail.
   - **Mood swings.** Teens may have more mood swings. This may strain relationships.
   - **Risk of substance abuse.** Some people say stress is the reason they started smoking or drinking. Substance use actually increases stress.

5. What are some of the ways that stress affects your health?

____

____

____

____

____

Reading Tutor, Lesson 1 *(continued)*

USE WITH CHAPTER 8, PAGES 198–204.

Taking Control of Chronic Stress *(page 204)*

Chronic stress is *stress associated with long-term problems that are beyond a person's control.* It can cause upset stomach, headache, trouble sleeping, and anxiety. Here are some of the ways to deal with the effects of stress.

- **Engage in physical activity.** Physical activity helps calm you down.
- **Look for support among your friends and family.** Talk about what is bothering you.
- **Find a hobby or activity that relaxes you.** Learn something new.
- **Avoid using tobacco, alcohol, or other drugs.** Use of these substances can lead to addiction.

6. What are some of the ways that you can deal with chronic stress?

____

____

____

____

____

Managing Stress and Anxiety: Managing Stress

Vocabulary

stress-management skills	Skills that help an individual handle stress in a healthful, effective way *(page 208)*
relaxation response	A state of calm that can be reached if one or more relaxation techniques are practiced regularly *(page 209)*

Drawing from Experience

Do you get nervous when you must take an exam? What are the things that give you stress? When do you feel that you need to relax? How do you think healthy behavior might lower your level of stress? Think about these questions as you read Lesson 2.

In the last lesson, you learned about the effects of stress. In this lesson, you will learn about managing stress.

Reading Tutor, Lesson 2 *(continued)*

USE WITH CHAPTER 8, PAGES 205–209.

Organizing Your Thoughts

Use the chart below to help you take notes as you read the summaries that follow. In the first box, list some of the things that help you identify causes of stress. In the next box, list some of the ways you can avoid and manage stress. In the last box, list some stress-management skills.

Ways to Identify Stress	Ways to Avoid and Manage Stress	Stress-Management Skills

Reading Tutor, Lesson 2 *(continued)*

USE WITH CHAPTER 8, PAGES 205–209.

Read to Learn

Read each passage carefully. Write in complete sentences to answer the following questions.

Identifying Personal Causes of Stress *(page 205)*

It is important to figure out the source of your stress. Here are some stressors.

- **Life events.** These may be getting a driver's license, graduation, moving, new family members, illness, or parents' divorce.
- **Physical stressors.** These may be pollution, noise, injury, lack of rest, drug use, or too much dieting.
- **Daily hassles.** These may be time pressures, too many responsibilities, deadlines, and conflicts.

1. What are some of the things that may trigger your stress?

Avoiding Stress with Refusal Skills *(page 206)*

You may be able to avoid some stress. Walk away from a tense situation. Calm down. Say no when it is necessary to avoid stress, conflict, or threat.

2. What are some of the ways to use refusal skills to avoid stress?

Reading Tutor, Lesson 2 *(continued)*

USE WITH CHAPTER 8, PAGES 205–209.

Ways to Manage Stress *(pages 206–208)*

You can manage stress by changing the way you react to a stressor. Here are some other ways to manage stress.

- **Plan ahead.** Decide what steps to take. Here are some steps to reduce test anxiety.
  1. Study a little each night to plan for a test.
  2. Outline, number, and highlight points.
  3. Do some deep breathing during the test.
  4. Answer all the questions that you are sure of. Go back and answer the other ones.
  5. Check your mistakes after you get your test back.
- **Get plenty of sleep.** Lack of sleep can affect your attention. It can affect your schoolwork, athletics, or your relationships. Get eight to nine hours of sleep each night. This will help you face your day. You will think more clearly. You will look and feel better.
- **Get regular physical activity.** Your body has excess nervous energy when you are under stress. Physical activity can help release this energy. Try jogging or walking or cleaning.
- **Eat nutritious foods.** Here are some nutrition tips to help you when you deal with stress.
  1. **Eat regular meals.** Reactions to stress may be to snack all day or not eat at all.
  2. **Limit "comfort" foods.** These foods are usually high in fat and sugar.
  3. **Limit caffeine.** It raises your blood pressure. It can add to your stress level.
- **Avoid tobacco, alcohol, and other drugs.**

3. What are some of the ways that you can manage stress?

____

____

____

____

____

Reading Tutor, Lesson 2 *(continued)*

USE WITH CHAPTER 8, PAGES 205–209.

Stress-Management Techniques *(pages 208–209)*

Stress-management skills are *skills that help an individual handle stress in a healthy, effective way*. Here are some successful techniques.

- **Redirect your energy.** Work on a project. Go jogging. Release your nervous energy.
- **Relax and laugh.** The **relaxation response** is *a state of calm that you can reach if you use one or more relaxation techniques regularly*. Breathe deeply. Think pleasant thoughts. Laugh.
- **Keep a positive outlook.** The way you think can affect the way you feel.
- **Seek out support.** Talk with a parent, teacher, or friend. Talk can make you feel better.

4. What are some of the techniques that you can use to manage stress?

____

____

____

____

____

Lesson 3

Reading Tutor

USE WITH CHAPTER 8, PAGES 210–213.

Managing Stress and Anxiety: Anxiety and Teen Depression

Vocabulary

anxiety	The condition of feeling uneasy or worried about what may happen *(page 210)*
depression	A prolonged feeling of helplessness, hopelessness, and sadness *(page 211)*

Drawing from Experience

Does anything make you anxious? Have you ever felt depressed or "blue"? Where can you go to get help for a friend who has serious anxiety or depression? Think about these questions as you read Lesson 3.

In the last lesson, you learned about managing stress. In this lesson, you will learn about anxiety and teen depression.

Reading Tutor, Lesson 3 *(continued)*

USE WITH CHAPTER 8, PAGES 210–213.

Organizing Your Thoughts

Use the chart below to help you take notes as you read the summaries that follow. In the first box, list some of the factors about anxiety. In the other, list some of the factors about depression.

Anxiety	Depression

Reading Tutor, Lesson 3 *(continued)*

USE WITH CHAPTER 8, PAGES 210–213.

Read to Learn

Read each passage carefully. Write in complete sentences to answer the following questions.

What Is Anxiety? *(pages 210–211)*

Anxiety is *the condition of feeling uneasy or worried about what may happen.* Some anxious feelings may be normal. They can motivate you to work hard and do better. Other times, they may keep you from doing your best. Here are some of the symptoms.

- Feelings of fear or dread.
- Sweating or trembling. Being restless or having tense muscles.
- Rapid heart rate or dizziness. Shortness of breath.

Some teens have a form of anxiety that makes them want to be perfect. They strive for perfect grades. They want to be the best on the team. They believe nothing they do is good enough. You can avoid this type of anxiety if you have a realistic outlook.

You can use stress-management skills to reduce your stress. Direct your energy to physical activity. Use relaxation exercises. Get support from family and friends.

1. What is anxiety? What are some of the symptoms of anxiety?

___

___

___

___

___

What Is Depression? *(pages 211–213)*

It is normal to feel sad sometimes. Here are some things you can try to feel better.

- Write your feelings in a journal.
- Draw, dance, or do some other creative activity.
- Talk about your feelings with your family or friends.
- Do something nice for someone else.

Depression is a *prolonged feeling of hopelessness and sadness.* There are two types.

- **Reactive depression** is a response to a stressful event such as the death of a friend. It lasts longer than the "blues," but it will go away in time.

- **Major depression** is a medical condition. It is severe and it may last a long time.

Symptoms may be an irritable or restless mood, staying away from family and friends, or a change in appetite or weight. It may also be feeling guilty or worthless. It is normal to have some of these symptoms once in a while. It is not normal to have more than one of them at the same time and for two weeks or more.

2. What are the two types of depression?

____

____

____

____

____

Getting Help for Anxiety and Depression *(page 213)*

You can treat mild anxiety or depression by talking to others or doing more physical activity. Symptoms may be worse if the person begins to lose interest in things he or she used to like to do, has mood changes, cannot sleep, or loses energy. It is time to get help if anxiety or depression begins to interfere with a person's life.

A doctor can treat these disorders. Talk to a parent or other adult. Get help from a counselor, school psychologist, or other health care professional.

3. Where can you get help for a friend who has serious anxiety or depression?

____

____

____

____

____

Name Class Date

Lesson 4 **Reading Tutor**

USE WITH CHAPTER 8, PAGES 214–217.

Managing Stress and Anxiety: Being a Resilient Teen

Vocabulary

resiliency	The ability to adapt effectively and recover from disappointment, difficulty, or crisis *(page 214)*
protective factors	Conditions that shield individuals from the negative consequences of exposure to risk *(page 216)*

Drawing from Experience

Have you ever felt disappointed? How soon were you able to bounce back? What do you think it means to be resilient? Think about these questions as you read Lesson 4.

In the last lesson, you learned about anxiety and teen depression. In this lesson, you will learn about what it means to be resilient.

Reading Tutor, Lesson 4 *(continued)*

USE WITH CHAPTER 8, PAGES 214–217.

Organizing Your Thoughts

Use the chart below to help you take notes as you read the summaries that follow. In the first box, list some of the factors that affect resiliency. In the other box, list some of the kinds of protective factors.

Factors That Affect Resiliency	Protective Factors

Reading Tutor, Lesson 4 *(continued)*

USE WITH CHAPTER 8, PAGES 214–217.

Read to Learn

Read each passage carefully. Write in complete sentences to answer the following questions.

What Is Resiliency? *(page 214)*

Resiliency is *the ability to adapt and recover from disappointment, difficulty, or crisis*. Some people find it easier than others to bounce back when they have been hurt. People who are resilient are able to deal with problems in healthy ways.

1. What is resiliency?

____

____

____

____

____

Factors That Affect Resiliency *(pages 215–216)*

Having some of the developmental assets can add to your resiliency. The factors that affect resiliency can be broken into two parts.

- **External factors.** These are your family, your school, your community, and your peers. They are school or volunteer projects or a youth group.
- **Internal factors.** These are factors you have some control over. You can make these factors strong to add to your resiliency. Here are some of your internal factors.
  - **Commitment to learning.** Be active in your school. It builds your self-esteem. It gives you a sense of belonging to the school.
  - **Positive values.** Show your values in your words and actions. Avoid risk behavior. Show that you are responsible for your health. You will feel good about yourself.
  - **Social competency.** This means that you have empathy and friendship skills. You are able to resist negative peer pressure.
  - **Positive identity.** This gives you a sense of control over what occurs to you. You are more likely to have good self-esteem and a sense of purpose.

Reading Tutor, Lesson 4 *(continued)*

USE WITH CHAPTER 8, PAGES 214–217.

2. What are some of the factors that affect teen resiliency?

____

____

____

____

____

Resiliency and Your Protective Factors *(pages 216–217)*

Developmental assets can save you from the risk of drug use, sexual activity, and gangs. **Protective factors** are *conditions that shield teens from the negative results of exposure to risk.*

Teens can make their external protective factors stronger. A good relationship with adults in your family can lead to better family communication. Here are some of the ways to improve your internal protective factors.

- Be a part of activities at school.
- Commit to learn. Read for fun at least three hours per week.
- Stand up for your beliefs. Do not act against your values.
- Be honest with yourself and others.
- Resist negative peer pressure. Avoid harmful situations.
- Learn about people from other cultures.
- Have a sense of purpose.
- Have a positive outlook.

3. What are some of the ways to build resiliency by making your internal protective factors strong?

____

____

____

____

____

Name Class Date

CHAPTER 9
Lesson 1

Reading Tutor

USE WITH CHAPTER 9, PAGES 224–229.

Mental and Emotional Problems: Mental Disorders

Vocabulary

mental disorder	An illness of the mind that can affect the thoughts, feelings, and behaviors of a person, preventing him or her from leading a happy, healthful, and productive life *(page 224)*
anxiety disorder	A condition in which real or imagined fears are difficult to control *(page 225)*
post-traumatic stress disorder	A condition that may develop after a person's exposure to a terrifying event that threatened or caused physical harm *(page 226)*
mood disorder	An illness, often with an organic cause, that involves mood extremes that interfere with everyday living *(page 226)*
conduct disorder	A pattern of behavior in which the rights of others or basic social rules are violated *(page 228)*

Drawing from Experience

Do you know anyone who has a phobia? Have you ever heard of bipolar disorder? What do you know about mental illness? How can you show care for someone who is not the same as you are? Think about these questions as you read Lesson 1.

In the last chapter, you learned how to manage stress and anxiety. In this lesson, you will learn about mental disorders.

Reading Tutor, Lesson 1 *(continued)*

USE WITH CHAPTER 9, PAGES 224–229.

Organizing Your Thoughts

Use the chart below to help you take notes as you read the summaries that follow. In the first box, define mental disorder. In the other box, list some of the types of mental disorders.

Definition of Mental Disorder	Types of Mental Disorders

Reading Tutor, Lesson 1 *(continued)*

USE WITH CHAPTER 9, PAGES 224–229.

Read to Learn

Read each passage carefully. Write in complete sentences to answer the following questions.

What Are Mental Disorders? *(pages 224–225)*

A **mental disorder** is *an illness of the mind. It can affect the thoughts, feelings, and behaviors of a person. It keeps him or her from having a happy, healthful, and productive life.*

People who have mental disorders are often not able to cope with life changes. About 20 percent of the U.S. population have some form of mental disorder.

Some people do not seek help for mental illness. They may be embarrassed or ashamed. Some people think that having a mental illness is a stigma. A stigma is a mark of shame. Mental illness requires medical attention.

1. What is a mental disorder?

____

____

____

____

____

Types of Mental Disorders *(pages 225–229)*

Mental disorders may be organic or functional. An organic disorder comes from an illness or an injury that affects the brain. Brain tumors, infections, drugs, or injury may lead to this.

A functional disorder is not brain damage. It has a psychological basis. It may come from heredity, stress, fear, or lack of coping skills. It may also come from abuse, illness, divorce, or another reason.

Here are some of the types of disorders.

- **Anxiety disorder.** An anxiety disorder is *a condition in which real or imagined fears are hard to control.* One of the traits is chronic fear. There are four types.
  - **Phobia.** This is a strong and real fear of a certain thing. A person with agoraphobia has a fear of open places. He or she may stay in the home all day.
  - **Obsessive-compulsive disorder.** This is a pattern of repeating actions. The person may feel the urge to wash his or her hands over and over.

- **Panic.** This is a sudden feeling of terror or "panic attacks." Fear gets in the way of the person's ability to enjoy life.
- **Post-traumatic stress disorder.** This is *a condition that may occur after a terrifying event. The person may have felt threatened or had physical harm.*

- **Mood disorders.** A mood disorder is *an illness, often with an organic cause, with mood swings that cut into day-to-day life.*
  - **Clinical depression.** This is a chemical imbalance. It affects the person's attention level, sleep, and coping skills.
  - **Bipolar** or **manic-depressive disorder** is extreme mood changes, energy levels, and actions. Here are some of the depressive traits.
    - Irritability. Thoughts about death. Physical complaints. Low energy. Overeating.

    Here are some of the manic traits.
    - Severe mood changes. High self-esteem. High energy. Talks too much. Attention moves back and forth. Use of alcohol or drugs.
- **Eating disorders.** An eating disorder involves an obsession with thinness and body image. Some types are anorexia and bulimia.
- **Conduct disorders.** This is *a type of behavior that violates the rights of others or basic social rules*. Some examples are lying, stealing, aggression, and more. Teens with this disorder need treatment to be able to grow into adulthood and to hold a job.
- **Schizophrenia.** This is a severe mental disorder. The person loses contact with reality. It leads to odd actions, delusions, and a lack of good health habits.
- **Personality disorders.** This is a disorder in which people have a hard time getting along with others. Here are three types.
  - **Antisocial personality disorder.** People with this are irritable and aggressive.
  - **Borderline personality disorder.** People with this have poor self-esteem. They engage in risk behavior. They have trouble with friendships.
  - **Passive-aggressive personality disorder.** People with this do not like to cooperate. They do not want to be told what to do.

2. What are some of the types of mental disorders?

____

____

____

____

____

USE WITH CHAPTER 9, PAGES 230–233.

Mental and Emotional Problems: Suicide Prevention

Vocabulary

alienation	Feeling isolated and separated from everyone else *(page 230)*
suicide	The act of intentionally taking one's own life *(page 230)*
cluster suicides	A series of suicides occurring within a short period of time and involving several people in the same school or community *(page 233)*

Drawing from Experience

What are some of the warning signs of suicide? Where can you go to get help if you think someone is thinking about suicide? Think about these questions as you read Lesson 2.

In the last lesson, you learned about mental disorders. In this lesson, you will learn about suicide.

Reading Tutor, Lesson 2 *(continued)*

USE WITH CHAPTER 9, PAGES 230–233.

Organizing Your Thoughts

Use the chart below to help you take notes as you read the summaries that follow. In the first box, list some of the suicide risk factors. In the other box, list some of the ways to prevent suicide.

Suicide Risk Factors	Ways to Prevent Suicide

Reading Tutor, Lesson 2 *(continued)*

USE WITH CHAPTER 9, PAGES 230–233.

Read to Learn

Read each passage carefully. Write in complete sentences to answer the following questions.

Suicide Risk Factors *(page 230)*

Alienation is *feeling isolated and separated from everyone else.* People who feel this way may try to get away from the pain. **Suicide** is *the act of intentionally taking one's own life.*

Most people who kill themselves are depressed, have a mental disorder, or are on drugs or alcohol. Here are some other risk factors.

- A history of abuse
- A history of suicide tries
- A family history of emotional disorders or suicide

1. What are some of the risk factors for suicide?

____

____

____

____

____

____

____

Preventing Suicide *(pages 231–233)*

Take a teen seriously if he or she talks about taking his or her life. Never bargain with someone who is thinking about suicide. Seek adult help right away. Here are some of the warning signs of suicide.

- An obsession with death. Staying away from friends.
- Change in personality or looks. Odd, bizarre behavior.
- Huge sense of guilt, shame, or rejection. A drop in schoolwork or sports success.
- Giving away personal items. Substance abuse. Physical complaints.
- Boredom. Violent acts. Running away. Unable to accept praise.
- Statements such as "I want to die." "They'll be sorry when I'm gone."

Reading Tutor, Lesson 2 *(continued)*

USE WITH CHAPTER 9, PAGES 230–233.

Here are some steps to take with someone who seems to be suicidal.

- **Start a meaningful talk.** Show interest. Show you care. Listen and be patient.
- **Show support and ask questions.** Tell the person you understand their feelings. Let him or her know that suicide is not the answer. Most survivors are very glad they did not die.
- **Try to get the person to seek help.** Urge the person to talk to a counselor or parent or other trusted adult. Offer to go with the person to get help.

Cluster suicides are a *series of suicides occurring within a short period of time. They involve several people in the same school or community*. They are often the result of a pact among two or more teens or young adults.

Here are some guidelines to stop cluster suicides.

- Get counseling for close friends of suicide victims. They are also at risk.
- Media should not glorify the suicide.

2. What are some of the ways that you can help prevent suicide?

____

____

____

____

____

____

____

USE WITH CHAPTER 9, PAGES 234–237.

Mental and Emotional Problems: Getting Help

Vocabulary

psychotherapy	An ongoing dialogue between a patient and a mental health professional *(page 237)*
behavior therapy	A treatment process that focuses on changing unwanted behaviors through reward and reinforcements *(page 237)*
cognitive therapy	A treatment method designed to identify and correct distorted thinking patterns that can lead to feelings and behaviors that may be troublesome, self-defeating, or self-destructive *(page 237)*
group therapy	Treating a group of people who have similar problems and who meet regularly with a trained counselor *(page 237)*
biomedical therapy	The use of certain medications to treat or reduce the symptoms of a mental disorder *(page 237)*

Drawing from Experience

Why do some people find it hard to seek help for mental problems? How do you know when it is time to get help? Who can you go to for information? Think about these things as you read Lesson 3.

In the last lesson, you learned about preventing teen suicide. In this lesson, you will learn about getting help for mental or emotional problems.

Reading Tutor, Lesson 3 *(continued)*

USE WITH CHAPTER 9, PAGES 234–237.

Organizing Your Thoughts

Use the chart below to help you take notes as you read the summaries that follow. In the first box, list when to get help. In the next box, list the signs that a person needs professional help. In the last box, list some of the therapy methods.

When to Get Help	Professional Help	Therapy Methods

Reading Tutor, Lesson 3 *(continued)*

USE WITH CHAPTER 9, PAGES 234–237.

Read to Learn

Read each passage carefully. Write in complete sentences to answer the following questions.

Knowing When to Get Help *(page 234)*

It can be hard to ask for help for mental or emotional problems. You may feel embarrassed or shy. You may need to get help if your problem occurs for days or weeks. You may need to get help if it begins to affect your daily life. Seek help for the following.

- You feel trapped with no way out. You worry all the time.
- Your feelings affect your sleep, eating habits, schoolwork, job, or friendships.
- Your family and friends tell you that they have concerns.
- You are using alcohol or other types of drugs.
- You are acting aggressive or violent.

1. What are some of the reasons to seek help for mental problems?

____

____

____

____

____

____

Signs That Professional Help Is Needed *(pages 235–236)*

Mental disorders may get worse if you do not get any treatment. Here are some of the signs that you may need professional help.

- You feel sad for no reason for a long period of time.
- You often have angry outbursts.
- You have lots of fear, anxiety, or anger at the world.
- You change your eating or sleeping habits for no reason.
- You withdraw from your social life.

You can seek help from a parent, teacher, coach, or counselor. Here are some of the types of mental health professionals.

- **Psychiatrist.** This is a doctor who diagnoses and treats mental disorders. He or she can prescribe medicine.

- **Neurologist.** This is a doctor for organic disorders of the brain and nervous system.
- **Clinical psychologist.** This is a person who diagnoses and treats emotional and behavior disorders by means of counseling. He or she does not prescribe medicine.
- **Counselor.** This is a person who helps people with personal and education matters.
- **Psychiatric social worker.** This person guides and treats people with emotional problems in a mental hospital, health clinic, or family service agency.
- **School psychologist.** This is a person who assesses learning, emotional, and behavior problems in schoolchildren.

Some people are afraid to get help for mental problems. Here are some facts to help them.

- Asking for help does not mean that you are weak. Asking for help is a sign of strength.
- Most mental disorders will not get better if you do not get treatment. Ask for help.
- Sharing your feelings with a health care provider is not painful. It can be a big relief.

2. What are some of the signs that a person may need help for mental problems?

____

____

____

____

____

____

Therapy Methods *(page 237)*

Here are some of the most common types of mental health therapy.

- **Psychotherapy** is an ongoing talk between a patient and a mental health professional.
- **Behavior therapy** is *a process for changing behaviors by reward and praise.*
- **Cognitive therapy** is *a method to find and correct thinking patterns that can lead to behavior that may be troubling or self-destructive.*

Reading Tutor, Lesson 3 *(continued)*

USE WITH CHAPTER 9, PAGES 238–241.

- **Group therapy** is *treating a group of people who have similar problems.*
- **Biomedical therapy** is *the use of medicine to treat a mental disorder.*

3. What are some of the types of mental health therapy?

____

____

____

____

____

____

Name Class Date

Lesson 4

USE WITH CHAPTER 9, PAGES 238–241.

Mental and Emotional Problems: Understanding Death and Grief

Vocabulary

coping	Dealing successfully with difficult changes in your life *(page 239)*
grief response	An individual's total response to a major loss *(page 239)*
mourning	The act of showing sorrow or grief *(page 240)*

Drawing from Experience

Have you ever lost a pet? Have you ever broken up with a friend? Has someone in your family died? How did you deal with your loss? How can you show support to a friend who has had a loss? Think about these questions as you read Lesson 4.

In the last lesson, you learned how to get help for mental health problems. In this lesson, you will learn how to cope with death and grief.

Reading Tutor, Lesson 4 *(continued)*

USE WITH CHAPTER 9, PAGES 238–241.

Organizing Your Thoughts

Use the chart below to help you take notes as you read the summaries that follow. In the first box, list the steps of the grieving process. In the other box, list some of the ways to cope with death and crises.

Steps of the Grieving Process	Ways to Cope with Death and Crises

Reading Tutor, Lesson 4 *(continued)*

USE WITH CHAPTER 9, PAGES 238–241.

Read to Learn

Read each passage carefully. Write in complete sentences to answer the following questions.

Different Kinds of Loss *(page 238)*

Loss can be very painful. It is important to learn to cope with loss. It is a part of life. Here are some of the different types of loss.

- You miss a chance to play in a play-off game because you are hurt.
- You break up with a good friend.
- Your pet dies or gets lost.
- A friend or family member passes away.
- You have to move and change schools.

1. What are some of the types of loss?

____

____

____

____

____

Expressions of Grief *(pages 239–240)*

Coping is *dealing successfully with difficult changes in your life.* A **grief response** is *a person's total response to a major loss.* Here are the steps of the grieving process.

- **Denial or numbness.** The person cannot believe that the loss has occurred.
- **Emotional releases.** The person knows there is a loss. He or she often cries.
- **Anger.** The person feels that the loss is not fair. He or she may lash out at others.
- **Bargaining.** The person may promise to change if only what is lost can return.
- **Depression.** The person feels deep sadness and he or she feels hopeless.
- **Remorse.** The person thinks a lot about what he or she could have done to prevent the loss.
- **Acceptance.** The person faces the reality of the loss.
- **Hope.** The person can think about the loss with less pain. He or she can look to the future.

2. What are the steps of the grieving process?

____

____

____

Coping with Death *(pages 240–241)*

Mourning is *the act of showing sorrow or grief*. Support from family and friends is important. You can help a friend go through the grieving process just by being there to listen. Here are some of the ways to help a person cope with death.

- Remember the good things about the person.
- Think about the good times you had with the person.
- Talk with others about the person.
- Write a letter to say good-bye to the person.
- See a grief counselor or therapist for help with the grief process.

3. What are some of the ways that a person can cope with death?

____

____

____

Coping with Disasters and Crises *(page 241)*

Natural disasters or sudden events can make people feel upset and afraid. Here are some of the ways to help people cope with these feelings.

- Spend time with others and talk about your feelings.
- Get back to your daily routine as soon as possible.
- Eat nutritious food. Get enough rest and sleep.
- Do something positive for your community. Help with cleanup. Help raise money for aid.

4. What are some of the things that you can do to cope with disasters or crises?

____

____

____

USE WITH CHAPTER 10, PAGES 248–253.

Skills for Healthy Relationships: Foundations of Healthy Relationships

Vocabulary

relationship	A bond or connection you have with other people *(page 248)*
friendship	A significant relationship between two people that is based on caring, trust, and consideration *(page 249)*
citizenship	The way you conduct yourself as a member of the community *(page 249)*
role	A part you play in a relationship *(page 250)*
communication	The ways in which you send messages to and receive messages from others *(page 250)*
cooperation	Working together for the good of all *(page 250)*
compromise	A problem-solving method that involves each participant's giving up something to reach a solution that satisfies everyone *(page 251)*

Drawing from Experience

What kind of role do you have in your family? What kind of role do you have with your friends? What are the traits of a good relationship? Think about these questions as you read Lesson 1.

In the last chapter, you learned about mental and emotional problems. In this lesson, you will learn how to build a healthy relationship.

Reading Tutor, Lesson 1 *(continued)*

USE WITH CHAPTER 10, PAGES 248–253.

Organizing Your Thoughts

Use the chart below to help you take notes as you read the summaries that follow. In the first box, list some of the kinds of healthy relationships. In the other box, list some of the ways to build a healthy relationship.

Types of Healthy Relationships	Ways to Build a Healthy Relationship

Reading Tutor, Lesson 1 *(continued)*

USE WITH CHAPTER 10, PAGES 248–253.

Read to Learn

Read each passage carefully. Write in complete sentences to answer the following questions.

Healthy Relationships *(pages 248–250)*

A **relationship** is *a bond or connection you have with other people*. A healthy relationship is based on shared values and interests and mutual respect. Here are some of the types of relationships.

- **Family relationships** last for your whole life. Your immediate family is your parents or guardians and siblings. Your extended family is your grandparents, uncles, aunts, and cousins. A healthy family relationship will benefit all sides of your health triangle.
- A **friendship** is *a relationship between two people based on caring, trust, and consideration*. Your friends can be any age. You choose them for different reasons. Good friends share similar values.
- **Citizenship** is *the way you conduct yourself as a member of the community*. You show good citizenship by obeying laws and by being a helpful neighbor. You work to improve your school and community.
- **Roles with family and friends**. A **role** is *a part you play in a relationship*. You may be a son or a daughter or a team member. You may be a volunteer or a girlfriend or a boyfriend. You may play many of these roles at the same time. A role can change. You may have a role as a fellow student with someone and that role will change if you begin to date each other.

1. What are some of the common types of relationships?

Reading Tutor, Lesson 1 *(continued)*

USE WITH CHAPTER 10, PAGES 248–253.

Building Healthy Relationships *(pages 250–251)*

People need certain skills to build a healthy relationship. Here are the Three Cs.

- **Communication** is *ways of sending and receiving messages*. You may do this with words, gestures, facial expressions, or behavior.
- **Cooperation** is *working together for the good of all*. Working and helping each other can build strong relationships.
- **Compromise** is *a problem-solving method in which each person gives up something to reach a solution that satisfies everyone*. This "give-and-take" can strengthen a relationship. Be sure not to go against your values just to reach a solution.

Here are some of the traits of a healthy relationship.

- **Mutual respect and consideration.** You show respect even when you disagree. You are tolerant of each other's point of view. You care about each other's rights and feelings.
- **Honesty.** You trust each other enough to be open and honest about your feelings. Dishonesty can ruin a friendship.
- **Dependability.** You can be trusted. You are reliable. You are there when the other person needs you.
- **Commitment.** You are willing to work with each other. You are willing to give up something for each other. You are loyal.

2. What are some of the skills and traits that you need to build a healthy relationship?

Character and Healthy Relationships *(pages 252–253)*

Your character is the way you think, feel, and act. It has the most influence on your relationships with others. Your friends have values that are like yours. Your values are the beliefs and ideals that guide the way you live.

Here are the six main traits of good character.

- **Trustworthiness.** You are honest, reliable, and loyal. You do not cheat or lie or steal.
- **Fairness.** You play by the rules. You take turns and share. You listen and are open-minded.
- **Respect.** You use good manners. You treat other people and property with care.
- **Caring.** You are kind and compassionate. You put in time to help others.
- **Responsibility.** You do what others expect of you. You are accountable for your actions.
- **Citizenship.** You do your share to improve your school and community. You obey laws.

3. What are the six main traits of good character?

Name Class Date

Lesson 2

Reading Tutor

USE WITH CHAPTER 10, PAGES 254–261.

Skills for Healthy Relationships: Communicating Effectively

Vocabulary

"I" message	A statement in which a person describes how he or she feels by using the pronoun "I" *(page 256)*
active listening	Paying close attention to what someone is saying and communicating *(page 256)*
body language	Nonverbal communication through gestures, facial expressions, behaviors, and posture *(page 258)*
prejudice	An unfair opinion or judgment of a particular group of people *(page 260)*
tolerance	The ability to accept others' differences and allow them to be who they are without expressing disapproval *(page 260)*
constructive criticism	Nonhostile comments that point out problems and encourage improvement *(page 260)*

Drawing from Experience

Are you a good listener? Can you communicate without using any words? Are you open to other people's ideas? Can you criticize a friend without hurting his or her feelings? Think about these questions as you read Lesson 2.

In the last lesson, you learned about building relationships. In this lesson, you will learn how to communicate well.

Reading Tutor, Lesson 2 *(continued)*

USE WITH CHAPTER 10, PAGES 254–261.

Organizing Your Thoughts

Use the chart below to help you take notes as you read the summaries that follow. In the first oval, list the styles of communication. In the next oval, list some of the types of speaking skills. In the next oval, list some listening skills. In the next oval, list some of the types of body language. In the next oval, list some of the barriers to communication. In the last oval, list some of the ways to give feedback and praise.

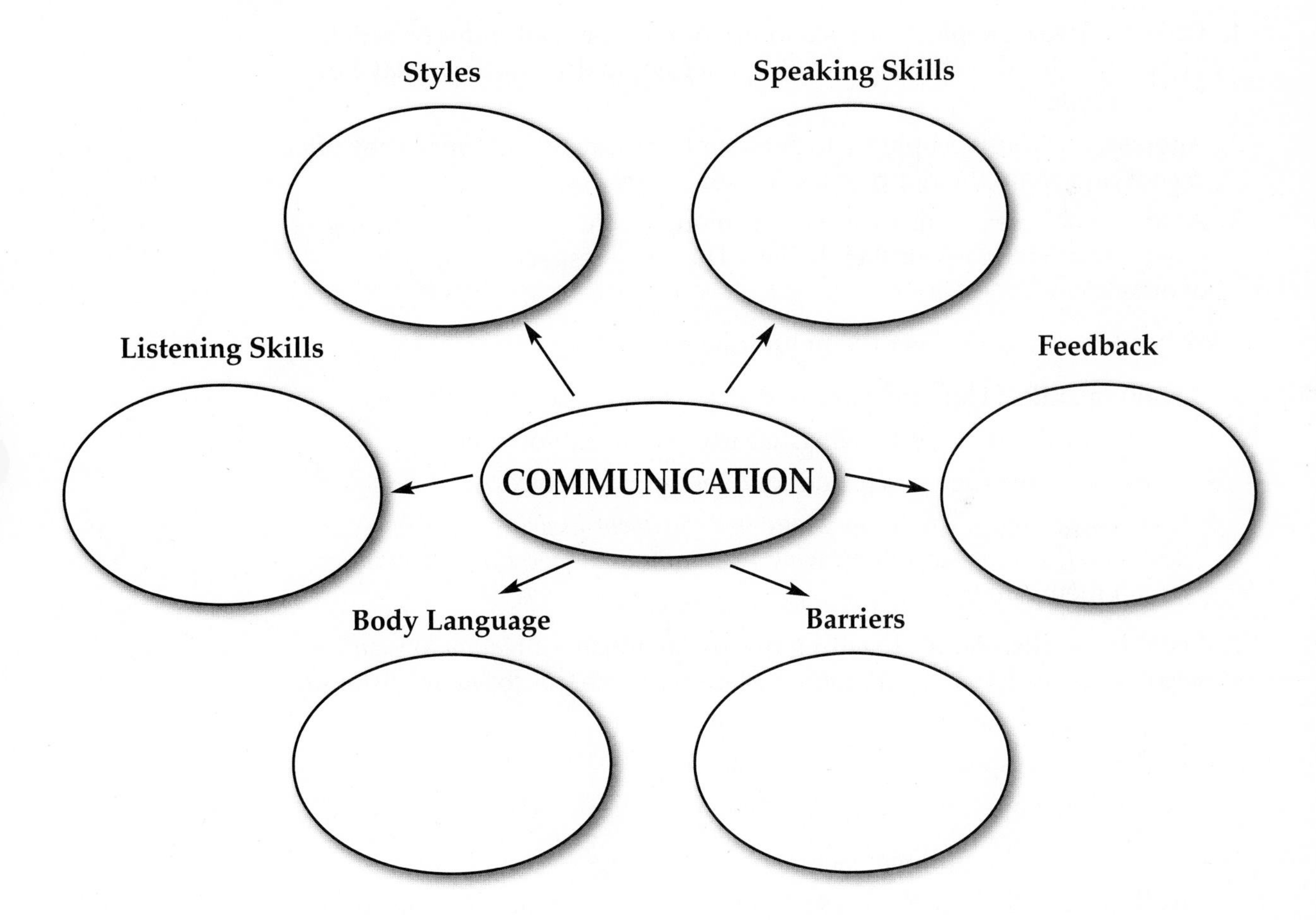

USE WITH CHAPTER 10, PAGES 254–261.

Read to Learn

Read each passage carefully. Write in complete sentences to answer the following questions.

Effective Communication ***(pages 254–258)***

People have different ways of saying things. Here are the three styles of communication.

1. **Passive.** These people do not stand up for their own attitudes or beliefs. They will often do what they would prefer not to do rather than say how they really feel.
2. **Aggressive.** These people try to get their own way by bullying. They often do not care about the rights or feelings of others.
3. **Assertive.** These people express their thoughts clearly without hurting others. They stand up for their beliefs. They also respect the rights of others.

We need three basic skills to communicate well.

1. **Speaking skills.** Here are some of the skills you need to speak well.
   - State your thoughts and feelings clearly. Say what you mean.
   - Be aware of the tone, pitch, and loudness of your voice.
   - Use "I" messages. An **"I" message** is *a statement in which a person describes how he or she feels by using the pronoun "I."* Do not blame others or call them names.
2. **Listening skills. Active listening** means *paying close attention to what someone is saying and communicating.* Here are some tips for active listening.
   - Make direct eye contact.
   - Lean in to the speaker. Nod your head.
   - Do not interrupt the speaker.

   Here are some other techniques for active listening.
   - **Reflective listening.** Rephrase or summarize what the other person has said.
   - **Clarifying.** Ask the speaker what he or she thinks.
   - **Encouraging.** Nod your head and say things like "I see" or "I understand."
   - **Empathizing.** Empathy means you are able to feel what the other person is feeling.

Reading Tutor, Lesson 2 *(continued)*

USE WITH CHAPTER 10, PAGES 254–261.

3. **Body Language. Body language** is *nonverbal communication through gestures, facial expressions, behaviors, and posture.* Words and movement must match for a clear message.
   - You may nod your head if you agree.
   - You may look at the floor if you are shy.
   - You may lean forward if you are interested.

1. What are the three basic skills we need to communicate well?

____

____

____

____

____

Eliminating Communication Barriers *(pages 259–260)*

Here are some of the things that may block clear communication.

- **Image and identity issues.** Many teens are searching for who they are.
- **Unrealistic expectations.** The listener may get defensive.
- **Lack of trust.** You may fear the other person will tell others what you said in private.
- **Prejudice.** This is *an unfair opinion or judgment of a particular group of people.*
- **Tolerance** is *the ability to accept others' differences and allow them to be who they are.*
- **Gender stereotyping.** This is a type of prejudice about the genders. You are doing this if you say all men like sports or all women like to cook.

2. What are some of the things that may block communication?

____

____

____

____

____

Reading Tutor, Lesson 2 *(continued)*

USE WITH CHAPTER 10, PAGES 254–261.

Constructive Feedback *(page 260)*

Constructive criticism means *nonhostile comments that point out problems to help a person improve.*

- Do not do this in an aggressive way.
- Use "I" messages to explain how you feel.
- Point out what the person is doing and suggest a better way to do it.

3. What is constructive criticism?

___

___

___

___

___

Acknowledgments and Compliments *(page 261)*

Appreciation makes you feel good about yourself. It also makes you feel good about the person who is giving you the praise. Being able to give and receive honest respect can build healthy relationships. It can show others that you care about them.

- You might tell a parent how much you liked a meal.
- You might tell a friend that he or she is a good artist.
- You might congratulate a team that beat your team.

These comments can show others that you are a good sport and you have good character.

4. What are some of the benefits of giving praise to others?

___

___

___

___

___

USE WITH CHAPTER 10, PAGES 262–267.

Skills for Healthy Relationships: Resolving Conflict

Vocabulary

conflict	Any disagreement, struggle, or fight *(page 262)*
interpersonal conflicts	Disagreements between groups of any size, from two people to entire nations *(page 262)*
conflict resolution	The process of ending a conflict in a manner that satisfies everyone involved *(page 264)*
negotiation	The use of communication and often compromise to settle a disagreement *(page 266)*
mediation	A process in which specially trained people help others resolve their conflicts peacefully *(page 267)*
confidentiality	Respecting the privacy of another and keeping details secret *(page 267)*
peer mediators	Students trained to help other students find fair resolutions to conflicts and disagreements *(page 267)*

Drawing from Experience

Have you ever had a conflict with a friend? What caused the conflict? How did you deal with it? Could you have resolved it any other way? Think about these questions as you read Lesson 3.

In the last lesson, you learned how to communicate well. In this lesson, you will learn about ways to resolve conflict.

Name Class Date

Reading Tutor, Lesson 3 *(continued)*

USE WITH CHAPTER 10, PAGES 262–267.

Organizing Your Thoughts

Use the chart below to help you take notes as you read the summaries that follow. In the first box, list some of the causes of conflict. In the next box, list some of the ways to resolve conflict. In the last box, list the parts of the mediation process.

Causes of Conflict	Ways to Resolve Conflict	The Mediation Process

Reading Tutor, Lesson 3 *(continued)*

USE WITH CHAPTER 10, PAGES 262–267.

Read to Learn

Read each passage carefully. Write in complete sentences to answer the following questions.

Understanding Conflict *(pages 262–264)*

Conflict is *any disagreement, struggle, or fight*. It is a normal part of life. **Interpersonal conflicts** are *disagreements between groups of any size, from two people to entire nations*. Conflicts can begin in many ways. Here are some of the common causes of conflict.

- **Power struggles.** You think you should be able to decide when you come home at night.
- **Loyalty.** A friend takes someone else's side in an argument.
- **Jealousy/envy.** Your friend makes the team and you do not.
- **Property disputes.** You get mad when your sister borrows your clothes without asking.
- **Territory and space.** You get mad when your brother uses your room to watch TV.

You can choose to face a conflict or ignore it. Here are some things to think about.

- Think about your health and safety.
- You are not a coward if you walk away from a dangerous situation. It is the smart and safe thing to do.
- You can resolve minor conflicts with compromise.
- Do not compromise if it goes against your values.

1. What are some of the common causes of conflict?

____

____

____

____

Conflict Resolution *(pages 264–266)*

Conflict resolution is *the process of solving a disagreement in a manner that satisfies everyone involved*. Here are some tips for resolving conflicts.

- Take time to calm down and think over the situation.
- Take turns telling each side of the story. Do not interrupt. Use "I" messages.
- Ask questions to clarify. Understand each person's position.

Reading Tutor, Lesson 3 *(continued)*

- Think about possible solutions.
- Agree on a solution that is good for each side.
- Follow up to see if the solution worked out for each side.

You must show respect to yourself and others to resolve a conflict. Stand up for your own beliefs. Listen to others with an open mind. Respect and tolerance can help prevent and resolve conflicts.

Negotiation is *the use of communication and often compromise to settle a disagreement.* Here are some ways to prepare for a successful negotiation.

- Make sure the issue is important to you.
- Check your facts. Make sure the parties based their conflict on fact.
- Your goal is to find a solution. Do not try to prove who is right.
- Practice what you will say. Write it down.

Here are some steps to take when you negotiate.

- Choose a calm time to work out the problem. Find a quiet place to meet.
- Work together to find a solution. Do not look at the other person as the enemy.
- Keep an open mind. Listen to the other person.
- Be flexible.
- Take responsibility for your role in the conflict.
- Give the other person an "out." Talk about it later if the person seems upset.

2. What are some of the tips for resolving conflicts?

____

____

____

____

____

The Mediation Process *(page 267)*

Mediation is *a process in which specially trained people help others resolve their conflicts peacefully.* Here are some of the facts about this process.

- The mediation takes place in a neutral location.
- The mediator keeps strict **confidentiality.** This means *respecting the privacy of both parties and keeping details secret.*

- The mediator asks each person to tell his or her side.
- The mediator gives a summary for each side. Each side can clarify any points.
- Then each side can speak to the other with the mediator.
- The mediator asks each side to sign an agreement. It works out the problem within a certain time frame.

Many schools have programs to resolve conflicts that take place at school. **Peer mediators** are *students trained to help other students find fair resolutions to conflicts and disagreements.*

3. What are some of the facts about mediation?

Name Class Date

USE WITH CHAPTER 11, PAGES 274–279.

Family Relationships: The Role of the Family

Vocabulary

family	The basic unit of society *(page 274)*
extended family	Your immediate family and other relatives such as grandparents, aunts, uncles, and cousins *(page 277)*
sibling	A brother or sister *(page 278)*
affirmation	Positive feedback that helps others feel appreciated and supported *(page 278)*

Drawing from Experience

Who are the people in your family? How does your family support you? What is your role in your family? What can you do to build a strong family? Think about these questions as you read Lesson 1.

In the last chapter, you learned about skills for healthy relationships. In this lesson, you will learn about the role of the family.

Reading Tutor, Lesson 1 *(continued)*

USE WITH CHAPTER 11, PAGES 274–279.

Organizing Your Thoughts

Use the chart below to help you take notes as you read the summaries that follow. In the first box, list some of the ways that a family is important. In the other box, list some of the ways that you can make your family stronger.

Ways the Family Is Important	Ways to Make a Family Strong

Reading Tutor, Lesson 1 *(continued)*

USE WITH CHAPTER 11, PAGES 274–279.

Read to Learn

Read each passage carefully. Write in complete sentences to answer the following questions.

What Is a Family? *(page 274)*

The **family** is *the basic unit of society*. The family provides a safe and caring place for its members. A teen learns values from his or her family.

Healthy families have love and respect for one another. They talk and listen to each other. They support and care for each other. A strong family is a protective factor that helps teens avoid risky behaviors.

1. What is a family?

____

____

____

____

The Importance of Family *(pages 275–276)*

Your family relationships can affect all three sides of your health triangle.

- **Physical health.** The family provides food, clothes, and a home to its members. The family teaches healthy behavior and safety skills.
- **Mental/emotional health.** The family cares for and supports each other. The family helps members have a positive self-concept.
- **Social health.** The family teaches communication skills and how to get along with others.
  - The family teaches values. Good values form good character. Good values help you to be a positive part of society.
  - The family passes along its traditions. Adults teach you religious beliefs. They teach you the family culture and history.

2. How do families affect the three sides of the health triangle?

____

____

____

____

Reading Tutor, Lesson 1 *(continued)*

USE WITH CHAPTER 11, PAGES 274–279.

Dynamics of Family Roles and Responsibilities *(pages 277–278)*

Your **extended family** is *your immediate family and other relatives such as grandparents, aunts, uncles, and cousins*. Each family member has a role in the family. Parents set limits and protect the health and safety of their children. Grandparents may pass along family history. Aunts or uncles may give advice.

Children and teens also have a role in the family. A **sibling** is *a brother or sister*. A teen may care for a sibling while parents are at work. Having a role in the family can give a teen high self-esteem.

3. What are some of the roles of family members?

____

____

____

____

Strengthening Family Relationships *(pages 278–279)*

Here are some of the ways to make your family strong.

- **Show care and love.** Show **affirmation.** This is *positive feedback that helps others feel appreciated*. Show that you care when a family member is feeling down.
- **Show support.** Be a good listener when someone is having a hard time.
- **Show trust.** Care for each other. Be honest. Keep your promises. Be loyal.
- **Show commitment.** Be willing to work with each other. Make sacrifices for the family.
- **Be responsible.** Think before you act. Avoid risky actions. Be accountable for what you do.
- **Spend time together.** Eat meals with each other. Plan fun activities. Take family trips.
- **Respect individuality.** Have respect for each other. Accept different tastes and ideas.
- **Work with each other to solve problems.** Work out your problems. Plan events together.
- **Be sensitive to others' needs.** Deal with stress by helping each other. Respect privacy.

Reading Tutor, Lesson 1 *(continued)*

USE WITH CHAPTER 11, PAGES 274–279.

4. What are some of the ways to make your family strong?

Family Relationships: Change and the Family

Vocabulary

separation	A decision between married individuals to live apart from each other *(page 281)*
divorce	A legal end to a marriage contract *(page 281)*
custody	A legal decision about who has the right to make decisions affecting the children in a family and who has the responsibility of physically caring for them *(page 281)*
grief	The sorrow caused by the loss of a loved one *(page 282)*
resiliency	The ability to adapt effectively and recover from disappointment, difficulty, or crisis *(page 285)*

Drawing from Experience

Have you ever had a big change in your family? Has your family ever moved to a new home? Do any of your friends have parents who are divorced? How do families cope with big changes? Think about these questions as you read Lesson 2.

In the last lesson, you learned about the role of the family. In this lesson, you will learn about change in the family.

Reading Tutor, Lesson 2 *(continued)*

USE WITH CHAPTER 11, PAGES 280–285.

Organizing Your Thoughts

Use the chart below to help you take notes as you read the summaries that follow. In the first box, list some of the types of changes in family structure. In the next box, list some of the types of changes in family circumstances. In the last box, list some of the ways to cope with family changes.

Changes in Structure	Changes in Circumstances	Coping with Family Changes

Read to Learn

Read each passage carefully. Write in complete sentences to answer the following questions.

Families and Change *(page 280)*

Change is a normal part of life. It can be a major cause of stress in a family. Family communication can solve most minor problems. Big problems require families to use coping skills to deal with the issues.

There are two major types of change. The first is change in the structure of the family. The second is change in the circumstances of the family.

1. What are the two major types of change in a family?

___

___

___

___

Changes in Family Structure *(pages 281–282)*

Family structure changes when someone new joins the family or when the family loses a member. Here are some of the types of change in family structure.

A. Separation and divorce. Marriage is a commitment to share life with each other. Sometimes there are problems that the couple is not able to work out.

- **Separation** is *a decision between married persons to live apart from each other.*
- **Divorce** is *a legal end to a marriage contract.*
- **Custody** is *a legal decision about who has the right to make decisions for the children in a family and who will physically care for them.*
- Here are some ideas for dealing with stress when parents get divorced.
  - Remind yourself that you did not cause the problem.
  - Do not feel that you have to pick sides.
  - Talk to your parents about your feelings.
  - Eat nutritious foods, get physical activity, and deal with your stress.
  - Join a support group for children of divorce. You are not alone.

Reading Tutor, Lesson 2 *(continued)*

USE WITH CHAPTER 11, PAGES 280–285.

B. Remarriage. Stepparents and children need to get used to each other. Everyone in a blended family needs to communicate and respect each other.

C. Death of a family member. Grief is *the sorrow caused by the loss of a loved one*. Here are some of the ways to cope with the death of a family member.

- **Focus on happy memories.** Think of the good times.
- **Accept your feelings.** It is normal to feel hurt.
- **Join a support group.** Talk about your pain with others.
- **Seek help from a grief counselor.**

2. What are some of the types of change in family structure?

____

____

____

____

____

____

Changes in Family Circumstances *(pages 283–284)*

Here are some of the types of change in family circumstances.

- **Moving.** Teens may worry about making new friends and going to a new school.
- **Financial problems.** Loss of a job, medical problems, and unpaid bills can cause worry in a family.
- **Illness and disability.** This can disrupt a family's normal activities. Other family members may need to stay home to take care of the person who is ill.
- **Drug and alcohol abuse.** Substance abuse can affect the health of the whole family. Seek help from trusted adults.

Reading Tutor, Lesson 2 *(continued)*

USE WITH CHAPTER 11, PAGES 280–285.

3. What are some of the types of change in family circumstances?

____

____

____

____

____

____

Coping with Family Changes *(pages 284–285)*

It is important to deal with the stress that family changes can cause. Here are some of the ways to cope with family changes.

- Do what you can to help. Take on some added chores. Helping can make you feel better.
- Read books about the subject or talk to people who have faced a similar problem.
- Use stress-management techniques. Be active. Get sleep. Eat nutritious meals. Relax.

An important trait of a healthy family is **resiliency.** This is *the ability to adapt and recover from disappointment or crisis.*

4. What are some of the ways that you can cope with family changes?

____

____

____

____

____

____

Name Class Date

Lesson 3 — Reading Tutor

USE WITH CHAPTER 11, PAGES 286–290.

Family Relationships: Dealing with Family Crises

Vocabulary

domestic violence	Any act of violence involving family members *(page 286)*
emotional abuse	A pattern of behavior that attacks the emotional development and sense of worth of an individual *(page 287)*
physical abuse	The intentional infliction of bodily harm or injury on another person *(page 287)*
sexual abuse	Any sexual contact that is forced upon a person against his or her will *(page 287)*
spousal abuse	Domestic violence directed at a spouse *(page 287)*
child abuse	Domestic abuse directed at a child *(page 288)*
neglect	Failure to provide for a child's physical or emotional needs *(page 288)*
cycle of violence	Pattern of repeating violent or abusive behaviors from one generation to the next *(page 289)*

Drawing from Experience

What do you know about abuse? Do you know anyone who has been a victim of abuse? What are the effects of abuse? What can you do to prevent it? Think about these questions as you read Lesson 3.

In the last lesson, you learned about change in the family. In this lesson, you will learn how to deal with family crises.

Reading Tutor, Lesson 3 *(continued)*

USE WITH CHAPTER 11, PAGES 286–290.

Organizing Your Thoughts

Use the chart below to help you take notes as you read the summaries that follow. In the first box, list some of the types of family abuse. In the other box, list some of the ways to break the cycle of violence and avoid abuse.

Types of Family Abuse	Ways to Break the Cycle and Avoid Abuse

Reading Tutor, Lesson 3 *(continued)*

USE WITH CHAPTER 11, PAGES 286–290.

Read to Learn

Read each passage carefully. Write in complete sentences to answer the following questions.

Family Violence *(pages 286–289)*

Domestic violence is *any act of violence involving family members.* It is a criminal act. Here are the main forms of abuse in the home.

- **Emotional abuse** is *behavior that attacks the emotional growth and sense of worth of a person.* This is bullying, name-calling, or threats of physical harm.
- **Physical abuse** is *doing bodily harm or injury to another person.* This might be slapping, punching, or kicking.
- **Sexual abuse** is *any sexual contact forced upon a person against his or her will.* It includes words and touching that are not welcome.

Spousal abuse is *domestic violence aimed at a spouse.* It may occur in all kinds of families. It can harm all sides of the person's health triangle. It is important for the abused person to leave the harmful situation and seek help.

Child abuse is *domestic abuse aimed at a child.* **Neglect** is *the failure to provide for a child's physical or emotional needs.* A child who lives in an abusive home may try to run away. This is not a safe solution. Ask for help from a trusted adult.

Victims of abuse may feel that they do not have the power to change the situation. They must get to a safe place and ask for help. Here are some long-term effects of abuse.

- It is hard for the abused person to trust others. It is hard to have a healthy relationship.
- The person has chronic physical pain.
- The person neglects, hurts, or tries to kill him- or herself.
- The person is depressed, is worried, cannot sleep, or has an eating disorder.
- The person abuses alcohol or other drugs.

1. What are some of the types of family violence and abuse?

___

___

___

___

___

Reading Tutor, Lesson 3 *(continued)*

USE WITH CHAPTER 11, PAGES 286–290.

Breaking the Cycle of Violence *(page 289)*

The **cycle of violence** is *a pattern of repeating violent or abusive behaviors from one generation to the next.* An abused child may become an adult who abuses others. You can help break this cycle.

- Tell a trusted adult. Ask this person to help you.
- Call an abuse hot line. They can help you find a counselor to talk to.
- Report the abuse to the police.

2. What are the ways that you can help break the cycle of violence?

___

___

___

___

___

Avoiding Domestic Violence *(page 290)*

There are some things you can do to avoid and prevent abuse. Here are the Three Rs.

- **Recognize.** Abuse takes many forms. It may be physical, emotional, or sexual abuse or neglect.
- **Resist.** Stand up for yourself. Run away from the abuser and seek help from a trusted adult.
- **Report.** Tell a trusted adult if someone is abusing you. Tell a trusted adult if you see someone is abusing a friend or someone else.

3. What are some of the ways that you can avoid or prevent abuse?

___

___

___

___

___

Name Class Date

Lesson 4 **Reading Tutor**

USE WITH CHAPTER 11, PAGES 291–295.

Family Relationships: Community Support Systems

Vocabulary

crisis center	A facility that handles emergencies and provides referrals to an individual needing help *(page 291)*
foster care	A temporary arrangement in which a child is placed under the guidance and supervision of a family or an adult who is not related to the child by birth *(page 292)*
family counseling	Therapy to restore healthy relationships in a family *(page 294)*
mediator	A person who helps others resolve issues to the satisfaction of both parties *(page 294)*

Drawing from Experience

Where could you go to get help if your family was in trouble? What resources offer help to families? Do you think it would be hard to ask for help? What can you do to keep your family healthy? Think about these questions as you read Lesson 4.

In the last lesson, you learned how to deal with family crises. In this lesson, you will learn about community support groups.

Reading Tutor, Lesson 4 *(continued)*

USE WITH CHAPTER 11, PAGES 291–295.

Organizing Your Thoughts

Use the chart below to help you take notes as you read the summaries that follow. In the first box, list some of the sources of help for families. In the other box, list some of the ways to keep your family healthy.

Sources of Help for Families	Ways to Maintain a Healthy Family

Reading Tutor, Lesson 4 *(continued)*

USE WITH CHAPTER 11, PAGES 291–295.

Read to Learn

Read each passage carefully. Write in complete sentences to answer the following questions.

Help for Families *(pages 291–294)*

A **crisis center** is *a place that handles emergencies. It gives referrals to a person who needs help*. Some communities also have crisis hot lines. These are numbers that you can call to get help 24 hours a day.

Here are some of the sources of help for families in need.

- **Community services.** Some of these services help people get food, clothes, and shelter. Some help find medical care, jobs, or parent classes.
  - **Help for children.** Abused children may go into **foster care.** This is *a temporary arrangement where a child stays with a family not related to the child.*
  - **Help for victims of spousal abuse.** Shelters and safe houses give food, clothes, and shelter to women in crisis and their children.
- **Support groups.** These are meetings in which people share their problems. They get advice from others who are in similar situations. They get comfort from knowing that they are not alone.
- **Counseling. Family counseling** is *therapy to restore healthy relationships in a family*. Family members meet with counselors to talk about issues and find solutions. Family members may also get individual counseling.
- **Mediation.** A **mediator** is *a person who helps others resolve issues to the satisfaction of both parties*. Mediation helps families communicate and get along with each other.

1. What are some of the sources of help for families in need?

Reading Tutor, Lesson 4 *(continued)*

USE WITH CHAPTER 11, PAGES 291–295.

Maintaining Healthy Families *(pages 294–295)*

Each member of a family can do his or her part to keep the family healthy. Here are some of the ways to make a family strong.

- **Cooperate.** Be polite. Do your chores without your parents asking you to.
- **Show appreciation.** Say "Thank you." Do not take others for granted.
- **Be a good communicator.** Listen. Do not interrupt. Do not raise your voice.
- **Offer help.** Show concern. Offer your support.
- **Be empathetic.** Try to see things from the other person's point of view.
- **Work to resolve conflict.** Use the Three Cs: Communicate. Cooperate. Compromise.
- **Know when to get outside help.** Know what type of situation needs professional help. Know where to go to get services.

2. What are some of the ways that you can help keep your family healthy?

USE WITH CHAPTER 12, PAGES 302-306.

Peer Relationships: Safe and Healthy Friendships

Vocabulary

peers	People of similar age who share similar interests *(page 302)*
friendship	A significant relationship between two people that is based on caring, trust, and consideration *(page 303)*
platonic friendship	A friendship with a member of the opposite gender in which there is affection, but the two people are not considered a couple *(page 303)*
clique	A small circle of friends, usually with similar backgrounds or tastes, who exclude people viewed as outsiders *(page 304)*
stereotype	An exaggerated and oversimplified belief about an entire group of people, such as an ethnic or religious group, or a gender *(page 305)*

Drawing From Experience

Who are your peers? Who are your friends? Are there any cliques in your school? Do you belong to a clique? How do you choose your friends? What makes someone a good friend? Think about these questions as you read Lesson 1.

In the last chapter, you learned about family relationships. In this lesson, you will learn about peer relationships.

Reading Tutor, Lesson 1 *(continued)*

USE WITH CHAPTER 12, PAGES 302-306.

Organizing Your Thoughts

Use the chart below to help you take notes as you read the summaries that follow. In the first box, list some of the types of peer relationships. In the other box, list some of the ways that you can form a healthy friendship.

Types of Peer Relationships	Ways to Form a Healthy Friendship

Reading Tutor, Lesson 1 *(continued)*

USE WITH CHAPTER 12, PAGES 302-306.

Read to Learn

Read each passage carefully. Write in complete sentences to answer the following questions.

Types of Peer Relationships *(pages 302-305)*

Peers are *people of a similar age who share similar interests*. You begin to meet more people as you get older. You meet people of all ages and races.

A **friendship** is *a significant relationship between two people.* Friends care for, respect, and trust each other. You can share your thoughts them. There are several kinds of friendships.

- A **platonic friendship** is *a friendship with a member of the opposite gender in which there is affection but the two people are not a couple.*
- A casual friendship is between peers who share something in common. This may be a classmate or a teammate. You share interests but you may not form close bonds with each other.
- A close friendship has strong ties. Close friends share thoughts and feelings. They trust and support each other. They work out problems. Here are more traits of friends.
    - They share values, interests, and beliefs on basic issues.
    - They have open and honest communication.
    - They share joys, troubles, and dreams.
    - They have mutual respect, caring, and support.
    - They have concern for each other's safety and well being.

A **clique** is *a small circle of friends, usually with similar backgrounds, who exclude people they see as outsiders*. They may have prejudices or exclude people because of a stereotype.

- **Prejudice** is making judgments about others without knowing them.
- A **stereotype** is *an exaggerated belief about an entire group of people, such as an ethnic or religious group or a gender*.

1. What are some of the types of friendship?

____

____

____

____

____

____

Forming Healthy Friendships *(pages 305-306)*

You will have many chances to make friends during your life. Choose friends who are positive and have a healthy attitude. Choose friends who share your values and who urge you to do better.

Avoid choosing friends who will influence you to try risky activities. A healthy friendship will add to your life in a positive way.

You build friendships on common values and interests. Here are some ways to build a healthy friendship.

- **Be loyal.** Friends do not do things to purposely hurt each other.
- **Encourage each other.** Friends give support. They help each other through hard times.
- **Respect each other.** Avoid taking friends for granted. Be on time. Keep your promises.

2. What are some of the ways to build a healthy friendship?

____

____

____

____

____

____

Name Class Date

Lesson 2 — Reading Tutor

USE WITH CHAPTER 12, PAGES 307-312.

Peer Relationships: Peer Pressure and Refusal Skills

Vocabulary

peer pressure	The influence that people your age may have on you *(page 307)*
harassment	Persistently annoying others *(page 308)*
manipulation	An indirect, dishonest way to control or influence others *(page 308)*
assertive	Standing up for your rights and beliefs in firm but positive ways *(page 310)*
refusal skills	Communication strategies that can help you say no when you are urged to take part in behaviors that are unsafe, unhealthful, or that go against your values *(page 310)*
passive	A tendency to give up, give in, or back down without standing up for rights and needs *(page 312)*
aggressive	Overly forceful, pushy, hostile, or otherwise attacking in their approach *(page 312)*

Drawing From Experience

Has a friend ever helped you do better in school or on a team? Has anyone ever tried to get you to do something against your values? Does peer pressure affect you? Do you know how to say no when you need to? Think about these questions as you read Lesson 2.

In the last lesson, you learned about friendships. In this lesson, you will learn about peer pressure and how to say no.

Reading Tutor, Lesson 2 *(continued)*

USE WITH CHAPTER 12, PAGES 307-312.

Organizing Your Thoughts

Use the chart below to help you take notes as you read the summaries that follow. In the first box, list the kinds of peer pressure. In the other box, list some of the ways to say no to negative peer pressure.

Types of Peer Pressure	Ways to Say No

Reading Tutor, Lesson 2 *(continued)*

USE WITH CHAPTER 12, PAGES 307-312.

Read to Learn

Read each passage carefully. Write in complete sentences to answer the following questions.

Peer Pressure *(pages 307-309)*

Peer pressure is *the influence that people your age may have on you*. It can be positive or negative.

Positive peer pressure can benefit all sides of your health triangle. It can motivate you to try new activities. Friends who do not use tobacco or alcohol may influence you to avoid substance abuse. You can also affect others. You can be a role model and inspire others to do positive things.

Negative peer pressure can put you at risk. Members of a clique may be rude to others. They may engage in activities that go against your values.

- **Harassment** is *persistently annoying others*. It may include name-calling and bullying.
- **Manipulation** is *an indirect, dishonest way to control others*. Here are some methods.
  - Mocking or teasing others in hurtful ways.
  - Using "guilt trips" to get what you want.
  - Bargaining—offer to make a deal to get what you want.
  - Using flattery or praise to get what you want.
  - Bribing—promising money or favors if the person will do what you ask.
  - Making threats—promising violence or some other negative consequence.
  - Using blackmail—threatening to tell some embarrassing information.

2. What are the types of peer pressure? What is manipulation?

Reading Tutor, Lesson 2 *(continued)*

USE WITH CHAPTER 12, PAGES 307-312.

Resisting Negative Peer Pressure *(pages 309-312)*

One way to resist negative peer pressure is to avoid it. Make friends with people who share your values and interests. Friends who respect you will be less likely to pressure you into doing something that will risk your health.

Being **assertive** means *standing up for your rights in firm but positive ways.*

Refusal skills are *strategies that help you say no when faced with something that you do not want to do or that goes against your values.* There are three steps.

1. **Step 1: State Your Position.** Say no. State your position simply and firmly. Give a reason why. Use body language.
   - Shake your head no.
   - Raise your hands in a stop signal.
   - Walk away.
2. **Step 2: Suggest Alternatives.** Suggest going to the movies instead of a party where there will not be adult supervision.
3. **Step 3: Stand Your Ground.** Peers may still try to get you to change your mind. Make it clear that you mean what you say. Use strong body language and maintain eye contact.

Being assertive takes practice. An assertive response is the most effective way to deal with peer pressure. Here are some other common responses.

- **Passive** people have *a tendency to give up, give in, or back down without standing up for their own rights and needs.* Others may see them as pushovers.
- **Aggressive** people are *overly forceful, pushy, or hostile in their approach.* Others may react by staying away from them or fighting back.

2. What are some of the ways that you can resist negative peer pressure?

____

____

____

____

____

Lesson 3 **Reading Tutor**

USE WITH CHAPTER 12, PAGES 313–317.

Peer Relationships: Dating and Setting Limits

Vocabulary

infatuation	Exaggerated feelings of passion for another person (page 313)
affection	A feeling of fondness for someone (page 313)
curfew	A set time at which you must be home at night (page 317)

Drawing From Experience

Have you ever been on a date? Have you ever gone out in a group? What kinds of activities did you do? What kinds of limits did you set? Think about these questions as you read Lesson 3.

In the last lesson, you learned about peer pressure. In this lesson, you will learn about dating.

Organizing Your Thoughts

Use the chart below to help you take notes as you read the summaries that follow. In the first box, list some of the facts about dating and what to do on a date. In the other box, list some of the limits to set in a dating relationship.

Dating and What to Do on a Date	Setting Limits

Reading Tutor, Lesson 3 *(continued)*

USE WITH CHAPTER 12, PAGES 313–317.

Read to Learn

Read each passage carefully. Write in complete sentences to answer the following questions.

Dating *(pages 313-316)*

Dating can be a way to get to know a person of the opposite gender. A teen may feel attraction for someone else in several ways.

- **Infatuation** is *an exaggerated feeling of passion for another person*. These feelings are natural but they are not real affection.
- **Affection** is *a feeling of fondness for someone*. This comes after you know a person well. You can express this by talking to each other, holding hands, and spending time together.

Not everyone dates. Some teens may be shy. Some may have other interests. Some may not date because of family values. Some teens go out with groups of friends of both genders. This lets teens develop social skills. Group dates ease the pressure of being alone with someone new.

What you do on a date will depend on who you are with and what you like to do. Here are some activities you might choose.

- **The movies.**
- **Dinner or a school dance.**
- **Sports or athletic activities.** You might try skating, miniature golf, or horseback riding.
- **Community activities.** You might try going to the zoo or the museum or a festival.
- **Charitable activities.** You can participate in a walk-a-thon or a fund-raiser.

Avoid risk situations by knowing where you are going on a date. Find out who will be there. Tell your parents when you expect to be home. Have some money with you. Here are more tips.

- **Avoid places where alcohol and other drugs are present.**
- **Avoid being alone with a date at home or in an isolated place.**

3. What is dating? What kinds of activities can you do on a date?

____

____

____

____

Dating Relationships *(page 316)*

Some teens choose to have an ongoing dating relationship with only one person. This may limit your chances to get to know others. Ending dating relationships may be hard. One person may want to end the relationship and the other does not. Being open and honest can help resolve this type of problem.

2. What are some of the facts about dating relationships?

____

____

____

____

____

Setting Limits *(page 317)*

Your parents may set limits on your dating. Limits can protect your health and safety. A **curfew** is *a set time at which you must be home at night*. You and your parents should fix limits and agree upon them ahead of time.

You will learn to set your own limits as you get older. Here are some types of limits.

- Set a limit on the age of the person you date.
- Set limits with your date about the places you go and how you will get there.
- Set limits before you leave on a date so that you avoid risky situations.
- Be clear and firm about your decision to practice abstinence.

3. What are some of the types of limits you might set regarding dating?

____

____

____

____

____

Name Class Date

Lesson 4 **Reading Tutor**

USE WITH CHAPTER 12, PAGES 318–323.

Peer Relationships: Abstinence: A Responsible Decision

Vocabulary

abstinence	A deliberate decision to avoid harmful behaviors, including sexual activity before marriage and the use of tobacco, alcohol, and other drugs *(page 318)*
sexually transmitted diseases (STDs)	Infectious diseases spread from person to person through sexual contact *(page 318)*
priorities	Those goals, tasks, and activities that you judge to be more important than others *(page 319)*
self-control	A person's ability to use responsibility to override emotions *(page 319)*

Drawing from Experience

What do you know about teen pregnancy? What do you know about STDs? What can you do if someone pressures you to have sex? Why is abstinence the best choice for teens? Think about these questions as you read Lesson 4.

In the last lesson, you learned about dating and setting limits. In this lesson, you will learn about abstinence.

Reading Tutor, Lesson 4 *(continued)*

USE WITH CHAPTER 12, PAGES 318–323.

Organizing Your Thoughts

Use the chart below to help you take notes as you read the summaries that follow. In the first box, list some of the ways to help you commit to abstinence. In the next box, list some of the reasons to practice abstinence. In the last box, list the ways to say no to sexual activity.

Commit to Abstinence	Reasons to Abstain	Ways to Say No

Name Class Date

Reading Tutor, Lesson 4 *(continued)*

USE WITH CHAPTER 12, PAGES 318–323.

Read to Learn

Read each passage carefully. Write in complete sentences to answer the following questions.

Abstinence Until Marriage *(pages 318–319)*

Abstinence is *a choice to avoid high-risk behaviors. These include sexual activity before marriage and the use of tobacco, alcohol, and other drugs.* Many teens choose to abstain from sexual activity because it is the only sure way to avoid pregnancy and STDs. **STDs** or **sexually transmitted diseases** are *infections spread from person to person by sexual contact.*

Priorities are *those goals, tasks, and activities that you judge to be more important than others.* Making abstinence from sexual activity a priority can take away risk. It can help you meet your goals. It takes planning and self-control. **Self-control** is *a person's ability to use responsibility to override emotions.*

Here are some tips to help you abstain.

- **Establish your priorities.** Think about your goals and your values.
- **Set limits on how you express affection.** Set your limits in advance.
- **Share your thoughts with your partner.** Be open and honest about your priorities.
- **Talk with a trusted adult.** He or she may be able to suggest ways to deal with your feelings.
- **Avoid high-pressure situations.** Go out on dates in a group. Avoid deserted places.
- **Do not use alcohol or other drugs.** They interfere with your ability to think.

1. What are some of the tips to help you abstain from sexual activity?

____

____

____

____

____

Reading Tutor, Lesson 4 *(continued)*

USE WITH CHAPTER 12, PAGES 318–323.

Reasons to Practice Abstinence *(pages 320–322)*

Sexual activity has many short-term and long-term consequences.

- **Legal issues**
  - It is not legal for an adult to have sexual contact with anyone under the age of consent.
  - People can go to jail for breaking the law.
  - They get a label as sex offenders. This label can harm them for the rest of their lives.
- **Effects on physical health**
  - One result of sexual activity may be unplanned pregnancy. Teen pregnancy risks the health of the teen mother and the baby.
  - Another result of sexual activity may be sexually transmitted diseases (STDs). Doctors can treat some STDs. Many do not have a cure. Others, such as AIDS can be fatal.
- **Effects on emotional health**
  - Having sex outside of marriage goes against the values of many people.
  - Teens may lie to their parents. They may feel guilty.
  - Teens who face unplanned pregnancy and parenthood may feel great stress.
- **Effects on social health**
  - Sexually active teens risk their reputation. They go against family values. They go beyond the limits their parents set for their safety.
  - An unplanned pregnancy can make teens drop out of school. They may need to give up their social lives to meet the needs of their child.

2. What are some of the reasons to practice abstinence from sexual activity?

___

___

___

___

___

Reading Tutor, Lesson 4 *(continued)*

USE WITH CHAPTER 12, PAGES 318–323.

Using Avoidance Techniques and Refusal Skills *(pages 322–323)*

Learn how to say no to sexual activity. Share your decision to abstain with your girlfriend or boyfriend. Here are some refusal lines that may help you.

- Your date says, "If you love me, you will." You say, "If you care about me, you won't pressure me."
- Your date says, "Everyone's doing it." You say, "No, everyone is not. I'm sticking to my values."
- Your date says, "Don't be such a baby." You say, "It's the mature, responsible decision to wait."
- Your date says, "My feelings won't change. I'll still respect you." You say, "Maybe, but I won't respect myself."

Make sure your body language matches your words. Do not be afraid of hurting the other person's feelings. It is possible to say no and still be friends.

3. What are some of the ways to say no to sexual activity?

USE WITH CHAPTER 13, PAGES 330–334.

Violence Prevention: Personal Safety

Vocabulary

body language	Nonverbal communication through gestures, facial expressions, behaviors, and posture *(page 332)*
self-defense	Any strategy for protecting oneself from harm *(page 332)*
assertive	Standing up for your rights and beliefs in firm but positive ways *(page 332)*

Drawing from Experience

Do you avoid unsafe areas? Do you lock your front door? How can you protect yourself from harm? Do you know self-defense? What does it mean to be assertive? Think about these things as you read Lesson 1.

In the last chapter, you learned about your peers. In this lesson, you will learn about personal safety.

Name Class Date

USE WITH CHAPTER 13, PAGES 330–334.

Organizing Your Thoughts

Use the chart below to help you take notes as you read the summaries that follow. In the first box, list some of your protective factors. In the next box, list some of the strategies for staying safe. In the last box, list some of the ways to keep your community safe.

Your Protective Factors	Ways to Stay Safe	Safety in the Community

Reading Tutor, Lesson 1 *(continued)*

USE WITH CHAPTER 13, PAGES 330–334.

Read to Learn

Read each passage carefully. Write in complete sentences to answer the following questions.

Your Protective Factors *(pages 330–331)*

Individual and social protective factors can reduce a teen's risk of violence.

1. **Individual protective factors**
   - The teen has no history of violent behavior.
   - The teen gets along with others.
   - The teen is smart.
   - The teen has a nonviolent attitude.
   - The teen is a female.
2. **Family protective factors**
   - Parents monitor the teen's behavior.
   - Parents assess peers in a positive way.
   - The teen has a warm relationship with parents or other adults.
3. **Peer/school protective factors**
   - The teen's peers and friends avoid high-risk behavior.
   - The teen is committed to school.
   - The teen has a good attitude.
4. **Community protective factors**
   - The teen has a strong economic opportunity.
   - The teen helps out in the community.

1. What are some of the protective factors that can reduce a teen's risk of violence?

____

____

____

____

____

Reading Tutor, Lesson 1 *(continued)*

USE WITH CHAPTER 13, PAGES 330–334.

Strategies for Staying Safe *(pages 331–333)*

There are behaviors you can practice to stay safe. Here are some smart precautions.

- Avoid unsafe areas.
- Do not carry your purse or wallet in an easy-to-grab place.
- Walk briskly. Always look like you know where you are going and what you are doing.
- Avoid walking alone at night. Avoid doorways. Walk under lights near the curb.
- Park your car in a well-lit area. Have your keys out as you near your car. Lock the doors.
- Let your family know where you are going and when you will be home.
- Do not get into an elevator alone with a stranger.
- Get on and off the bus in a well-lit area.
- Ask a person who gives you a ride to not leave until you are in your home.
- Avoid the use of alcohol and other drugs.

You can protect yourself from harm by using body language and self-defense.

- **Body language** is *nonverbal communication by gesture, facial expression, behavior, and posture.* Make direct eye contact, use a strong voice, hold your head high, and walk with a firm stride.
- **Self-defense** is *any strategy for protecting oneself from harm.* Taking a self-defense class can add to your sense of safety.
- **Assertive** means *standing up for your rights and beliefs in firm but positive ways.* Show that you are not an easy target.

Here are some tips for keeping your home safe.

- Lock doors with a bolt.
- Make sure windows have a lock.
- Never open the door to someone you do not know.
- Do not tell callers you are home alone.
- Do not give out personal information over the phone.

Reading Tutor, Lesson 1 *(continued)*

2. What are some of the ways that you can keep yourself and your home safe?

____

____

____

____

____

Safety in the Community *(page 334)*

Many communities take steps to make the neighborhoods safer. Here are some of the steps.

- **Increased police patrol.** More officers are put on street patrol.
- **Neighborhood Watch programs.** Neighbors report suspicious activity to the police.
- **After-school programs.** These are safe places where teens can use their time well.
- **Improved lighting in parks and playgrounds.** This can lower crime in the area.

3. What are some of the ways that you can make your community a safer place?

____

____

____

____

____

Name Class Date

Lesson 2 — Reading Tutor

USE WITH CHAPTER 13, PAGES 335–340.

Violence Prevention: Keeping Schools Safe

Vocabulary

violence	Threatened or actual use of physical force or power to harm another person or to damage property *(page 335)*
bullying	The act of seeking power or attention through the psychological, emotional, or physical abuse of another person *(page 336)*
sexual harassment	Uninvited and unwelcome sexual contact directed at another person *(page 336)*
gang	A group of people who associate with one another to take part in criminal activity *(page 337)*
peer mediation	A process in which trained students help other students find fair ways to resolve conflict and settle their differences *(page 339)*

Drawing from Experience

Do you feel safe at school? Are you concerned about violence? Do you know anyone who is in a gang? What kinds of safety measures are in place at your school? What can you do to promote safety in your school? Think about these questions as you read Lesson 2.

In the last lesson, you learned about personal safety. In this lesson, you will learn about safety in your school.

Reading Tutor, Lesson 2 *(continued)*

USE WITH CHAPTER 13, PAGES 335–340.

Organizing Your Thoughts

Use the chart below to help you take notes as you read the summaries that follow. In the first box, list some of the school safety issues. In the other box, list some of the ways to reduce the risk of violence.

School Safety Issues	Ways to Reduce the Risk of Violence

Reading Tutor, Lesson 2 *(continued)*

USE WITH CHAPTER 13, PAGES 335–340.

Read to Learn

Read each passage carefully. Write in complete sentences to answer the following questions.

Issues of School Safety *(pages 335–337)*

Schools are usually safe places, but violence does occur. **Violence** is *the threatened or actual use of physical force or power to harm another person or to damage property*. Here are some of the factors that play a role in school violence.

Bullying is *seeking power by emotional or physical abuse of another person*. Bullies often try to anger or scare their victims. You may need to report the problem to a teacher or parent. No one should tolerate bullying.

Sexual harassment is *uninvited and unwelcome sexual conduct aimed at another person*. It is not legal and it must be reported to a teacher or parent at once. Here are some types of sexual harassment.

- Making sexual comments or jokes
- Writing sexual messages on notes or walls
- Spreading sexual rumors
- Spying on someone who is dressing
- Pulling off someone's clothes
- Exposing body parts
- Touching that is not appropriate

A **gang** is *a group of people who associate with one another to take part in crimes*. Gangs may vandalize property, rob others, and sell drugs. Gang members may bring guns to school. They risk the safety of all the other students.

1. What are some of the factors that play a role in school violence?

____

____

____

____

____

Reading Tutor, Lesson 2 *(continued)*

USE WITH CHAPTER 13, PAGES 335–340.

Reducing the Risk of Violence *(pages 337–340)*

Keeping schools safe is a priority in a community. Here are some of the warning signs of violence. Tell a teacher if you see any of these signs in another student and you think he or she may become violent.

- The teen has a hard time controlling anger.
- The teen disobeys school rules.
- The teen engages in risk behaviors.
- The teen creates violent artwork or writing.
- The teen talks about weapons or violence all the time.
- The teen destroys property.
- The teen uses alcohol or other drugs.
- The teen harms animals.
- The teen makes threats or plans to hurt others.
- The teen brings or talks about bringing a weapon to school.

You can take a stand and help to keep your school a safe place. Here are some tips.

- Do not carry a weapon. Report people who carry weapons.
- Report any violent acts or threats of violence to adults or police.
- Use conflict-resolution skills.
- Use refusal skills to avoid unsafe situations.
- Choose your friends wisely. Have friends who share your values.
- Avoid spending time with peers who show any of the warning signs of violence.
- Tell a parent or other adult if you fear that you are in danger. Avoid being alone.
- Join a S.A.V.E. (Students Against Violence Everywhere) chapter.
- Schools also have policies in place to make sure students are safe. Here are some of them.
- Some schools have a zero-tolerance policy. This means that the school will expel any students who bring weapons or drugs to school.
- Some schools have metal detectors or look in lockers for weapons or drugs.

Reading Tutor, Lesson 2 *(continued)*

USE WITH CHAPTER 13, PAGES 335–340.

- Some schools have "closed" campuses. They lock all doors except the main door.
- Some schools have security guards.
- Some schools use **peer mediation.** This is when *trained students help other students find fair ways to resolve conflict*. Here are the steps.
  1. **Make introductions.** The mediator explains that he or she will stay neutral.
  2. **Set ground rules.** The sides agree not to interrupt. They agree to listen to each other.
  3. **Hear each side.** Each party gets to speak. The other side may ask questions.
  4. **Find solutions.** The parties talk about each idea. They agree upon a solution.
  5. **Close the session.** The mediator goes over the agreement.

Parents are also concerned about safety in schools. Parents can work with the police and business leaders to promote safety in schools. Community members can volunteer to watch hallways or rest rooms. Everyone can work with each other to provide a safe place for teens.

2. What are some of the ways to reduce the risk of violence in schools?

____

____

____

____

____

Name Class Date

Lesson 3 **Reading Tutor**

USE WITH CHAPTER 13, PAGES 341–347.

Violence Prevention: Protecting Yourself from Violence

Vocabulary

assailant	A person who commits a violent act against another *(page 341)*
prejudice	An unfair opinion or judgment of a particular group of people *(page 342)*
assault	An unlawful attack on a person with the intent to harm or kill *(page 344)*
random violence	Violence committed for no particular reason *(page 344)*
homicide	The willful killing of one human being by another *(page 344)*
sexual violence	Any form of unwelcome sexual conduct directed at an individual, including sexual harassment, sexual assault, and rape *(page 345)*
sexual assault	Any intentional sexual attack against another person *(page 346)*
rape	Any form of sexual intercourse that takes place against a person's will *(page 346)*

Drawing from Experience

Have you ever seen an act of violence? Do you think violent movies can influence real life? What are some of the reasons for violence? What can you do to help prevent violence? Think about these questions as you read Lesson 3.

In the last lesson, you learned about school safety. In this lesson, you will learn about the causes and effects of violence.

Reading Tutor, Lesson 3 *(continued)*

USE WITH CHAPTER 13, PAGES 341–347.

Organizing Your Thoughts

Use the chart below to help you take notes as you read the summaries that follow. In the first box, list some of the reasons why violence occurs. In the next box, list some of the influences on violence. In the last box, list some of the types of violence.

Why Violence Occurs	Influences on Violence	Types of Violence

Reading Tutor, Lesson 3 *(continued)*

USE WITH CHAPTER 13, PAGES 341–347.

Read to Learn

Read each passage carefully. Write in complete sentences to answer the following questions.

Why Violence Occurs *(pages 341–342)*

Violence may occur for many reasons. The victim may know his or her **assailant.** This is *a person who commits a violent act against another*. Here are some common causes of violence.

- **Need to control others.** Some people use violence to get what they want.
- **Way of expressing anger.** Some people who cannot deal with anger may lash out.
- **Prejudice.** This is *an unfair judgment of a particular group of people.*
- **Retaliation.** Some people use violence to get back at others.

1. What are some of the reasons that violence occurs?

___

___

___

___

___

Influences on Violence *(pages 342–343)*

Here are several factors that may contribute to violence.

- **Weapons availability.** Many teen homicides involve guns. More than one-fifth of high school students reported that they had carried a weapon. People who own guns legally should keep them unloaded and in a locked place.
- **The media.** Violence is a common theme in movies, video games, songs, and on TV. Teens who see this violence may not feel upset when they see violent acts in real life.
- **Alcohol and other drugs.** People who use alcohol and drugs do not think clearly. Drug users may turn to violence to get money to buy drugs. Drive-by shootings may be drug-related. Drunk drivers kill many people every year.
- **Mental/emotional issues.** People who have a negative self-concept may use violence to prove they have worth. Some people use it as an act of revenge. People who have trouble dealing with their anger can get anger management counseling.

Reading Tutor, Lesson 3 *(continued)*

USE WITH CHAPTER 13, PAGES 341–347.

2. What are some of the factors that may influence violence?

____

____

____

____

____

Types of Violence *(pages 344–346)*

Teens are more likely to be crime victims than adults are. Teens also carry out violent acts. Here are some of the types of violent crime.

1. Assault and homicide.

- An **assault** is *an attack on a person with the intent to harm or kill.*
- **Random violence** is *violence committed for no particular reason.*
- **Homicide** is *the willful killing of one human being by another.*
- Here are safety tips to protect yourself from crime.
  - Throw your purse or wallet away from you if an attacker wants your money. Run the other way.
  - Go to a place where there are other people if someone is following you.

2. Sexual violence is *any form of unwelcome sexual conduct aimed at a person, such as sexual harassment, sexual assault, and rape.* All forms are illegal.

- **Sexual assault** is *any intentional sexual attack against another person.*
- **Rape** is *any form of sexual intercourse that takes place against a person's will.*
- Here are safety tips to escape and survive a sexual attack.
  - Try to run for help.
  - Scream or yell, "Fire!"
  - Try to disable or stun your attacker.
  - Be alert and try to escape.

Reading Tutor, Lesson 3 *(continued)*

USE WITH CHAPTER 13, PAGES 341–347.

3. What are some of the types of violence?

Gang-Related Violence *(page 347)*

Teens commit many crimes that are gang-related. Teens may join gangs to be part of a group. Most gangs are involved in violent activities. Teens who join gangs are at risk for arrest, injury, or death. Resist pressure to join a gang. Leave when you see gang members.

4. What are some of the facts about gang violence?

Name Class Date

Lesson 4

Reading Tutor

USE WITH CHAPTER 13, PAGES 348–353.

Violence Prevention: Preventing and Overcoming Abuse

Vocabulary

abuse	The physical, mental/emotional, or sexual mistreatment of one person by another *(page 348)*
physical abuse	The intentional infliction of bodily harm or injury on another person *(page 349)*
verbal abuse	Using words to mistreat or injure another person *(page 349)*
stalking	The repeated following, harassment, or threatening of an individual to frighten or cause him or her harm *(page 349)*
date rape	When one person in a dating relationship forces the other person to participate in sexual intercourse *(page 350)*

Drawing from Experience

Do you know any victims of abuse? What is date rape? How can you protect yourself from abuse? What can you do to help victims of abuse? Think about these questions as you read Lesson 4.

In the last lesson, you learned about the causes and effects of violence. In this lesson, you will learn about abuse.

Reading Tutor, Lesson 4 *(continued)*

USE WITH CHAPTER 13, PAGES 348–353.

Organizing Your Thoughts

Use the chart below to help you take notes as you read the summaries that follow. In the first box, list some of the types of abuse. In the next box, list some of the facts about dating violence. In the last box, list some of the ways to overcome abuse and get help for abusers.

Types of Abuse	Dating Violence Facts	Help for Victims/Abusers

Reading Tutor, Lesson 4 *(continued)*

USE WITH CHAPTER 13, PAGES 348–353.

Read to Learn

Read each passage carefully. Write in complete sentences to answer the following questions.

Types of Abuse *(pages 348–349)*

Abuse is the *physical, mental/emotional, or sexual mistreatment of one person by another*. Abuse takes many forms and affects many people. All forms of abuse are illegal.

Physical abuse is *the intentional infliction of bodily harm or injury on another person*. The abuser may slap, punch, kick, bite, shake, beat, or shove another person. The abuse is not the victim's fault. No one deserves abuse.

Emotional abuse is a pattern of behavior that attacks a person's emotional growth and sense of worth. It may include verbal abuse and stalking.

- **Verbal abuse** is *using words to mistreat or hurt another person*. Name-calling, insults, and threats are some of the types of this abuse. The victim may feel stupid or helpless.
- **Stalking** is *the repeated following, harassment, or threatening of a person to scare or cause him or her harm*. The abuser may follow a person, stand outside his or her home, and make many phone calls.

1. What are some of the types of abuse?

Dating Violence *(pages 350–351)*

Dating violence is abuse in dating relationships. It includes all forms of abuse. People in a healthy relationship respect and care about each other. Here are some signs of dating abuse.

- Expressions of jealousy
- Attempts to control a partner's behavior
- Use of insults or put-downs to manipulate a partner
- Use of guilt to control a partner

Reading Tutor, Lesson 4 *(continued)*

USE WITH CHAPTER 13, PAGES 348–353.

Date rape is *when one person in a dating relationship forces the other person to have sexual intercourse.* Acquaintance rape is when a casual friend forces you to have sex. All forms of rape cause lasting hurt and emotional scars.

- Date rape drugs are GHB and Rohypnol. The rapist puts the drug in the victim's food or drink. The victim may black out and be an easy target for rape. Get your own drink and do not leave it alone when you are at a party.

2. What are some of the signs of dating abuse?

____

____

____

____

Overcoming Abuse *(page 352)*

Victims of abuse have not done anything that is wrong. It is vital to report the abuse. Call the police and get medical help. Get counseling. Here are some of the sources of help for victims of abuse or rape.

- Parents and guardians
- A teacher, a coach, or a counselor
- A clergy member
- The police
- A doctor or the hospital emergency room
- A battered women's shelter
- A rape crisis center
- A therapist
- Support groups

3. What are some of the sources of help for a victim of abuse or rape?

____

____

____

____

Reading Tutor, Lesson 4 *(continued)*

USE WITH CHAPTER 13, PAGES 348–353.

Help for Abusers *(page 353)*

The victim and the abuser need to get help. Some of the people who abuse others were also victims of abuse at one time. The cycle of violence may go on from one generation to another. It is very important to get help for the abuser and to break this cycle of harm.

Here are some of the possible ways to break the cycle of violence.

- Have classes for parents on family life and child development.
- Provide counseling for all victims of abuse and violence.
- Have treatment programs for abusers.

4. What are some of the possible ways to help break the cycle of violence?

Personal Care and Healthy Behaviors: Healthy Skin, Hair, and Nails

Vocabulary

epidermis	The outer, thinner layer of the skin that is composed of living and dead cells *(page 360)*
dermis	The thicker layer of the skin beneath the epidermis that is made up of connective tissue and contains blood vessels and nerves *(page 360)*
melanin	A pigment that gives the skin, hair, and iris of the eyes their color *(page 361)*
sebaceous glands	Structures within the skin that produce an oily secretion called sebum *(page 361)*
sweat glands	Structures within the dermis that secrete perspiration through ducts to pores on the skin's surface *(page 361)*
melanoma	The most serious form of skin cancer *(page 364)*
hair follicle	A structure that surrounds the root of a hair *(page 365)*
dandruff	A condition that can occur if the scalp becomes too dry and dead skin cells are shed as sticky, white flakes *(page 365)*

Drawing from Experience

Have you ever had a sunburn? Do you wear sunscreen when you are out in the sun? Do you ever "break out" or get acne? How often do you wash your hair? How do you care for your nails? Think about these questions as you read Lesson 1.

In the last chapter, you learned about preventing violence and abuse. In this lesson, you will learn about healthy skin, hair, and nails.

Reading Tutor, Lesson 1 *(continued)*

USE WITH CHAPTER 14, PAGES 360–366.

Organizing Your Thoughts

Use the chart below to help you take notes as you read the summaries that follow. In the first box, list the parts of the skin. In the next box, list the ways to care for your skin. In the third box, list some of the facts about your hair. In the last box, list some facts about your nails.

Parts of the Skin	Ways to Care for the Skin

Your Hair	Your Nails

Reading Tutor, Lesson 1 *(continued)*

USE WITH CHAPTER 14, PAGES 360–366.

Read to Learn

Read each passage carefully. Write in complete sentences to answer the following questions.

Structure and Function of the Skin *(pages 360–362)*

The skin has two main layers.

1. The **epidermis** is *the outer, thinner layer of the skin that is made of living and dead cells.*
2. The **dermis** is *the thicker layer of the skin beneath the epidermis that is made of connective tissue and contains blood vessels and nerves.*

Here are some of the substances that the cells of the epidermis produce.

- Keratin is a protein that makes the nails tough.
- Lipids are substances that make your skin waterproof.
- **Melanin** is *a pigment that gives the skin, hair, and iris of the eyes their color.* People with fair skin have less melanin and are at more risk for harm from the sun.

Here are some of the parts of the dermis.

- **Sebaceous glands** *produce an oily secretion called sebum.* Sebum helps keep skin and hair from drying out.
- Blood vessels supply cells with blood and nutrients. They ease the removal of waste. They also help regulate body heat.
- **Sweat glands** *secrete perspiration through ducts to pores on the skin's surface.* They also regulate body heat.

1. What are some of the parts of the skin?

___

___

___

___

Healthy Skin *(pages 362–365)*

Take care of your skin as a part of your daily routine.

- Wash your face every morning and evening. Use mild soap and water.
- Take a bath or a shower every day. Avoid touching your face with your hands.
- Eat a well-balanced diet. Vitamin A is good for the skin. Eat vegetables, liver, and milk.

Reading Tutor, Lesson 1 *(continued)*

USE WITH CHAPTER 14, PAGES 360–366.

The sun can harm your skin. UV rays cause your skin to make more melanin. Your skin will get tan or sunburn. Your skin will get wrinkled and leathery over time. You may get skin cancer. Here are some ways to protect your skin.

- **Always wear sunscreen on the exposed areas of your skin.** Use SPF 15 or higher.
- **Wear clothes that protect your skin.** Wear hats and long sleeves and sunglasses.

Body piercing and tattoos carry health risks. Bacteria can enter the body through breaks in the skin. Hepatitis B and C and HIV can pass into the body through dirty needles. Tattoos and piercing may also affect your social life. They may make a poor impression on an employer or others.

Here are some of the common types of skin problems.

- **Acne** occurs when pores in the skin clog up. Redness occurs. Pus may form. Wash your face gently twice a day. Avoid oily products.
- **Warts** are from a virus that infects the surface layers of the skin. They are usually on the hands, feet, and face.
- **Vitiligo** is when patches of the skin lose all pigment. There is no known cure for this.
- **Boils** form when bacteria infect hair follicles. Redness occurs and pus forms. The doctor may drain the pus and give you antibiotics. Keep skin clean to prevent boils.
- **Moles** are spots that have extra melanin. Most moles do not cause harm. Some moles may lead to skin cancer.

Melanoma is the most serious form of skin cancer.

The ABCs of melanoma. Check your moles to find early signs of cancer.

A = **Asymmetry** means the mole does not have matching halves.

B = **Border irregularity** means the mole does not have smooth edges.

C = **Color** is very black or an uneven color.

D = **Diameter** is wider than a pea.

2. What are some of the most common types of skin problems?

____

____

____

____

Reading Tutor, Lesson 1 *(continued)*

USE WITH CHAPTER 14, PAGES 360–366.

Your Hair *(pages 365–366)*

You have hair on almost every surface of your skin. A **hair follicle** is a *structure that surrounds the root of a hair*. Hair protects the skin and eyes. A well-balanced diet is the basis for healthy hair. Washing and brushing your hair will also keep your hair healthy.

Here are some of the common types of hair problems.

- **Dandruff** is *a condition that can occur if the scalp becomes too dry*. The scalp sheds dead skin cells as sticky, white flakes. You can treat it with dandruff shampoo.
- **Head lice** are tiny insects that live in scalp hair. They can spread by contact. Do not use combs or hats that belong to others. You can treat it with medicated shampoo.

3. What are some of the common types of hair problems?

____

____

____

____

____

Your Nails *(page 366)*

Your fingernails and toenails are made of dead cells that contain keratin. Nails protect your fingers and toes.

Keep your nails clean and trimmed. Use a nail file to smooth nails. Keep cuticles pushed back. Clip toenails straight across.

4. What are some of the ways to take care of your nails?

____

____

____

____

____

Name Class Date

Lesson 2

Reading Tutor

USE WITH CHAPTER 14, PAGES 367–370.

Personal Care and Healthy Behaviors: Care of Teeth and Mouth

Vocabulary

periodontium	The area immediately around the teeth *(page 367)*
pulp	The tissue that contains the blood vessels and nerves of a tooth *(page 368)*
plaque	A sticky, colorless film that acts on sugar to form acids that destroy tooth enamel and irritate gums *(page 368)*
periodontal disease	An inflammation of the periodontal structures *(page 370)*
tartar	The hard, crustlike substance formed when plaque hardens *(page 370)*

Drawing from Experience

Do you brush and floss your teeth after you eat? Do you have any fillings? How often do you see your dentist? Why do you think it is important to take good care of your teeth? Think about these questions as you read Lesson 2.

In the last lesson, you learned about your skin, hair, and nails. In this lesson, you will learn about the care of your teeth and mouth.

Reading Tutor, Lesson 2 *(continued)*

USE WITH CHAPTER 14, PAGES 367–370.

Organizing Your Thoughts

Use the chart below to help you take notes as you read the summaries that follow. In the first box, list the parts of your teeth. In the next box, list the way to care for your teeth. In the last box, list some of the problems of the teeth and the mouth.

Parts of the Teeth	Ways to Care for Teeth	Problems of the Teeth and Mouth

Reading Tutor, Lesson 2 *(continued)*

USE WITH CHAPTER 14, PAGES 367–370.

Read to Learn

Read each passage carefully. Write in complete sentences to answer the following questions.

Your Teeth *(pages 367–368)*

The **peridontium** is *the area immediately around the teeth*. It is made of the gums, the periodontal ligament, and the jawbone.

A tooth is made of three main parts. These are the **crown**, the **neck**, and the **root.**

- The crown is the visible part of the tooth. Enamel covers the crown. Enamel is made of **calcium**. It protects the teeth.
- Dentin is the layer under the enamel. Dentin is tissue that adds to the shape and hardness of a tooth and acts as a barrier to protect the pulp.
- The **pulp** is *the tissue that contains the blood vessels and nerves of a tooth*. It extends into the root canal. It gives nutrients to the tooth.

1. What are some of the parts of the tooth?

____

____

____

____

____

Healthy Teeth and Mouth *(pages 368–369)*

It is very important to keep your teeth clean. **Plaque** is *a sticky, colorless film that acts on sugar to form acids that destroy tooth enamel and irritate gums*. A cavity may form in the tooth if the enamel breaks down.

Good oral hygiene can prevent tooth decay.

- Brush your teeth to remove the plaque.
- Floss your teeth to get the plaque that your brush cannot reach.
- Have your dentist clean and check your teeth on a regular basis.

A well balanced diet can also help prevent tooth decay. Phosphorous, calcium, and vitamin C help keep your teeth strong and your gums healthy. Avoid sugary snacks and avoid all tobacco products.

Reading Tutor, Lesson 2 *(continued)*

USE WITH CHAPTER 14, PAGES 367–370.

2. What are some of the ways to keep your teeth and mouth healthy?

___

___

___

___

Problems of the Teeth and Mouth *(page 370)*

Here are some of the types of problems that affect the teeth and mouth.

- Halitosis is bad breath. Poor oral hygiene, smoking, bacteria on the tongue, decayed teeth, gum disease, or some foods may cause bad breath.
- **Periodontal disease** is *an inflammation of the periodontal structures.* Bacteria cause it. Gum disease begins with a buildup of plaque. **Tartar** is *the hard, crustlike substance that forms when plaque hardens.*
- Malocclusion means "bad bite." This might mean crowded teeth or upper and lower jaws that are out of alignment. You can correct this by wearing braces.

3. What are some of the problems of the teeth and mouth?

___

___

___

___

___

Name Class Date

Lesson 3

Reading Tutor

USE WITH CHAPTER 14, PAGES 371–375.

Personal Care and Healthy Behaviors: Eye Care

Vocabulary

lacrimal gland	The gland that secretes tears into ducts that empty into the eye *(page 371)*
sclera	The tough, white part of the eye *(page 372)*
cornea	A transparent tissue that bends and focuses light before it enters the lens *(page 372)*
choroid	A thin structure that lines the inside of the sclera *(page 372)*
retina	The light-sensitive membrane on which images are cast by the cornea *(page 372)*

Drawing from Experience

Do you wear glasses? How often do you get your eyes checked? Do you wear protective eyewear when needed? How can you take care of your eyes? Think about these things as you read Lesson 3.

In the last lesson, you learned about the care of your teeth and mouth. In this lesson, you will learn about caring for your eyes.

Reading Tutor, Lesson 3 *(continued)*

USE WITH CHAPTER 14, PAGES 371–375.

Organizing Your Thoughts

Use the chart below to help you take notes as you read the summaries that follow. In the first box, list the parts of the eye and how it works. In the other box, list some of the things to do to keep your eyes healthy and some of the kinds of eye problems.

Parts of the Eye and Vision	Healthy Eyes and Eye Problems

Reading Tutor, Lesson 3 *(continued)*

USE WITH CHAPTER 14, PAGES 371–375.

Read to Learn

Read each passage carefully. Write in complete sentences to answer the following questions.

Your Eyes *(page 371)*

Most of the sensory information that your brain receives comes from your eyes. Your eyes sit in sockets at the front of your skull. Your eyebrows, eyelashes, and eyelids protect your eyes.

The **lacrimal gland** is *the gland that secretes tears into ducts that empty into the eye.* Tears move across the eye as you blink. People blink more than six million times a year. Tears are made of water, salt, and mucus that protect the eye against germs.

1. What is the lacrimal gland? How does it protect your eye?

____

____

____

____

____

Parts of the Eye *(pages 372–373)*

The two main parts of the eye are the optic nerve and the three layers of the eyeball wall.

- The outer layer of the eyeball wall is the sclera and the cornea.
  - The **sclera** is *the tough, white part of the eye.* It supports and shapes the eyeball.
  - The **cornea** is *a transparent tissue that bends and focuses light before it enters the lens.*
- The middle layer of the eye is the choroid.
  - The **choroid** is *a thin layer that lines the inside of the sclera.*
  - The **iris** is the colored part of the eye that holds the pupil.
  - The **pupil** is the hole that light goes in to reach the inner eye.
- The inner layer is the retina.
  - The **retina** is *the light-sensitive membrane on which the cornea casts images.*
  - **Rods** allow us to see in dim light.

Reading Tutor, Lesson 3 *(continued)*

USE WITH CHAPTER 14, PAGES 371–375.

- **Cones** work in bright light and let us see color.
- The **optic nerve** sends impulses to the brain.
- The **lens** of the eye is behind the iris and pupil. It is transparent and it refines the focus of images on the retina.
- The **aqueous humor** is the watery fluid between the cornea and the lens.
- **Vitreous humor** is a gelatin-like substance between the lens and the retina.

2. What are some of the parts of the eye?

____

____

____

____

____

Vision *(page 373)*

Your eye begins to work when light passes through the cornea, pupil, and lens to reach the retina. The cornea focuses the light rays. The lens refines the light rays. Muscles in the eye shape the lens to focus on a near or far object. Light turns on the cones and rods in the retina. A nerve impulse goes to the brain through the optic nerve.

The retina makes a sharp image if your vision is normal. You can check your vision by reading an eye chart. To have 20/20 vision means you can stand 20 feet away from an eye chart and read the top eight lines.

3. What does 20/20 vision mean?

____

____

____

____

____

Reading Tutor, Lesson 3 *(continued)*

USE WITH CHAPTER 14, PAGES 371–375.

Healthy Eyes *(pages 373–374)*

Here are some tips to help you keep your eyes healthy.

- **Eat a well-balanced diet.** Eat foods that have vitamin A. Lack of vitamin A may cause night blindness.
- **Protect your eyes.** Wear safety goggles. Keep dirty hands away from your eyes. Wear sunglasses. Never look directly into the sun.
- **Have regular eye exams.** See the eye doctor.
- **Rest your eyes.** Look up and away from close work every ten minutes to reduce eyestrain.

4. What are some of the ways that you can help keep your eyes healthy?

____

____

____

____

____

Eye Problems *(pages 374–375)*

The two main types of eye problems are vision problems and diseases of the eye. Here are some of the common kinds of vision problems. You can correct most of these problems with glasses, contact lenses, or laser surgery.

- **Myopia** means nearsighted. It is when a person cannot see distant objects clearly.
- **Hyperopia** means farsighted. It is when a person cannot see close-up objects clearly.
- **Astigmatism** is a curved cornea or lens. The eye is not able to focus. Things look blurry.
- **Strabismus** is weak eye muscles that cause the eyes to turn inward or outward.

Reading Tutor, Lesson 3 *(continued)*

USE WITH CHAPTER 14, PAGES 371–375.

Here are some of the kinds of diseases of the eye.

- **Conjunctivitis** is pinkeye. It is a redness and swelling of the lining of the eyelids.
- **Detached retina** occurs when a part of the retina separates from the choroid. It is a serious threat to your vision. You can treat it with laser surgery.
- **Glaucoma** is high pressure in your eye that harms the retina and the optic nerve. It may result in loss of sight. Regular eye exams are the best way to find it early.
- **Cataracts** occur when the lens of the eye gets cloudy. Sight is blurry or foggy. You can treat it with surgery.
- **Macular degeneration** occurs when the macula portion of the retina begins to fail. It is the leading cause of vision loss in older people. There is no cure.

5. What are some of the types of vision problems and diseases of the eye?

Name Class Date

USE WITH CHAPTER 14, PAGES 376–379.

Personal Care and Healthy Behaviors: Ears and Hearing Protection

Vocabulary

external auditory canal	A passageway about one inch long that leads to the remaining portion of the outer ear, the eardrum *(page 376)*
auditory ossicles	Three small bones linked together that connect the eardrum to the inner ear *(page 377)*
labyrinth	The inner ear *(page 377)*
tinnitus	A condition in which a ringing, buzzing, whistling, roaring, hissing, or other sound is heard in the ear in the absence of external sound *(page 379)*

Drawing from Experience

Do you ever listen to really loud music? Do you get earaches when you are sick? How is hearing important in your life? What can you do keep your ears healthy? Think about these questions as you read Lesson 4.

In the last lesson, you learned about your eyes. In this lesson, you will learn about your ears and how to care for your hearing.

Reading Tutor, Lesson 4 *(continued)*

USE WITH CHAPTER 14, PAGES 376–379.

Organizing Your Thoughts

Use the chart below to help you take notes as you read the summaries that follow. In the first box, list some of the parts of the ear and how the ear works. In the other box, list some of ways to care for your ears and some of the kinds of problems of the ear.

Parts of the Ear and Hearing	Healthy Ears and Ear Problems

Reading Tutor, Lesson 4 *(continued)*

USE WITH CHAPTER 14, PAGES 376–379.

Read to Learn

Read each passage carefully. Write in complete sentences to answer the following questions.

Parts of the Ear *(pages 376–377)*

The ear has three main sections.

1. **The outer ear.**
   - The part of the ear you see is the **auricle.**
   - It sends sound waves into the **external auditory canal.** This is a *tunnel about one inch long that leads to the remaining portion of the outer ear, the eardrum*. Tiny hairs and glands line the eardrum. They make wax to protect the ear.
   - The **eardrum** is the tympanic membrane. It acts as a barrier between the outer and middle ear.
2. **The middle ear.**
   - The **auditory ossicles** are *three small bones that connect the eardrum to the inner ear*. They are the smallest bones in the body.
   - The middle ear is connected to the throat by the **eustachian tube.** It equalizes pressure when you yawn.
3. **The inner ear.**
   - *The inner ear* is the **labyrinth.** It is a network of passages with three main parts.
   - The **cochlea** is the area of hearing in the inner ear.
   - The **vestibule** and **semicircular canals** control the body's balance.

1. What are some of the parts of the ear?

____

____

____

____

____

Hearing and Balance *(page 377)*

A nerve impulse goes to your brain when a sound wave enters your inner ear. Your brain reads the impulse as a sound. Sound waves enter the external auditory canal. The eardrum vibrates. The fluid in the cochlea moves. Receptor cells send a nerve impulse to the brain.

Reading Tutor, Lesson 4 *(continued)*

USE WITH CHAPTER 14, PAGES 376–379.

Receptor cells in your **vestibule** and **semicircular canals** send signals to the brain about your sense of balance. Your brain sends signals to your muscles to adjust to keep your balance.

2. What are the parts of the ear that control your sense of balance?

____

____

____

____

____

Healthy Ears *(page 378)*

Here are some of the ways to keep your ears healthy.

- Keep your ears clean.
- Wear a helmet when you play sports.
- Wear a hat that covers the auricles and the earlobes in cold weather.
- Keep foreign objects out of your ears.
- Get medical help right away when you have an ear infection.
- Have an ear exam and have your hearing tested.

Avoid loud noise. Exposure to loud noise can lead to hearing loss and deafness over time.

3. What are some of the ways that you can keep your ears healthy?

____

____

____

____

____

Reading Tutor, Lesson 4 *(continued)*

USE WITH CHAPTER 14, PAGES 376–379.

Problems of the Ear *(page 379)*

There are two types of hearing loss.

- **Conductive hearing loss.** This occurs when sound waves do not pass from the outer to the inner ear. Middle ear infections may lead to rupture of the eardrum. Fluid may build up in the middle ear.
- **Sensorineural hearing loss.** This occurs when there is damage to the cochlea, auditory nerve, or brain.

Tinnitus is *a ringing, buzzing, or other sound heard in the ear when there is no external sound.* It can occur from age, high blood pressure, or loud noise. Protect your ears by wearing earplugs at loud events or near loud machines.

4. What are some of the types of problems that occur in the ear?

Skeletal, Muscular, and Nervous Systems: The Skeletal System

Vocabulary

axial skeleton	The 80 bones of the skull, spine, ribs, vertebrae, and sternum, or breastbone *(page 387)*
appendicular skeleton	The 126 bones of the upper and lower limbs, shoulders, and hips *(page 387)*
cartilage	A strong, flexible connective tissue *(page 387)*
ossification	The process by which bone is formed, renewed, and repaired *(page 387)*
ligament	A band of fibrous, slightly elastic connective tissue that attaches bone to bone *(page 389)*
tendon	A fibrous cord that attaches muscle to bone *(page 389)*

Drawing from Experience

What do you know about your skeletal system? How many bones does the human body have? What role does your skeleton play in your total health? Think about these questions as you read Lesson 1.

In the last chapter, you learned about your personal care. In this lesson, you will learn about the skeletal system.

Reading Tutor, Lesson 1 *(continued)*

USE WITH CHAPTER 15, PAGES 386–389.

Organizing Your Thoughts

Use the chart below to help you take notes as you read the summaries that follow. In the first box, list some of the ways that the skeletal system works. In the other box, list some of the parts of the skeletal system.

Functions of the Skeletal System	Parts of the Skeletal System

Read to Learn

Read each passage carefully. Write in complete sentences to answer the following questions.

Functions of the Skeletal System *(page 386)*

Your skeletal system gives your body structure. Here are some of the functions of the skeleton.

- It gives support for your upper body and head.
- It is a strong and mobile framework that muscles can act on.
- It protects your internal tissues and organs.
- It stores minerals that are vital to the body.
- Bone marrow makes new blood cells.

1. What are some of the functions of the skeletal system?

____

____

____

Structure of the Skeleton *(pages 387–389)*

Your skeletal system has 206 bones. There are two main types of bones.

- The **axial skeleton** is made of *the 80 bones of the skull, spine, ribs, vertebrae, and sternum, or breastbone.*
- The **appendicular skeleton** is made of the other *126 bones of the upper and lower limbs, shoulders, and hips.*

An outer layer of hard, **compact bone** covers all bones. **Spongy bone** is under the compact bone. **Red bone marrow** fills the cavities in the spongy bone. Here are some of the types of bones.

- **Long bones.** These are the bones in your arms and legs. The **diaphysis** is the main column of a long bone. It is made of compact bone. There is a narrow cavity in the diaphysis that holds yellow bone marrow. The **epiphysis** is the end of a long bone. It forms joints with other bones. It holds red blood cells.
- **Short bones.** These are the bones in your ankles and wrists. They are about equal in length and width.
- **Flat bones.** These are the bones in the skull and the shoulder blade. They are thinner and much flatter than other bones.
- **Irregular bones.** These are the bones in your face and your vertebrae. They have unusual shapes.

Reading Tutor, Lesson 1 *(continued)*

USE WITH CHAPTER 15, PAGES 386–389.

Cartilage is *a strong, flexible connective tissue.* Here are some of the places where the body has cartilage.

- At the ends of long bones
- At the end of the nose
- In the outer ear
- As a cushion in the knee
- An embryo's skeleton is made of cartilage. It later hardens. This **ossification** is *the process by which bone forms, renews, and repairs.*

Joints are points where bones meet. Here are some of the types of joints.

- **Ball-and-socket joints** allow a wide range of movement. The head of one bone fits into the cavity of another bone. Some of these are the hip and the shoulder.
- **Hinge joints** allow a joint to bend and straighten. Some of these are the elbow, knee, ankle, and fingers.
- **Pivot joints** allow limited rotation or turning of the head.
- **Ellipsoidal joints** such as the wrist have an oval-shaped part that fits into a curved space. Gliding joints allow bones to slide over each other.

Here are some of the parts of the skeletal system that help the body move.

- A **ligament** is *a band of fibrous, slightly elastic connective tissue. It attaches bone to bone.*
- A **tendon** is *a fibrous cord. It attaches muscle to bone.*

2. What are some of the types of bones in the human body?

____

____

____

____

Name Class Date

Lesson 2 | Reading Tutor

USE WITH CHAPTER 15, PAGES 386–389.

Skeletal, Muscular, and Nervous Systems: Care and Problems of the Skeletal System

Vocabulary

osteoporosis	A condition in which progressive loss of bone tissue occurs *(page 391)*
scoliosis	Lateral, or side-to-side, curvature of the spine *(page 391)*
repetitive motion injury	Damage to tissues caused by prolonged, repeated movements *(page 393)*

Drawing from Experience

Have you ever had a broken bone? Do you know anyone who has scoliosis? What kinds of nutrients can make your bones strong? How can you care for your skeletal system? Think about these questions as you read Lesson 2.

In the last lesson, you learned about the parts of the skeletal system. In this lesson, you will learn about the care of the skeletal system.

Reading Tutor, Lesson 2 *(continued)*

USE WITH CHAPTER 15, PAGES 390–393.

Organizing Your Thoughts

Use the chart below to help you take notes as you read the summaries that follow. In the first box, list some of the ways to care for your skeletal system. In the other box, list some of the problems of the skeletal system.

Ways to Care for Your Skeletal System	Problems of the Skeletal System

Read to Learn

Read each passage carefully. Write in complete sentences to answer the following questions.

Care of the Skeletal System *(page 390)*

The health of your skeletal system can affect your total health. Here are some of the ways that you can care for your skeletal system.

- Eat foods that have calcium, such as dark green leafy vegetables and milk.
- Eat foods that have vitamin D, such as fortified milk.
- Eat foods that have phosphorus, such as dairy foods, beans, whole grains, and liver.
- Do regular physical activity. Include weight-bearing exercises.
- Wear safety gear such as a helmet when you play sports.

1. What are some of the ways that you can care for your skeletal system?

____

____

____

____

Problems of the Skeletal System *(pages 391–393)*

Problems of the skeletal system may occur from injury, poor nutrition, or other factors. Here are some of the types of problems of the skeletal system.

- **Fractures.** A fracture is any type of break in a bone. Here are the types of fractures.
  - **Compound fracture.** The broken end of the bone breaks through the skin.
  - **Simple fracture.** The broken bone does not break through the skin.
  - **Hairline fracture.** The two parts of the bone do not separate.
  - **Transverse fracture.** The fracture is completely across the bone.
  - **Comminuted fracture.** The bone shatters into more than two pieces.

- **Osteoporosis.** This is *a progressive loss of bone tissue.* Bones become weak and brittle. It is very serious and it affects many older people. It is important to increase bone mass while you are a teen to lower the risk of this disease late in life.

Reading Tutor, Lesson 2 *(continued)*

USE WITH CHAPTER 15, PAGES 390–393.

- **Scoliosis.** This is *a lateral, or side-to-side, curve of the spine*. You may have it at birth or it may develop as you grow. The curve gets worse as you get older, so it is important to treat this early. You treat it by wearing a brace or having surgery.
- **Injuries to joints.** Injuries can occur for any of the following reasons.
  - **Dislocation.** This is when the ligaments of a joint tear as a bone slips out of place. The doctor may need to reset the joint until the injury heals.
  - **Torn cartilage.** This may happen if you twist a joint. You can treat it with surgery.
  - **Bursitis.** This is pain and swelling of the bursa, a fluid-filled sac. The shoulder and elbow have these sacs.
  - **Bunion.** This is the pain and swelling of the bursa in the first joint of the big toe. Some shoes make this worse. Large bunions may need surgery.
  - **Arthritis.** This is the pain and swelling of a joint. It may occur from an injury or from wear and tear on the joint. It may also come from an autoimmune disease.
- **Repetitive motion injury.** This is *harm to tissues caused by repeated movements*. Computer work, sewing, or assembly-line work may cause it. Carpal tunnel syndrome is an example of this condition. Swollen tendons in the wrist may cause a numb feeling in the hand. You can treat it by wearing a splint.

2. What are some of the types of problems of the skeletal system?

USE WITH CHAPTER 15, PAGES 394–398.

Skeletal, Muscular, and Nervous Systems: The Muscular System

Vocabulary

smooth muscles	Muscles that act on the lining of passageways and internal organs *(page 395)*
skeletal muscles	Muscles that are attached to bone and cause body movements *(page 395)*
flexor	The muscle that closes a joint *(page 395)*
extensor	The muscle that opens a joint *(page 395)*
cardiac muscle	A type of striated muscle that forms the wall of the heart *(page 395)*
muscle tone	The natural tension in the fibers of a muscle *(page 396)*
tendonitis	The inflammation of a tendon *(page 398)*
hernia	When an organ or tissue protrudes through an area of weak muscle *(page 398)*

Drawing from Experience

Have you ever sprained your ankle? Have you ever pulled a muscle? How do your muscles work to move your skeleton? How can you care for your muscular system? Think about these questions as you read Lesson 3.

In the last lesson, you learned how to care for the skeletal system. In this lesson, you will learn about the muscular system.

Reading Tutor, Lesson 3 *(continued)*

USE WITH CHAPTER 15, PAGES 394–398.

Organizing Your Thoughts

Use the chart below to help you take notes as you read the summaries that follow. In the first box, list some of the types of muscles. In the other box, list some of the problems of the muscular system.

Types of Muscles	Problems of the Muscular System

Read to Learn

Read each passage carefully. Write in complete sentences to answer the following questions.

Functions of the Muscular System *(page 394)*

There are two main types of muscles in your body.

- **Involuntary muscles** are the muscles that you do not control. They help you breathe, make your heart beat, and move food in your digestive system.
- **Voluntary muscles** are muscles that you control to do things, such as play the piano or throw a ball.

1. What are the two main types of muscles in your body?

____

____

____

____

Structure of the Muscular System *(pages 395–397)*

Muscles are lots of long fiber cells. Muscles contract or shorten and then extend or stretch when they work. There are three types of muscle tissue.

1. **Smooth muscles** are *muscles that act on the lining of passageways and internal organs*. These are involuntary muscles in the blood vessels, digestive tract, and passage to the lungs.
2. **Skeletal muscles** are *muscles that attach to the bones and cause the body to move*. These are voluntary muscles. The **flexor** is *the muscle that closes a joint*. The **extensor** is *the muscle that opens a joint*.
3. **Cardiac muscle** is *a type of striated muscle that forms the wall of the heart*. This is the muscle that contracts your heart.

Physical activity is the best way to have strong, healthy muscles. Muscles will shrink if you do not use them. **Muscle tone** is *the natural tension in the fibers of a muscle*. Here are some ways to care for your muscles.

- Be physically active.
- Practice good posture.
- Wear safety gear.

2. What are some of the types of muscles?

___

___

___

___

___

Problems of the Muscular System *(pages 397–398)*

Your muscles may be sore for a few days after you work out. Here are some of the other types of muscle problems.

- **Bruise.** This is an area of discolored skin. It appears after an injury causes blood vessels to break and leak under the skin. You can treat any swelling with ice.
- **Muscle strain or sprain.** A strain occurs when you stretch or tear a muscle. You can treat it with the R.I.C.E. (rest, ice, compression, elevation) method. A sprain is an injury to a ligament and needs medical help.
- **Tendonitis.** This is *the pain and swelling of a tendon*. Injury or aging may cause it. You can treat it with rest and medicine.
- **Hernia.** This occurs *when an organ or tissue protrudes through an area of weak muscle*. Lifting a very heavy object may cause it. You may need surgery to repair it.
- **Muscular dystrophy.** This is an inherited disorder that destroys skeletal muscle fibers over time. There is no cure.

3. What are some of the types of muscle problems?

___

___

___

___

___

USE WITH CHAPTER 15, PAGES 399–405.

Skeletal, Muscular, and Nervous Systems: The Nervous System

Vocabulary

neurons	Nerve cells *(page 400)*
cerebrum	The largest and most complex part of the brain *(page 402)*
cerebellum	The second largest part of the brain *(page 403)*
brain stem	A 3-inch stalk of nerve cells and fibers that connects the spinal cord to the rest of the brain *(page 403)*
reflex	A spontaneous response of the body to a stimulus *(page 404)*

Drawing from Experience

Do you ever get sweaty palms? Does your heart ever race? What do you know about your nervous system? What is a reflex? How does your body know what to do when you are asleep? Think about these questions as you read Lesson 4.

In the last lesson, you learned about the muscular system. In this lesson, you will learn about the nervous system.

Reading Tutor, Lesson 4 *(continued)*

USE WITH CHAPTER 15, PAGES 399–405.

Organizing Your Thoughts

Use the chart below to help you take notes as you read the summaries that follow. In the first box, list the parts and functions of the central nervous system. In the other box, list the parts and functions of the peripheral nervous system.

The Central Nervous System	The Peripheral Nervous System

Reading Tutor, Lesson 4 *(continued)*

USE WITH CHAPTER 15, PAGES 399–405.

Read to Learn

Read each passage carefully. Write in complete sentences to answer the following questions.

Function and Structure of the Nervous System *(page 399)*

The nervous system allows your brain to communicate with all the parts of your body. The nervous system has two main parts.

- The **central nervous system (CNS)** is the brain and the spinal cord.
- The **peripheral nervous system (PNS)** is the nerves that extend from the brain and spinal cord. It is the nerves that come from receptors in the skin that sense touch, heat, or pain.

The central nervous system gets messages from the peripheral nervous system. The brain reads the messages and sends out a response. The impulses travel up to 280 miles per hour. Your brain can tell you to let go of a hot pan before it burns you.

1. What are the two main parts of the nervous system?

____

____

Neurons *(page 400)*

Neurons are *nerve cells* that carry messages to and from the brain and the spinal cord. A neuron has three main parts.

- **Cell body.** This holds the nucleus or the control center of the cell.
- **Dendrites.** These extend from the cell body. They receive messages from other neurons and send impulses back to the cell body.
- **Axons.** These carry impulses away from the cell body to another neuron, muscle cell, or gland. Some axons have a myelin sheath cover. They carry messages faster than other axons.

There are three kinds of neurons. These are sensory neurons, motor neurons, and interneurons. Interneurons carry messages between the other neurons. Here is how the nerve impulse works.

- A nerve impulse begins when a sensory neuron is stimulated.
- The impulse travels to the CNS. The CNS reads the message with the help of an interneuron.
- A motor neuron carries the message to a muscle cell.

2. What are the three main parts of a neuron?

____

____

____

____

The Central Nervous System *(pages 401–404)*

The central nervous system has two main parts, the spinal cord and the brain.

1. The **spinal cord** is a long column of nerve tissue. It is about as thick as your finger. It extends about 18 inches down your back.

- **Vertebrae** are the bones that make up your spine.
- The **spinal meninges** are connective tissue that help protect the spinal cord.
- **Cerebrospinal fluid** is around the spinal cord. It absorbs shock and gives nourishment.

2. The **brain** controls all the activity of the body. It weighs about 3 pounds and it sits in the cavity of the skull. The brain uses about 20 percent of the body's oxygen. It can only last for four to five minutes without oxygen. The brain has three main parts. Each hemispere has four lobes.

- The **cerebrum** is *the largest and most complex part of the brain.* It is the center of thought, learning, and memory. It has two hemispheres, or halves. The right one controls the left side of the body. It is also the center for processing music and art and thinking about spatial relationships. The left one controls language, reason, and math analysis. Each hemisphere has four lobes.
  - The **frontal lobe** controls voluntary movement, language, intellect, and personality.
  - The **parietal lobe** controls sensory feelings of heat, cold, pain, touch, and place.
  - The **occipital lobe** controls the sense of vision.
  - The **temporal lobe** controls the senses of hearing and smell, memory, and judgment.
- The **cerebellum** is *the second largest part of the brain.* Its job is to coordinate the movement of the skeleton. It maintains the body's balance and posture. It allows the body to perform a series of moves, such as serving a volleyball.

Reading Tutor, Lesson 4 *(continued)*

USE WITH CHAPTER 15, PAGES 399–405.

- The **brain stem** is *a 3-inch stalk of nerves and fibers that connects the spinal cord to the rest of the brain.* Sensory and motor impulses pass through the brain stem. It has five parts.
  - **Medulla oblongata.** This is the lower part of the brain stem. It regulates heartbeat, respiratory rate, and reflexes like coughing. It affects hearing and tongue movement.
  - **Pons.** This is above the medulla. It is a path to connect nerve impulses to the other areas of the brain. It helps regulate breathing. It controls the eye and face muscles.
  - **Midbrain.** This is the highest part of the brain stem. It helps control eyeball movement and pupil size. It affects reflexes such as turning your head at a loud noise.
  - **Thalamus.** This is a relay center for sensory impulses. It receives information from the eyes, ears, and touch receptors in the skin.
  - **Hypothalamus.** This regulates body heat, appetite, and sleep. It controls secretions from the **pituitary gland**. This gland controls metabolism, sexual growth, and emotions.

3. What are some of the parts of the central nervous system and the brain?

____

____

____

____

The Peripheral Nervous System *(pages 404–405)*

The peripheral nervous system (PNS) is made of all the nerves that are not part of the CNS. It carries messages between the CNS and the rest of the body. It has two main parts.

- **The autonomic nervous system** controls involuntary acts like digestion and heart rate. It is a network of nerves divided into two main parts.
  - The **sympathetic nervous system** controls the "fight-or-flight" response. This prepares your body to react. It also controls reflexes. A **reflex** is *a spontaneous response of the body to a stimulus.*
    - **Steps of a reflex action.**
      1. **Stimulus.** Your hand touches a hot stove.
      2. The **sensory neuron** contacts a connecting neuron in the spinal cord.
      3. The **connecting neuron** contacts a **motor neuron** that sends an impulse to the muscles.
      4. **Reflex.** The muscle responds. It pulls your hand away from the heat.
    - The **parasympathetic nervous system** slows down body functions during rest times. It slows the heartbeat, opens blood vessels, and lowers blood pressure.
- **The somatic nervous system** relays messages to and from the CNS. Sensory neurons relay messages from receptors in the eyes, ears, nose, tongue, and skin to the CNS. Motor neurons carry impulses from the CNS to skeletal muscles.

4. What are the main parts of the peripheral nervous system?

____

____

____

____

____

Name Class Date

Lesson 5

Reading Tutor

USE WITH CHAPTER 15, PAGES 406–409.

Skeletal, Muscular, and Nervous Systems: Care and Problems of the Nervous System

Vocabulary

epilepsy	A disorder of the nervous system that is characterized by recurrent seizures—sudden episodes of uncontrolled electrical activity in the brain *(page 409)*
cerebral palsy	A group of nonprogressive neurological disorders that are the result of damage to the brain before, during, or just after birth or in early childhood *(page 409)*

Drawing from Experience

Do you wear a helmet when you ride your bike? Have you ever had a concussion? Do you know anyone who has epilepsy? What are some of the ways that you can take care of your nervous system? Think about these questions as you read Lesson 5.

In the last lesson, you learned about the nervous system. In this lesson, you will learn how to care for the nervous system.

Reading Tutor, Lesson 5 *(continued)*

USE WITH CHAPTER 15, PAGES 406–409.

Organizing Your Thoughts

Use the chart below to help you take notes as you read the summaries that follow. In the first box, list some of the ways to care for the nervous system. In the other box, list some of the problems and diseases of the nervous system.

Care of the Nervous System	Nervous System Problems/Diseases

Reading Tutor, Lesson 5 *(continued)*

USE WITH CHAPTER 15, PAGES 406–409.

Read to Learn

Read each passage carefully. Write in complete sentences to answer the following questions.

Care of the Nervous System *(page 406)*

Any injury to the nervous system may lead to problems in other areas of the body. Here are some of the ways to care for your nervous system.

- Use helmets and other safety gear to protect your brain and spinal cord.
- Eat a well-balanced diet. Get physical activity. Get plenty of sleep.
- Check the depth of water before you dive. Look for rocks.
- Avoid the use of alcohol and other drugs.

1. What are some of the ways that you can care for the nervous system?

____

____

____

____

Problems of the Nervous System *(pages 407–408)*

Many of the problems of the nervous system are the result of head or spinal cord injuries. These injuries may be from falls, sports accidents, car crashes, or a blow to the head.

- **Head injury.** Any direct blow to the head can cause injury.
  - **Concussion** is the most common type of brain injury. It may cause a short loss of consciousness.
  - **Contusion** is a bruising of the brain tissues. It may cause harmful swelling.
  - **Coma** is a state of unconsciousness from which you cannot wake a person.
- **Spinal injury.** Any injury to the spine is serious and needs medical care.
  - **Swelling of the spinal cord** can cause a loss of nerve function for a short time.
  - **Paraplegia** is a paralysis of the legs. It can be the result of an injury to the lower part of the spinal cord.
  - **Quadriplegia** is a paralysis of the arms and legs. It may be the result of an injury to the upper part of the spinal cord.

Reading Tutor, Lesson 5 *(continued)*

USE WITH CHAPTER 15, PAGES 406–409.

2. What are some of the types of head and spinal cord injuries?

____

____

____

____

____

Degenerative Diseases *(page 408)*

These diseases cause cells to break down over time. Here are some of the more common types of degenerative diseases.

- **Parkinson's disease** destroys nerve cells in the area of the brain that controls skeletal movement. It gets worse as time goes on. Muscles get stiff and rigid. The person has muscle tremors. There is no cure for this disease.
- **Multiple sclerosis** destroys the myelin sheath that covers the axons of neurons in the CNS. The scar tissue blocks nerve impulses. Voluntary control of muscles begins to get worse. The body attacks its own cells.
- **Alzheimer's disease** occurs when protein deposits clog the neurons. The neurons are not able to carry impulses. This may cause confusion, loss of memory, and mental illness. There is no cure.

3. What are some of the more common types of degenerative diseases?

____

____

____

____

____

Reading Tutor, Lesson 5 *(continued)*

USE WITH CHAPTER 15, PAGES 406–409.

Other Disorders and Problems *(page 409)*

Here are some of the other types of problems of the nervous system.

- **Epilepsy** is *a disorder of the nervous system. It causes recurrent seizures. These are sudden episodes of uncontrolled electrical activity in the brain.* It may result from head injury, brain damage, drugs, or other causes. Medicine can help a person lead a normal life.
- **Cerebral palsy** is *a group of nonprogressive neurological disorders. These are the result of damage to the brain before, during, or just after birth or in early childhood.* Some of the causes include infection and head injury among others. You can treat it with therapy, leg braces, and medicine.

4. What are some of the other types of problems of the nervous system?

USE WITH CHAPTER 16, PAGES 416–422.

Cardiovascular and Respiratory Systems: The Cardiovascular System

Vocabulary

plasma	The fluid in which other parts of the blood are suspended *(page 418)*
hemoglobin	The oxygen-carrying protein in blood *(page 418)*
arteries	Blood vessels that carry blood away from the heart *(page 419)*
capillaries	Small vessels that carry blood between arterioles and small vessels called venules *(page 419)*
veins	Blood vessels that return blood to the heart *(page 419)*
platelets	Cells that prevent the body's loss of blood *(page 420)*
lymph	The clear fluid that fills the spaces around body cells *(page 421)*
lymphocytes	Specialized white blood cells that provide the body with immunity *(page 421)*

Drawing from Experience

What do you know about your cardiovascular system? Do you ever feel your heart pound? Have you ever taken your pulse? Do you know what type of blood you have? Think about these questions as you read Lesson 1.

In the last chapter, you learned about the skeletal, muscular, and nervous systems. In this lesson, you will learn about the cardiovascular system.

Reading Tutor, Lesson 1 *(continued)*

USE WITH CHAPTER 16, PAGES 416–422.

Organizing Your Thoughts

Use the chart below to help you take notes as you read the summaries that follow. In the first box, list the parts of the cardiovascular system. In the other box, list the parts of the lymphatic system.

Parts of the Cardiovascular System	Parts of the Lymphatic System

Reading Tutor, Lesson 1 *(continued)*

USE WITH CHAPTER 16, PAGES 416–422.

Read to Learn

Read each passage carefully. Write in complete sentences to answer the following questions.

Functions of the Cardiovascular System *(page 416)*

The cardiovascular system is made up of your heart and all the blood vessels of the body. Here are some of the functions of this system.

- Pump and circulate the blood.
- Get nutrients to all of the cells of the body.
- Deliver oxygen to the lungs. Carry carbon dioxide out of the lungs.
- Take waste to the kidneys for removal from the body.

1. What are some of the functions of the cardiovascular system?

___

___

___

___

Structure of the Cardiovascular System *(pages 417–420)*

The main parts of this system are the heart, the blood, and the blood vessels.

- **The heart.** Your heart is the pump that makes the system work. It never rests. It is made of myocardium muscle tissue.
  - **The chambers of the heart.** Your heart has four parts. Each of the two upper chambers is an **atrium.** The two lower chambers are the **ventricles.** The wall that separates the chambers is the **septum.** The right atrium acts as a pacemaker. There are one-way valves that allow blood to flow through the chambers.
  - **The circulation in the heart.** Pulmonary circulation is the circulation of blood between the heart and the lungs.
    - Blood that holds carbon dioxide and waste flows to the heart in the vena cava blood vessels. The heart pumps the blood into the lungs.
    - The blood releases carbon dioxide in the lungs and picks up oxygen from inhaled air. The blood and oxygen return to the heart.
    - The heart pumps the blood and oxygen back into the body through the aorta artery.

Reading Tutor, Lesson 1 *(continued)*

- **The blood.** Blood delivers oxygen and nutrients to the cells. It carries away waste.
  - **Plasma** is *the fluid in which other parts of the blood are suspended.* It makes up 55 percent of blood. It is mostly water. It holds nutrients, protein, salt, and hormones.
  - **Red blood cells** make up about 40 percent of blood. They carry oxygen to the body. They form in the bone marrow and they contain **hemoglobin.** This is *the oxygen-carrying protein in blood.*
  - **White blood cells** and platelets make up 5 percent of blood. The main role of white blood cells is to fight infection. They form in the bone marrow and are a part of the body's immune system. The body makes more of these cells when an infection occurs.
- **The blood vessels.** There are three main types of blood vessels.
  - **Arteries** are the *blood vessels that carry blood away from the heart.*
    - **Pulmonary arteries** carry blood from the right ventricle to the lungs.
    - **Systemic arteries** like the aorta carry blood and oxygen from the left ventricle to all areas of the body.
    - As arteries move away from the heart they branch into smaller **arterioles.**
- **Capillaries** are *small vessels that carry blood between arterioles and small vessels called venules.* They form a network that reaches into all parts of the body. They also help to regulate body heat.
  - **Veins** are the *blood vessels that return blood to the heart.*
    - **Vena cava** veins carry blood from the body to the right atrium of the heart.
    - **Pulmonary veins** carry blood and oxygen from the lungs to the left atrium.

Platelets are *cells that stop the body's loss of blood.* They gather at the site of an injury. **Fibrin** are small threadlike fibers. A clump of fibrin, platelets, and blood cells forms a sticky mass. A clot forms and stops the loss of blood. A scab forms as the clot dries.

2. What are the three main types of blood vessels?

____

____

____

____

Reading Tutor, Lesson 1 *(continued)*

USE WITH CHAPTER 16, PAGES 416–422.

The Lymphatic System *(pages 421–422)*

The lymphatic system is a network of vessels that helps protect the body against pathogens.

- **Lymph** is *the clear fluid that fills the spaces around body cells.* It is made of water, protein, fats, and lymphocytes. **Lymphocytes** are *special white blood cells that provide the body with immunity.* There are two types.
  - **B cells** are lymphocytes that multiply when they come in contact with a pathogen or germ. Some B cells make antibodies and attack the germs. Other B cells form memory cells that will activate if the body meets the same germ again.
  - **T cells** are also lymphocytes that multiply when they come in contact with a pathogen. There are two main types.
    1. **Killer cells** destroy the infected cells.
    2. **Helper cells** help activate B cells and killer T cells.
- **Structure of the lymphatic system**
  - Small lymph vessels collect lymph and form larger vessels.
  - Two **lymphatic ducts** empty lymph into veins close to the heart. Lymph returns to the blood.
  - **Lymph nodes** are small beanlike organs that are in lymph vessels.
  - **White blood cells** in lymph nodes destroy bacteria and viruses.
  - The **spleen, thymus gland,** and **tonsils** are also part of the lymphatic system.

3. What are some of the types of lymphocytes?

____

____

____

____

____

____

____

Lesson 2 **Reading Tutor**

USE WITH CHAPTER 16, PAGES 423–427.

Cardiovascular and Respiratory Systems: Care and Problems of the Cardiovascular System

Vocabulary

blood pressure	A measure of the amount of force that the blood places on the walls of blood vessels, particularly large arteries, as it is pumped through the body *(page 424)*
congenital	A condition that is present at birth *(page 425)*
anemia	A condition in which the ability of the blood to carry oxygen is reduced *(page 426)*
leukemia	A form of cancer in which any one of the different types of white blood cells is produced excessively and abnormally *(page 426)*
Hodgkin's disease	A type of cancer that affects the lymph tissue *(page 427)*

Drawing from Experience

Has the doctor ever checked your blood pressure? Do you know anyone who has had his or her tonsils out? What are some of the ways that you can keep your cardiovascular system healthy? Think about these questions as you read Lesson 2.

In the last lesson, you learned about the cardiovascular system. In this lesson, you will learn about caring for your cardiovascular system.

Reading Tutor, Lesson 2 *(continued)*

USE WITH CHAPTER 16, PAGES 423–427.

Organizing Your Thoughts

Use the chart below to help you take notes as you read the summaries that follow. In the first box, list some habits that can help keep your systems healthy. In the next box, list some of the problems of the cardiovascular system. In the last box, list the problems of the lymphatic system.

Healthy Habits	Cardiovascular Problems	Lymphatic Problems

Reading Tutor, Lesson 2 *(continued)*

USE WITH CHAPTER 16, PAGES 423–427.

Read to Learn

Read each passage carefully. Write in complete sentences to answer the following questions.

Healthy Behaviors and the Cardiovascular and Lymphatic Systems *(pages 423–424)*

Healthy habits can prevent many of the problems that occur in your body systems. Here are some healthy habits that should be a part of your life.

- Eat a well-balanced diet that is low in fats, cholesterol, and salt.
- Keep a healthy weight.
- Do aerobic exercise for at least 30 minutes three to four times per week.
- Avoid the use of tobacco.
- Avoid illegal drugs.

Blood pressure is *the force that the blood places on the walls of blood vessels as it pumps through the body.*

- Doctors measure blood pressure with a sphygmomanometer. They wrap a cuff around your arm and inflate the cuff until it is tight. They listen with a stethoscope. They let out air until they can hear the blood beating in your arm. This is your systolic pressure. Then they let out the air until they no longer hear your blood. This is your diastolic pressure.
- The maximum pressure in your arteries is the **systolic pressure.** This is the top number of the fraction in a blood pressure reading.
- **Diastolic pressure** is when your blood pressure is at its lowest point. This is when your heart relaxes and refills. It is the bottom number of the fraction in a blood pressure reading.

High blood pressure is a reading of 140/90 or more. It puts strain on the heart. To prevent high blood pressure, keep a healthy weight, be active, and deal with stress. Avoid tobacco and drugs, and eat healthy low-salt foods.

1. What are some of the healthy habits that can help you care for your body systems?

____

____

____

____

Reading Tutor, Lesson 2 *(continued)*

USE WITH CHAPTER 16, PAGES 423–427.

Cardiovascular System Problems *(pages 425–426)*

Some of the problems of the cardiovascular system are inherited and some result from illness. Here are some of the types of problems.

- **Congenital heart defects.** *A condition that is present at birth* is **congenital.** You can treat some defects with medicine or surgery.
  - A **septal defect** is when a hole in the septum lets blood with oxygen mix with blood without oxygen. It can affect the pumping of the heart.
  - **Valve defects** keep the heart valves from working the right way.
  - A **narrow aorta** may reduce the amount of blood flowing to the body.
- **Cardiovascular disease (CVD).** This is a group of disorders that includes hypertension (high blood pressure), heart disease, and stroke. It is the number one killer of men and women.
- **Heart murmur.** These are abnormal sounds made as blood flows through the heart. Some are very slight and others may need surgery.
- **Varicose veins.** These form if the valves in the veins do not close tightly enough to prevent backflow of blood. They are usually in the legs and they can be very painful. You can prevent it with physical activity. You can treat it with surgery.
- **Anemia.** This is *a condition that reduces the ability of the blood to carry oxygen*. It may be a result of low hemoglobin or low numbers of red blood cells in the blood. **Iron deficiency** is the most common cause of anemia. Avoid it by eating foods high in iron. Some of these are red meat, liver, and egg yolks.
- **Leukemia.** This is *a form of cancer. The body produces any one of the types of white blood cells in excess and abnormally*. The white blood cells cannot work and the body cannot make enough other blood cells. You can treat this with cancer drugs or a bone marrow transplant.
- **Hemophilia.** This is an inherited disorder in which the blood does not clot properly. Clotting factors are missing from the person's blood. Internal and external bleeding is hard to control. You can treat this with injections of clotting factors.

2. What are some of the types of problems of the cardiovascular system?

____

____

____

____

Lymphatic System Problems *(page 427)*

Here are some of the types of lymphatic problems. They can be the result of heredity or illness.

- **Immune deficiency.** This occurs when the immune system can no longer protect the body from infection. This can be congenital or caused by HIV, the virus that causes AIDS.
- **Hodgkin's disease.** This is *a type of cancer that affects the lymph tissue* in lymph nodes and the spleen. Early detection is important. You can treat this with cancer drugs and surgery.
- **Tonsillitis.** This is an infection of the tonsils. Tonsils are a part of the immune system. You can treat it with antibiotics or surgery.

3. What are some of the types of problems of the lymphatic system?

Cardiovascular and Respiratory Systems: The Respiratory System

Vocabulary

respiration	The exchange of gases between the body and the environment *(page 428)*
diaphragm	The muscle that separates the chest from the abdominal cavity *(page 429)*
pharynx	The throat *(page 431)*
trachea	The windpipe *(page 431)*
bronchi	The airways that connect the trachea and the lungs *(page 431)*
larynx	The voice box *(page 431)*

Drawing from Experience

Do you know how the lungs work? How do you breathe when you are asleep? What do you know about your respiratory system? Think about these questions as you read Lesson 3.

In the last lesson, you learned how to care for your cardiovascular system. In this lesson, you will learn about the respiratory system.

Reading Tutor, Lesson 3 *(continued)*

USE WITH CHAPTER 16, PAGES 428–431.

Organizing Your Thoughts

Use the chart below to help you take notes as you read the summaries that follow. In the first box, list the functions of the respiratory system. In the other, list the parts of the respiratory system.

Functions of the Respiratory System	Parts of the Respiratory System

Reading Tutor, Lesson 3 *(continued)*

USE WITH CHAPTER 16, PAGES 428–431.

Read to Learn

Read each passage carefully. Write in complete sentences to answer the following questions.

Functions of the Respiratory System *(page 428)*

Respiration is *the exchange of gases between the body and the environment*. Your lungs fill with air and then empty without your conscious control. This process has two main parts.

- **External respiration** is the exchange of oxygen and carbon dioxide that takes place between air and blood in the lungs.
- **Internal respiration** is the exchange of gases between blood and body cells.

1. What are the two main parts of respiration?

____

____

____

____

Structure of the Respiratory System *(pages 429–431)*

The respiratory system is the lungs and a series of air passages. The nose and throat are the upper system. The larynx, trachea, bronchi, and lungs are the lower system. The **lungs** are the main organs of the respiratory system. They are in the chest cavity and the ribs protect them. The **diaphragm** is *the muscle that separates the chest from the abdominal cavity*. When you inhale:

- Air moves through the nose and throat. It goes into the lungs through the **trachea,** or windpipe.
- The trachea branches out into the **bronchi.** These are *the main airways that lead into each lung*.
- The bronchi split into a network of tubes. These are the **bronchioles.**
- At the end of each bronchiole are groups of **alveoli.** These are tiny air sacs in which the gas exchange of external respiration takes place.
- Your diaphragm contracts and expands your chest cavity. The pressure in your lungs falls lower than that outside of your body.

When you exhale, your muscles relax and the volume of your chest cavity decreases. Air flows out of your lungs and exits through the nose and mouth.

Reading Tutor, Lesson 3 *(continued)*

USE WITH CHAPTER 16, PAGES 428–431.

Other respiratory structures include the following.

- Mucus and hairlike **cilia** line the membranes of the nose and trachea.
- The cilia and mucus trap particles such as dust, bacteria, and viruses.
- Air passes through the **pharynx**, or *throat*.

The **larynx and the epiglottis** are not directly involved in respiration, but they have important functions.

- The **larynx** is the *voice box*. It connects the throat and the trachea. It holds the vocal chords. These are two bands of tissue that make sound when air forces them to vibrate.
- The **epiglottis** is a flap of cartilage above the larynx. It folds down to cut off the opening to the trachea when you swallow.

2. What are some of the parts of the respiratory system?

Name Class Date

Lesson 4

Reading Tutor

USE WITH CHAPTER 16, PAGES 432–435.

Cardiovascular and Respiratory Systems: Care and Problems of the Respiratory System

Vocabulary

bronchitis	An inflammation of the bronchi caused by infection or exposure to irritants such as tobacco smoke or air pollution *(page 433)*
pneumonia	An inflammation of the lungs commonly caused by a bacterial or viral infection *(page 433)*
pleurisy	An inflammation of the lining of the lungs and chest cavity *(page 433)*
asthma	An inflammatory condition in which the trachea, bronchi, and bronchioles become narrowed, causing difficulty in breathing *(page 434)*
sinusitis	An inflammation of the tissues that line the sinuses *(page 435)*
tuberculosis	A contagious bacterial infection that usually affects the lungs *(page 435)*
emphysema	A disease that progressively destroys the walls of the alveoli *(page 435)*

Drawing from Experience

Do you ever have trouble breathing when you exercise? Does the air affect you on a smoggy day? Do you know anyone who has asthma? What are some of the ways to care for your lungs? Think about these questions as you read Lesson 4.

In the last lesson, you learned about the respiratory system. In this lesson, you will learn how to care for this system.

Reading Tutor, Lesson 4 *(continued)*

USE WITH CHAPTER 16, PAGES 432–435.

Organizing Your Thoughts

Use the chart below to help you take notes as you read the summaries that follow. In the first box, list some habits to keep your respiratory system healthy. In the other, list some of the problems of the system.

Habits for a Healthy Respiratory System	Problems of the Respiratory System

Reading Tutor, Lesson 4 *(continued)*

USE WITH CHAPTER 16, PAGES 432–435.

Read to Learn

Read each passage carefully. Write in complete sentences to answer the following questions.

Health Behaviors and the Respiratory System *(pages 432–433)*

Practicing healthy habits can prevent many respiratory problems. Here are some healthy behaviors for you to follow.

- Choose not to smoke. Avoid all tobacco. It is the main cause of lung cancer. It can also cause many other health problems.
- Be physically active. Exercise increases the capacity of the lungs.
- Wash your hands often. Germs pass from your hands to your respiratory system when you touch your nose or mouth.
- Limit time in areas that have air pollution. It may contribute to respiratory infections, asthma, and lung cancer.

1. What are some of the healthy habits that can help you care for your respiratory system?

____

____

____

____

Respiratory System Problems *(pages 433–435)*

Colds and the flu are common respiratory problems. Here are some of the other types of disorders.

- **Bronchitis** is the *pain and swelling of the bronchi from infection or irritants such as smoke or air pollution*. You may cough, wheeze, or have shortness of breath. You can treat this with medicine and by avoiding the irritant.
- **Pneumonia** is the *pain and swelling of the lungs from a bacterial or viral infection*. You may have a cough, fever, chills, or chest pain. You can treat it with antibiotics.
- **Pleurisy** is the *pain and swelling of the lining of the lungs and chest cavity*. You may cough and have chest pain.
- **Asthma** is *a condition that causes the trachea, bronchi, and bronchioles to become narrowed. This makes it hard to breathe*. You may cough, wheeze, or have chest pain. You can treat this with a bronchodilator. This is a medicine that makes the air tubes wider.

Reading Tutor, Lesson 4 *(continued)*

USE WITH CHAPTER 16, PAGES 432–435.

- **Sinusitis** is the *pain and swelling of the tissues that line the sinuses*. The sinus is an air-filled cavity above the nose and the throat. You may have a headache and fever. You can treat this with drops or sprays or antibiotics.
- **Tuberculosis** is *a contagious bacterial infection. It usually affects the lungs.* You may have cough, fever, weakness, and weight loss. Treat this in the hospital with medication.
- **Emphysema** is *a disease that destroys the walls of the alveoli over time*. You may have trouble breathing and a chronic cough. There is no cure.

2. What are some of the types of respiratory problems?

Name Class Date

CHAPTER 17
Lesson 1

Reading Tutor

USE WITH CHAPTER 17, PAGES 442–446.

Digestive and Urinary Systems: The Digestive System

Vocabulary

digestion	The mechanical and chemical breakdown of foods for use by the body's cells *(page 442)*
absorption	The passage of digested food from the digestive tract into the cardiovascular system *(page 442)*
elimination	The expulsion of undigested food or body wastes *(page 442)*
mastication	The process of chewing *(page 443)*
peristalsis	A series of involuntary muscle contractions that move food through the digestive tract *(page 443)*
gastric juices	Secretions from the stomach lining that contain hydrochloric acid and pepsin, an enzyme that digests protein *(page 444)*
chyme	A creamy, fluid mixture of food and gastric juices *(page 444)*
bile	A yellow-green, bitter fluid important in the breakdown and absorption of fats *(page 445)*

Drawing from Experience

Why does your stomach growl when you are hungry? What happens to food after you swallow it? What do you know about your digestive system? Think about these questions as you read Lesson 1.

In the last chapter, you learned about the cardiovascular and respiratory systems. In this lesson, you will learn about the digestive system.

Reading Tutor, Lesson 1 *(continued)*

USE WITH CHAPTER 17, PAGES 442–446.

Organizing Your Thoughts

Use the chart below to help you take notes as you read the summaries that follow. In the first box, list the functions of the digestive system. In the other, list some of the parts of the system.

Functions of the Digestive System	Parts of the Digestive System

USE WITH CHAPTER 17, PAGES 442–446.

Read to Learn

Read each passage carefully. Write in complete sentences to answer the following questions.

Functions of the Digestive System *(pages 442–443)*

The digestive system has three main functions.

- **Digestion** is *the mechanical and chemical breakdown of foods for use by the body's cells.* The mechanical part is chewing food into small pieces. The chemical part is in the digestive juices that help break down the food.
- **Absorption** is *the passage of digested food from the digestive tract into the cardiovascular system.*
- **Elimination** is *ridding the body of undigested food or body wastes.*

1. What are the three main functions of the digestive system?

____

____

____

____

____

Structures of the Digestive System *(pages 443–446)*

The parts of the digestive system work with each other. They break food down and move it through the body. Here are some of the structures of the digestive system.

- **Teeth.** The teeth break the food you eat into small pieces. **Mastication** is *the process of chewing.* It breaks down the food so you can swallow it.
- **Salivary glands.** The salivary glands in the mouth make juices or saliva. In the saliva is an enzyme that breaks down sugar and starch into smaller bits. It makes the food easier to swallow.
- **Tongue.** The tongue forms food into a shape you can swallow. A muscle forces food into the **pharynx**, or throat. The **uvula** is a small flap of tissue at the back of the mouth that closes the opening to the nasal tubes. The **epiglottis** is a flap of tissue that closes the opening of the **trachea** to stop food from going down the wrong tube.
- **The esophagus.** The **esophagus** is a muscular tube about 10 inches long. It connects the pharynx to the stomach. **Peristalsis** is *a series of involuntary muscle contractions that move food through the digestive tract.*

Reading Tutor, Lesson 1 *(continued)*

USE WITH CHAPTER 17, PAGES 442–446.

- **The stomach.** The **stomach** is a hollow, saclike organ within a muscular wall. The stomach has three tasks.
  - **Mixing foods with gastric juices. Gastric juices** are *secretions from the stomach lining that contain hydrochloric acid and pepsin, an enzyme that digests protein.*
  - **Storing swallowed food and liquid.** The stomach holds food and liquid until they move into the small intestine.
  - **Moving food into the small intestine.** The food in the stomach turns into chyme. **Chyme** is *a creamy, fluid mixture of food and gastric juices.* The chyme moves into the small intestine.
- **The pancreas, liver, and gallbladder.** The juices of the **pancreas** make enzymes that break down the food in the small intestine. The **liver** makes bile. **Bile** is *a yellow-green, bitter fluid important in the breakdown and absorption of fats.* The body stores bile in the **gallbladder.** It secretes the bile into the bile duct when you eat. From there it goes to the intestine.
- **The small intestine.** This organ is 20 to 23 feet in length. It has three parts. These are the **duodenum, the jejunum,** and the **ileum.** The inner wall of the small intestine has millions of fingerlike **villi.** Capillaries cover the villi. The capillaries carry nutrients into the body. The food that is left over moves into the large intestine.
- **The large intestine.** The leftover parts of food pass into the large intestine, or colon. It is 5 to 6 feet in length. It absorbs water, vitamins, and salt. Solid wastes move through the colon. Bacteria in the colon turn the waste into feces. Feces leave the body through the anus during a bowel movement.

2. What are some of the parts of the digestive system?

____

____

____

____

____

____

____

____

____

____

Name Class Date

Lesson 2

Reading Tutor

USE WITH CHAPTER 17, PAGES 447–452.

Digestive and Urinary Systems: Care and Problems of the Digestive System

Vocabulary

indigestion	A feeling of discomfort in the upper abdomen *(page 448)*
heartburn	A burning sensation in the center of the chest that may rise from the bottom, or tip, of the breastbone up to the throat *(page 448)*
hiatal hernia	A condition in which part of the stomach pushes through an opening in the diaphragm *(page 448)*
appendicitis	An inflammation of the appendix *(page 450)*
peptic ulcer	A sore in the lining of the digestive tract *(page 451)*

Drawing from Experience

Have you ever had an upset stomach? Do you know anyone who has had his or her appendix removed by the doctor? How can you take care of your digestive system? Think about these questions as you read Lesson 2.

In the last lesson, you learned about the digestive system. In this lesson, you will learn how to care for the digestive system.

Reading Tutor, Lesson 2 *(continued)*

USE WITH CHAPTER 17, PAGES 447–452.

Organizing Your Thoughts

Use the chart below to help you take notes as you read the summaries that follow. In the first box, list some habits you can follow to keep your digestive system healthy. In the other box, list some of the problems of the digestive system.

Habits for a Healthy Digestive System	Problems of the Digestive System

Reading Tutor, Lesson 2 *(continued)*

USE WITH CHAPTER 17, PAGES 447–452.

Read to Learn

Read each passage carefully. Write in complete sentences to answer the following questions.

Health Behaviors and the Digestive System *(pages 447–448)*

Healthy eating habits can reduce your risk of digestive trouble. Here are some good health behaviors that will keep your digestive system healthy.

- Eat a well-balanced diet. Eat a variety of foods that are low in fat and high in fiber.
- Wash your hands before you prepare your food or before you eat.
- Eat slowly and chew your food well.
- Drink at least eight 8-ounce glasses of water every day.
- Avoid using food to deal with your emotions. Take a walk instead.

1. What are some of the habits that will keep your digestive system healthy?

____

____

____

____

____

Problems of the Digestive System *(pages 448–452)*

Here are some of the functional problems of the digestive system.

- **Indigestion** is *a feeling of discomfort in the upper abdomen.* Eating too much food, eating too fast, or eating spicy or high-fat foods may cause this.
- **Heartburn** is *a burning feeling in the center of the chest. It may rise from the bottom, or tip, of the breastbone up to the throat.* A backflow of stomach acid may cause this. It can also be a sign of a **hiatal hernia.** This is *a condition in which part of the stomach pushes through an opening in the diaphragm.*
- **Gas.** Too much gas can cause cramps or a feeling of fullness in the abdomen. Fats and proteins make less gas than carbohydrates.
- **Constipation** is when feces get dry and hard and bowel movements are difficult. Not drinking enough water or not eating enough fiber may be the cause. You can treat this by a change in your diet. A doctor may treat this with a laxative.

Reading Tutor, Lesson 2 *(continued)*

USE WITH CHAPTER 17, PAGES 447–452.

- **Nausea** is the feeling that comes before you vomit. Motion sickness, germs, some types of medicine, or dehydration may be the cause. Vomiting is a reflex in which the contents of the stomach come back up and out of the mouth.
- **Diarrhea** is the passage of watery feces. The large intestine is not able to absorb all of the water when food passes too quickly through the colon. A change in diet, eating too much, or emotions may be the cause. Drink lots of water to avoid dehydration. See a doctor if it does not go away.

Here are some of the structural problems of the digestive system.

- **Gallstones** form when cholesterol in the bile blocks the bile duct. You may have pain, nausea, vomiting, and fever. You can treat this with medicine or surgery.
- **Appendicitis** is the *pain and swelling of the appendix*. This is a 3- or 4-inch tube that extends from the top of the colon. You may have pain in the lower right side of the abdomen, fever, nausea, and loss of appetite. You treat this with medical care and surgery.
- **Gastritis** is the pain and swelling of the lining of the stomach. Stomach acid, tobacco, alcohol, infection, or some types of medicine may be the cause. You may have pain, loss of appetite, nausea, and vomiting. You can treat this by avoiding the irritant and with antibiotics.
- **Lactose intolerance** is when the body does not make enough of the enzyme lactase. Lactase breaks down the lactose in milk and other dairy food. Undigested lactose stays in the small intestine and causes cramps, bloating, gas, and diarrhea. You can treat this by avoiding dairy foods. Eat dark green vegetables, soy, and yogurt to get your calcium.
- **Peptic ulcer** is *a sore in the lining of the digestive tract*. Use of aspirin or a bacterial infection may be the cause. You may have nausea, vomiting, pain, and bleeding in the stomach. You can treat this with medicine and by avoiding the irritant.
- **Cirrhosis** is a scarring of the liver tissue. Heavy use of alcohol may be the cause. It can lead to liver failure and death. A liver transplant is the best chance to survive.
- **Crohn's disease** causes pain and swelling of the lining of the digestive tract. You may have diarrhea, weight loss, fever, and pain. Trouble in the immune system may be the cause.
- **Colon cancer** is the second leading cause of cancer death. It begins in the lowest part of the colon. It blocks the colon or bleeds. Early treatment gives you the best chance to survive.

Reading Tutor, Lesson 2 *(continued)*

USE WITH CHAPTER 17, PAGES 447–452.

- **Colitis** is pain and swelling in the colon. Bacteria or viruses may be the cause. You may have fever, pain, and diarrhea with blood.
- **Hemorrhoids** are veins in the rectum and anus that swell from pressure. Constipation or pregnancy may be the cause. You may have itching, pain, and bleeding. You can treat this with physical activity and a high-fiber diet.
- **Tooth decay** is harmful to the digestive process. Brush and floss your teeth every day.

2. What are some of the functional and structural problems of the digestive system?

USE WITH CHAPTER 17, PAGES 453–457.

Digestive and Urinary Systems: The Urinary System

Vocabulary

urine	Liquid waste material *(page 453)*
nephrons	Functional units of the kidneys *(page 454)*
ureters	Tubes that connect the kidneys to the bladder *(page 454)*
bladder	A hollow muscular organ that acts as a reservoir for urine *(page 455)*
urethra	The tube that leads from the bladder to the outside of the body *(page 455)*
cystitis	An inflammation of the bladder *(page 456)*
urethritis	An inflammation of the urethra *(page 456)*
hemodialysis	A technique in which an artificial kidney machine removes waste products from the blood *(page 457)*

Drawing from Experience

How many glasses of water do you drink every day? What causes you to get thirsty? Why do we need to drink so much water? How do you feel about organ donation? Think about these questions as you read Lesson 3.

In the last lesson, you learned about the care of the digestive system. In this lesson, you will learn about the urinary system.

Reading Tutor, Lesson 3 *(continued)*

USE WITH CHAPTER 17, PAGES 453–457.

Organizing Your Thoughts

Use the chart below to help you take notes as you read the summaries that follow. In the first box, list some of the parts of the urinary system. In the other box, list some of the types of urinary problems.

Parts of the Urinary System	Types of Urinary Problems

Read to Learn

Read each passage carefully. Write in complete sentences to answer the following questions.

Function of the Urinary System *(pages 453–455)*

The main job of the urinary system is to remove waste and extra fluid from the blood. **Urine** is *liquid waste material*. It exits the body through urination. Urine is made of water, body waste, and nitrogen. It becomes toxic if it stays in the body too long.

Here are some of the main parts of the urinary system.

- The **kidneys** are bean-shaped organs. They are about the size of a fist. They are near the middle of the back and below the rib cage.
  - **Nephrons** are the *working units of the kidneys*. Each nephron is made of these parts.
    - A **glomerulus** is a ball of small capillaries.
    - A **renal tubule** is a small tube that acts as a filtering funnel.

  The kidneys adjust the amount of salt, water, and other material in the urine. They check and alter the acid and alkaline levels. The pituitary gland emits antidiuretic hormone (ADH) when the body gets dehydrated. This causes thirst. It lets the kidneys balance the fluid level in the body.

- The **ureters** are *tubes that connect the kidneys to the bladder*. They are 8 to 10 inches long. The ureters work to force urine down and away from the kidneys. Some urine goes from the ureters to the bladder every 15 seconds.
- The **bladder** is *a hollow muscular organ that acts as a reservoir for urine*. It is in the pelvic cavity and ligaments hold it in place.
  - The **sphincter muscles** close tightly at the opening to the urethra until the bladder is ready to empty.
  - The **urethra** is *the tube that leads from the bladder to the outside of the body*.

1. What are some of the main parts of the urinary system?

____

____

____

____

____

Reading Tutor, Lesson 3 *(continued)*

USE WITH CHAPTER 17, PAGES 453–457.

Health Behaviors and the Urinary System *(pages 455–456)*

Here are some of the things that you can do to keep your urinary system healthy.

- Drink at least eight 8-ounce glasses of water each day. Limit soft drinks. Caffeine drinks cause more water to leave your body.
- Eat a well-balanced diet.
- Use good hygiene. Keep your body clean to lower your risk of infection.
- Have regular medical checkups. Report changes in urine to your doctor.

2. What are some of the ways that you can keep your urinary system healthy?

____

____

____

____

____

Problems of the Urinary System *(pages 456–457)*

Here are some of the types of problems that may occur in the urinary system.

- **Cystitis** is the *pain and swelling of the bladder*. A bacterial infection may be the cause. You may have to urinate more often. It may cause you to have burning pain, fever, or blood in the urine. You can treat this with antibiotics.
- **Urethritis** is the *pain and swelling of the urethra*. It has some of the same signs as cystitis.
- **Kidney problems** are serious. They can be very painful. You need to get medical help.
  - **Nephritis** is the pain and swelling of the nephrons. It may cause you to have fever, swelling, and changes in your urine.
  - **Kidney stones** form when salts in the urine turn into solid stones. They may be made of calcium. Small stones may pass through the urine. Large stones need medical help to break the stones apart.
  - **Uremia** is a decrease in blood filtering by the kidneys. It leads to very high levels of nitrogen in the blood. It can cause damage to your tissues.

- **Kidney failure** can be acute or sudden. It can be chronic or progress more slowly. Here are some of the types of treatment.
- **Hemodialysis** is *a procedure in which an artificial kidney machine removes waste products from the blood*. A needle with plastic tubing passes blood from the patient to the machine.
- **Peritoneal dialysis** uses the peritoneum to filter the blood. This is a thin membrane that surrounds the digestive organs. The doctor inserts a tube into the abdomen to remove the toxins.
- **Kidney transplant** is an option for chronic kidney failure. The doctor replaces your kidney with a healthy kidney from a donor.

3. What are some of the types of problems that occur in the urinary system?

Endocrine and Reproductive Systems: The Endocrine System

Vocabulary

endocrine glands	Ductless— or tubeless— organs or groups of cells that secrete hormones directly into the bloodstream *(page 464)*
hormones	Chemical substances that are produced in glands and help regulate many of your body's functions *(page 464)*
thyroid gland	Gland that produces hormones that regulate metabolism, body heat, and bone growth *(page 465)*
parathyroid glands	Glands that produce a hormone that regulates the body's calcium and phosphorous balance *(page 465)*
pancreas	A gland that serves both the digestive and the endocrine systems *(page 465)*
pituitary gland	Gland that regulates and controls the activities of all other endocrine glands *(page 465)*
gonads	The ovaries and testes *(page 466)*
adrenal glands	Glands that help the body recover from stress and respond to emergencies *(page 466)*

Drawing from Experience

Do you know what a hormone is? How can it affect your growth? What do you know about the endocrine system? What can you do to care for it? Think about these questions as you read Lesson 1.

In the last chapter, you learned about your digestive and urinary systems. In this lesson, you will learn about the endocrine system.

Reading Tutor, Lesson 1 *(continued)*

USE WITH CHAPTER 18, PAGES 464–467.

Organizing Your Thoughts

Use the chart below to help you take notes as you read the summaries that follow. In the first box, list some of the parts of the endocrine system. In the other box, list some of the problems and ways to care for the system.

Parts of the Endocrine System	Problems and Care of the Endocrine System

Reading Tutor, Lesson 1 *(continued)*

USE WITH CHAPTER 18, PAGES 464–467.

Read to Learn

Read each passage carefully. Write in complete sentences to answer the following questions.

Structure of the Endocrine System *(pages 464–466)*

The endocrine system is a network of glands within the body. **Endocrine glands** are *ductless organs or groups of cells that secrete hormones directly into the blood.*

Hormones are *chemicals that the body's glands produce. They help control many of your body's functions.* Hormones also cause changes in the body during puberty.

Here are some of the major glands.

- The **pituitary gland** is *the master gland. It controls the actions of all of the other glands.* It has three parts.
  - **Anterior lobe.** This lobe makes six hormones. One hormone triggers body growth. Others stimulate the thyroid gland, and the adrenal glands. This lobe also makes hormones that control the growth and the functions of the **gonads.** The **gonads** are *the ovaries and the testes.*
  - **Intermediate lobe.** This lobe secretes a hormone that controls the darkening of the skin.
  - **Posterior lobe.** This lobe secretes a hormone that controls the balance of water in the body.
- The **adrenal glands** are *glands that help the body recover from stress and react to emergencies.* They each have two parts.
  - The **adrenal cortex** secretes hormones that affect sodium levels, blood pressure, metabolism, immunity, and the body's response to stress.
  - The **adrenal medulla** secretes adrenaline. The hypothalamus controls this part of the adrenal glands. Adrenaline affects the body's response to emergencies.
- The **thyroid gland** is *a gland that makes hormones that control metabolism, body heat, and bone growth.*
- The **parathyroid glands** are *glands that make a hormone that controls the body's calcium and phosphorous balance.*
- The **testes** are the male reproductive glands.
- The **ovaries** are the female reproductive glands.
- The **hypothalamus** links the endocrine with the nervous system. It triggers the pituitary gland to secrete hormones.
- The **pineal gland** secretes melatonin. This controls sleep cycles and affects the onset of puberty.
- The **thymus gland** regulates the development of the immune system.
- The **pancreas** is *a gland that serves both the digestive and the endocrine systems.* It secretes two hormones that control the level of glucose in the blood. They are glucagon and insulin.

1. What are some of the types of glands that make up the endocrine system?

____

____

____

____

____

Problems of the Endocrine System *(pages 466–467)*

Here are some of the types of problems that may occur in the endocrine system.

- **Diabetes mellitus** is when the pancreas does not make enough or any insulin. It may cause high glucose levels. You have to urinate often. It may cause fatigue, loss of weight, and thirst.
- **Graves' disease** is hyperthyroidism. It is when the thyroid makes too much thyroxine. It may cause you to feel nervous and have weight loss, rapid heart rate, and thirst.

Having a low thyroxine level is hypothyroidism. It may cause you to be tired or have dry skin, weight gain, or constipation.

- **Cushing's disease** is the result of too many adrenal hormones. It may cause you to have a round face, a hump on your upper back, thin skin, and fragile bones.
- **Goiter** is an enlarged thyroid gland. A lack of iodine in the diet is what causes it. It is rare.
- **Growth disorders** are the result of too much growth hormone. Early treatment can help a teen reach a normal height.

It is very important to take care of all of your body systems.

- Eat a healthy diet. Get lots of sleep. Avoid stress.
- Have your doctor give you some tests to make sure your endocrine system is working right.

2. What are some of the types of trouble that may occur in the endocrine system?

____

____

____

____

____

Name Class Date

Lesson 2

Reading Tutor

USE WITH CHAPTER 18, PAGES 468–473.

Endocrine and Reproductive Systems: The Male Reproductive System

Vocabulary

reproductive system	The system of organs involved in producing offspring *(page 468)*
sperm	The male reproductive cells *(page 468)*
testosterone	The male sex hormone *(page 469)*
testes	Two small glands that produce sperm *(page 469)*
scrotum	An external skin sac that extends outside the body and contains the testes *(page 469)*
penis	A tube-shaped organ that extends from the trunk of the body just above the testes *(page 469)*
semen	A thick fluid containing sperm and other secretions from the male reproductive system *(page 469)*
sterility	The inability to reproduce *(page 472)*

Drawing from Experience

Which hormones affect the male reproductive system? What do you know about fertilization? Why is it important to take care of the male reproductive system? Think about these questions as you read Lesson 2.

In the last lesson, you learned about the endocrine system. In this lesson, you will learn about the male reproductive system.

Reading Tutor, Lesson 2 *(continued)*

USE WITH CHAPTER 18, PAGES 468–473.

Organizing Your Thoughts

Use the chart below to help you take notes as you read the summaries that follow. In the first box, list some of the parts of the male reproductive system. In the other box, list some of the problems and care of the male reproductive system.

Parts of the Male Reproductive System	Problems and Care of the Male Reproductive System

Reading Tutor, Lesson 2 *(continued)*

USE WITH CHAPTER 18, PAGES 468–473.

Read to Learn

Read each passage carefully. Write in complete sentences to answer the following questions.

Structure and Function of the Male Reproductive System *(pages 468–471)*

The **reproductive system** is *the system of organs involved in producing offspring.* **Sperm** are *the male reproductive cells.* A male reaches maturity between the ages of 12 and 15. The pituitary gland triggers release of the *male sex hormone* **testosterone.**

Here are the main parts of the external organs of the male reproductive system.

- The **testes** or **testicles** are *two small glands that make sperm.* These glands also secrete testosterone.
- The **scrotum** is *an external skin sac that holds the testes.*
- The **penis** is *a tube-shaped organ that extends from the trunk of the body just above the testes.* The penis gets large and erect when blood flow increases to the area. This is an erection. The penis releases semen.
  - The **foreskin** is a cover of loose skin over the tip of the penis. **Circumcision** is when a doctor takes off the foreskin during surgery.
- The **semen** is *a thick fluid containing sperm and other secretions from the male reproductive system.*
- **Ejaculation** may occur at the peak of sexual arousal. This is a series of contractions that results in the semen leaving the body.
- **Fertilization** is the joining of a male sperm cell and a female egg cell. It may occur if an ejaculation occurs during sexual intercourse.

Here are the parts of the internal organs of the male reproductive system.

- The **urethra** is the tube by which semen and urine leave the male body.
- The **seminal vesicles** make a fluid that mixes with the sperm.
- The **prostate gland** and the **Cowper's glands** make fluids that mix with the sperm to form semen.
- The **epididymis** is a coiled tube next to each testis where the sperm mature. The body also stores sperm in this tube.
- The **vas deferens** are tubes that extend from each epididymis to the urethra.

1. What are some of the parts of the male reproductive system?

____

____

____

____

Reading Tutor, Lesson 2 *(continued)*

USE WITH CHAPTER 18, PAGES 468–473.

Care of the Male Reproductive System *(pages 471–472)*

Here are some of the ways to take care of the male reproductive system.

- **Get checkups.** All males should have a medical checkup every 12 or 18 months.
- **Bathe often.** Males should shower or bathe every day.
- **Wear safety gear.** Use a protective cup or support during sports.
- **Do regular self-exams.** Check the scrotum and the testicles for any signs of cancer.
- **Practice abstinence.** Abstain from sexual activity before marriage to avoid STDs.

Here are some of the types of STDs that affect the male reproductive system.

- **Chlamydia** and **gonorrhea** are bacterial infections. They cause a discharge from the penis. They may cause burning when you urinate. They may also harm your ability to reproduce. A doctor can treat them with antibiotics.
- **Syphilis** is also a bacterial infection. It starts with a red sore. It can spread and harm the body organs. A doctor may be able to treat it with antibiotics.
- **Genital herpes** is caused by a virus. It causes blister-like sores to recur in the genital area. It has no cure. You can treat it with medicine.

2. What are some of the types of STDs that affect the reproductive male system?

____

____

____

____

Problems of the Male Reproductive System *(pages 472–473)*

Here are some of the types of problems of the male reproductive system.

- An **inguinal hernia** is when a part of the intestine pushes into the abdominal wall near the top of the scrotum. Lifting heavy objects can cause a tear in this area. It may cause a male to have a lump in the groin. You may need surgery to fix the hole in the muscle wall.
- **Sterility** is *the inability to reproduce.* It can be the result of too few sperm or sperm of poor quality. It may occur from toxins, lead, drugs, steroids, STDs, or other causes.

Reading Tutor, Lesson 2 *(continued)*

USE WITH CHAPTER 18, PAGES 468–473.

- **Testicular cancer** can affect males of any age. It occurs most often in males 14 to 40. Testes that do not drop down and a family history of this cancer may add to the risk. Males should do regular self-exams to check for any lumps or swelling or pain.
- The **prostate gland** can get large from an infection, a tumor, or aging. It may result in trouble with urination. It may lead to cancer. Early detection adds to the chance of a cure.

3. What are some of the types of problems of the male reproductive system?

Lesson 3 — Reading Tutor

USE WITH CHAPTER 18, PAGES 474–479.

Endocrine and Reproductive Systems: The Female Reproductive System

Vocabulary

ova	Female reproductive cells *(page 474)*
uterus	A hollow, muscular, pear-shaped organ inside a female's body *(page 474)*
ovaries	The female sex glands that store the ova and produce female sex hormones *(page 474)*
ovulation	The process of releasing a mature ovum into the fallopian tube each month *(page 474)*
fallopian tubes	A pair of tubes with fingerlike projections that draw in the ovum *(page 475)*
vagina	A muscular, elastic passageway that extends from the uterus to the outside of the body *(page 475)*
cervix	The opening to the uterus *(page 476)*
menstruation	Shedding of the uterine lining *(page 476)*

Drawing from Experience

Which hormones affect the female reproductive system? What do you know about the menstrual cycle? Why is it important to take care of the female reproductive system? Think about these questions as you read Lesson 3.

In the last lesson, you learned about the male reproductive system. In this lesson, you will learn about the female reproductive system.

Reading Tutor, Lesson 3 *(continued)*

USE WITH CHAPTER 18, PAGES 474–479.

Organizing Your Thoughts

Use the chart below to help you take notes as you read the summaries that follow. In the first box, list some of the parts of the female reproductive system. In the other box, list some of the problems and care of the female reproductive system.

Parts of the Female Reproductive System	Problems and Care of the Female Reproductive System

Read to Learn

Read each passage carefully. Write in complete sentences to answer the following questions.

Structure and Function of the Female Reproductive System *(pages 474–476)*

The *female reproductive cells* are the **ova.** The **uterus** is *a hollow, pear-shaped organ inside a female body*. It feeds and takes care of the fertilized ovum until it is born. Here are some of the other organs of the female reproductive system.

- **Ovaries** are *the female sex glands. They store the ova and make the sex hormones.* **Ovulation** is *the process of sending a mature ovum into the fallopian tube each month.*
- The **fallopian tubes** are *a pair of tubes with projections that draw in the ovum.*
- The **vagina** is *a muscular, elastic tube that goes from the uterus to the outside of the body.* Sperm from the male enter the female by way of the vagina.
- **Endometrium** tissue lines the walls of the uterus. The zygote imbeds itself in the wall of the uterus. It begins to grow.

Fertilization will occur if a sperm cell unites with an ovum. A **zygote** is a fertilized cell. The zygote enters the **uterus** when it leaves the fallopian tube.

Menstruation. The uterus gets ready for a pregnancy every month. The thick lining of the walls breaks down into blood and tissue if it does not occur.

- The **cervix** is *the opening to the uterus*. The blood and tissue pass through the cervix and out the vagina.
- **Menstruation** is the *shedding of the lining of the uterus*. It is a part of the **menstrual cycle.**
  - **Days 1–13.** A new egg is maturing in the ovary.
  - **Day 14.** The ovary sends the egg into one of the fallopian tubes.
  - **Days 15–20.** The egg goes down the tube to the uterus.
  - **Days 21–28.** Menstruation begins after seven days if the egg stays unfertilized.

Reading Tutor, Lesson 3 *(continued)*

USE WITH CHAPTER 18, PAGES 474–479.

Most females begin their first cycle by the age of 10 to 15.

1. What are some of the parts of the female reproductive system?

Care of the Female Reproductive System *(pages 476–477)*

Here are some of the ways to take care of the female reproductive system.

- **Bathe often.** Shower or bathe every day. Change tampons or sanitary pads every few hours when menstruating. Stay clean to avoid odor.
- **Practice abstinence.** Abstain from sexual activity before marriage. To avoid unplanned pregnancy and STDs.
- **Do breast self-exams.** Breast cancer is one of the leading causes of death for women. Early detection adds to the chance of a cure.

Lie down and place the right arm under the head. Use the fingers of the right hand to feel for any lumps. Go over the whole breast in a circle and up and down. Check the left breast with the right hand.

Repeat the exam when standing up. Check the armpit, the skin, and the nipples.

2. What are some of the ways to care for the female reproductive system?

Problems of the Female Reproductive System *(pages 477–479)*

Here are some of the types of problems that relate to the menstrual cycle.

- **Cramps** may occur at the start of a cycle. Light exercise or a heating pad may help.
- **Premenstrual syndrome (PMS)** is the result of a hormonal change. It may cause tension, bloating, weight gain, or mood swings one to two weeks before the start of a cycle. Light exercise and a good diet may help.

Reading Tutor, Lesson 3 *(continued)*

USE WITH CHAPTER 18, PAGES 474–479.

- **Toxic shock syndrome (TSS)** is a rare but very serious bacterial infection. It can affect the immune system and the liver. It may be fatal. Be sure to change tampons often to lower the risk of TSS. It may cause fever, vomiting, rash, and more. Get help right away.

Here are some of the types of problems that relate to infertility.

- **Endometriosis** is a very painful and chronic disease. It occurs when tissue that lines the uterus moves and grows in the ovaries, fallopian tubes, or pelvic cavity. Treatment may be pain medicine or surgery.
- **Pelvic inflammatory disease (PID)** is an infection of the fallopian tubes, ovaries, and pelvis. It can harm the female organs. STDs are often the cause of this disease.
- **Sexually transmitted diseases** are the most common cause of infertility. Avoiding sexual contact until marriage is the one sure way to stop STDs.

Here are some of the other types of disorders.

- **Vaginitis** is the most common infection for women. It often has a discharge, odor, or pain. It may have itching or burning. It can lead to PID.
- **Blocked fallopian tubes** are one of the main causes of infertility. They may be the result of PID, abdominal surgery, or STDs.
- **Ovarian cysts** are fluid-filled sacs on the ovary. Small cysts may go away on their own. Big cysts may need surgery.
- **Cervical, uterine, and ovarian cancers** occur in the female reproductive system. Early sexual activity and STDs add to the risk of getting cervical cancer. Checkups and pelvic exams are key for early treatment.

3. What are some of the types of problems of the female reproductive system?

Prenatal Development and Birth: The Beginning of the Life Cycle

Vocabulary

fertilization	The union of a male sperm cell and a female egg cell *(page 486)*
implantation	The attachment of the zygote to the uterine wall *(page 486)*
embryo	The cluster of cells that develop between the third and eighth weeks of pregnancy *(page 486)*
fetus	The developing group of cells after eighth week of pregnancy *(page 486)*
amniotic sac	A thin, fluid-filled membrane that surrounds and protects the developing embryo *(page 487)*
umbilical cord	A ropelike structure that connects the embryo and the mother's placenta *(page 487)*
placenta	A thick, blood-rich tissue that lines the walls of the uterus during pregnancy and nourishes the embryo *(page 487)*
labor	The final stage of pregnancy in which the uterus contracts and pushes the baby out of the mother's body *(page 490)*

Drawing from Experience

How does an unborn baby get food? How do twins form? Is there a way for parents to know the sex of their baby before it is born? Think about these questions as you read Lesson 1.

In the last chapter, you learned about the endocrine and reproductive systems. In this lesson, you will learn about the start of the life cycle.

Reading Tutor, Lesson 1 *(continued)*

USE WITH CHAPTER 19, PAGES 486–491.

Organizing Your Thoughts

Use the chart below to help you take notes as you read the summaries that follow. In the first box, list some of the changes that occur to an embryo as it grows. In the next box, list the stages of fetal growth. In the last box, list the stages of birth.

Growth of the Embryo	Stages of Fetal Growth	Stages of Birth

Reading Tutor, Lesson 1 *(continued)*

USE WITH CHAPTER 19, PAGES 486–491.

Read to Learn

Read each passage carefully. Write in complete sentences to answer the following questions.

Conception and Implantation *(page 486)*

The human body begins as one cell. The *union of a male sperm cell and a female egg cell* is **fertilization**, or conception. The cell is now a zygote. The zygote begins to divide as it travels to the uterus. The *attachment of the zygote to the uterine wall* is called **implantation.**

The *cluster of cells that develop between the third and eighth weeks of pregnancy* is called an **embryo.** The *developing group of cells after the eighth week of pregnancy* is called a **fetus.**

1. What is fertilization?

____

____

____

Embryonic Growth *(page 487)*

The cells continue to divide as an embryo grows. Three tissue layers become the body systems.

- One layer becomes the respiratory and digestive systems.
- The second layer forms into the muscles, bones, blood vessels, and skin.
- The third layer forms the nervous system, sense organs, and mouth.

Other structures form outside the embryo.

- The **amniotic sac** is *a thin, fluid-filled membrane that surrounds and protects the developing embryo.*
- The **umbilical cord** is *a ropelike structure that connects the embryo and the mother's placenta.*
- The **placenta** is *a thick, blood-rich tissue that lines the walls of the uterus during pregnancy and nourishes the embryo.*

Nutrients and oxygen pass from the mother's body to the embryo. Wastes from the embryo exit through the mother's blood. Tobacco, alcohol, and other drugs can also pass to the embryo from the mother's body.

2. What are some of the structures that form outside the embryo?

____

____

____

____

____

Fetal Development *(pages 488–489)*

The time from conception to birth is about nine months. The nine months are divided into three 3-month trimesters.

- **First Trimester (0–14 weeks)**
  - **0–2 weeks.** The spinal cord, brain, ears, arms, and heart form. The heart begins to beat.
  - **3–8 weeks.** The embryo is 1 inch long at 8 weeks. The mouth, nose, eyelids, hands, fingers, feet, and toes form. The nervous and cardiovascular systems work.
  - **9–14 weeks.** Sex organs, eyelids, fingernails, and toenails form. The fetus can make crying motions and suck its thumb.
- **Second Trimester (15–28 weeks)**
  - **15–20 weeks.** The fetus can blink. The body grows. Eyebrows and eyelashes form. The fetus can grasp and kick.
  - **21–28 weeks.** The fetus can hear. It sleeps and wakes. Weight goes up. The fetus is 12 inches long and weighs more than 1 pound. It may survive if born after 24 weeks.
- **Third Trimester (29 weeks–birth)**
  - **29–40 weeks.** The fetus uses all five senses and passes water from the bladder. The baby weighs 6 to 9 pounds after 266 days and is ready to be born.

3. What are some of the major changes to the fetus during the second trimester?

____

____

____

____

____

Reading Tutor, Lesson 1 *(continued)*

USE WITH CHAPTER 19, PAGES 486–491.

Stages of Birth *(pages 490–491)*

Labor is *the final stage of pregnancy. The uterus contracts and pushes the baby out of the mother's body*. There are three stages of labor.

1. **Stage 1: Dilation.** The uterus contracts. The cervix begins to dilate or widen. The baby's head is resting on the cervix in most cases. The contractions break the amniotic sac that surrounds the baby.
2. **Stage 2: Passage through the birth canal.** The baby passes through the birth canal and comes out of the mother's body. The baby takes its first breath. It cries to clear the lungs.
3. **Stage 3: Afterbirth.** The uterus contracts. The contractions push the placenta or afterbirth from the mother's body. The doctor cuts the umbilical cord to separate the placenta from the baby.

4. What are the three stages of labor or birth?

Prenatal Development and Birth: Prenatal Care

Vocabulary

prenatal care	Steps that a pregnant female can take to provide for her own health and for the health of her baby *(page 492)*
birthing center	A facility in which females with low-risk pregnancies can deliver their babies in a homelike setting *(page 492)*
fetal alcohol syndrome (FAS)	A group of alcohol-related birth defects that includes both physical and mental problems *(page 494)*
miscarriage	The spontaneous expulsion of a fetus that occurs before the twentieth week of a pregnancy *(page 496)*
stillbirth	A dead fetus expelled from the body after the twentieth week of a pregnancy *(page 496)*

Drawing from Experience

Do you know anyone who is pregnant? Why is it important for a mother-to-be to take care of her health? What are some of the ways that she can protect her unborn baby? Think about these questions as you read Lesson 2.

In the last lesson, you learned about start of the life cycle. In this lesson, you will learn about prenatal care.

Reading Tutor, Lesson 2 *(continued)*

USE WITH CHAPTER 19, PAGES 492–497.

Organizing Your Thoughts

Use the chart below to help you take notes as you read the summaries that follow. In the first box, list some of the ways a mother-to-be can stay healthy during pregnancy. In the other box, list some of the ways she can protect the health of her unborn baby.

Health of the Mother	Health of the Unborn Baby

Read to Learn

Read each passage carefully. Write in complete sentences to answer the following questions.

Importance of Prenatal Care ***(pages 492–493)***

Prenatal care is the *steps that a pregnant female can take to provide for her own health and the health of her baby*. The mother-to-be must decide where she will go for care.

- An **obstetrician** is a doctor who specializes in the care of a female and her unborn fetus.
- A **certified nurse-midwife** is an advanced practice nurse. He or she works in the area of prenatal care and the delivery of babies.
- A **birthing center** is *a facility in which women with low-risk pregnancies can deliver their babies. It has a homelike setting.*

The doctor or nurse-midwife gives the female a physical exam. He or she will keep track of the mother's weight and blood pressure. The parents may choose to see the baby on an ultrasound machine.

1. What are some of the choices a mother-to-be may have for prenatal care?

____

____

____

____

____

Proper Nutrition During Pregnancy ***(pages 493–494)***

A baby depends on its mother for good nutrition. A pregnant female needs more nutrients than at any other time in her life. Here are some of the nutrients she may need.

- **Calcium** helps build strong bones and teeth. It builds healthy nerves and muscles.
- **Protein** helps form muscle and most other tissue.
- **Iron** makes red blood cells. It also gets oxygen to the cells.
- **Vitamin A** helps cell and bone growth and eye development.
- **Vitamin B complex** aids in forming the nervous system.
- **Folic acid** is a critical part of spinal fluid. It helps close the tube that holds the spinal cord.

Reading Tutor, Lesson 2 *(continued)*

USE WITH CHAPTER 19, PAGES 492–497.

A mother-to-be must be careful not to gain too much weight. She may need about 300 extra calories a day. Healthy females should gain about 25 to 35 pounds while they are pregnant.

Too much weight can be a health risk for the mother and the baby. A mother who needs to lose weight should talk to her doctor. Losing too much weight may harm the fetus.

2. What are some of the nutrients a female may need to take while she is pregnant?

____

____

____

____

____

The Health of the Fetus *(pages 494–496)*

A pregnant female must be very careful. The things she puts into her body may affect the health of her fetus. Here are some of the major risks.

- **Alcohol.** Alcohol passes from a mother to her unborn baby. **Fetal alcohol syndrome (FAS)** is *a group of alcohol-related birth defects. It causes both physical and mental problems that last for a lifetime.*
- **Tobacco.** Smoking can cause low birth weight babies. It can also cause premature birth and infant death. Some studies show that it may affect the growth of a child.
- **Medicines and drugs.** Using drugs or medicines can harm an unborn baby. They may lead to birth defects or early labor. A baby can be born addicted to the drugs its mother takes. The mother should only use medicine under a doctor's orders.
- **Environmental hazards.** A mother-to-be should avoid these hazards.
  - **Lead** exposure may cause a miscarriage or mental disability in children.
  - **Smog** may cause birth defects, low birth weight, or infant death.
  - **Radiation** in Xrays can affect fetal growth. It may cause mental retardation.
  - **Cat litter** and cat feces may contain an organism that can cause miscarriage and health problems in a new baby.
  - **Household products** such as cleaning fluids may also pose a danger.

Reading Tutor, Lesson 2 *(continued)*

USE WITH CHAPTER 19, PAGES 492–497.

3. What are some of the harmful things a mother-to-be should avoid?

___

___

___

___

___

Complications During Pregnancy *(pages 496–497)*

Most females do not have any trouble during pregnancy. Here are some of the problems that may arise.

- **Miscarriage** is *the spontaneous expulsion of a fetus that occurs before the twentieth week of a pregnancy.*
- **Stillbirth** is *a dead fetus expelled from the body after the twentieth week of pregnancy.*
- **Ectopic Pregnancy** is when the zygote imbeds in the fallopian tube, abdomen, ovary, or cervix. It can occur when a female has an STD. It is a threat to the mother's life.
- **Preeclampsia** or toxemia can prevent the placenta from getting enough blood. The mother may have high blood pressure and swelling. It may cause low birth weight.

4. What are some of the problems that may occur during pregnancy?

___

___

___

___

___

Lesson 3

Reading Tutor

USE WITH CHAPTER 19, PAGES 498–503.

Prenatal Development and Birth: Heredity and Genetics

Vocabulary

heredity	The passing of traits from parents to their children *(page 498)*
chromosomes	Threadlike structures found within the nucleus of a cell that carry the codes for inherited traits *(page 499)*
genes	The basic units of heredity *(page 499)*
DNA	The chemical unit that makes up chromosomes *(page 499)*
genetic disorder	A disorder caused partly or completely by a defect in genes *(page 500)*
amniocentesis	A procedure in which a syringe is inserted through a pregnant female's abdominal wall into the amniotic fluid surrounding the developing fetus *(page 501)*
chorionic villi sampling (CVS)	A procedure in which a small piece of membrane is removed from the chorion, a layer of tissue that develops into the placenta *(page 501)*
gene therapy	The process of inserting normal genes into human cells to correct genetic disorders *(page 503)*

Drawing from Experience

Are you tall or short? Do you look like anyone else in your family? Do you have the same color of eyes? What do you know about genetic disorders? Think about these questions as you read Lesson 3.

In the last lesson, you learned about prenatal care. In this lesson, you will learn about heredity and genetics.

Reading Tutor, Lesson 3 *(continued)*

USE WITH CHAPTER 19, PAGES 498–503.

Organizing Your Thoughts

Use the chart below to help you take notes as you read the summaries that follow. In the first box, list some of the key facts about heredity and genetics. In the other box, list some of the types of genetic disorders.

Heredity and Genetics	Genetic Disorders

Reading Tutor, Lesson 3 *(continued)*

USE WITH CHAPTER 19, PAGES 498–503.

Read to Learn

Read each passage carefully. Write in complete sentences to answer the following questions.

Heredity *(pages 498–499)*

Heredity is *the passing of traits from parents to their children*. Some of the traits you inherit from your parents are your eye and hair color. Other factors may affect inherited traits. Height is an inherited trait, but a poor diet can stunt a child's growth.

Chromosomes are *threadlike structures within the nucleus of a cell. They carry the codes for human traits*. Most cells in the body have 46 chromosomes. **Genes** are *the basic units of heredity*. They occur in pairs. You inherit one gene of each pair from each parent.

DNA is *the chemical unit that makes up chromosomes*. All living things are made of DNA. DNA is made of bases. The order of the bases is the **genetic code.** Your genetic code controls all of your traits. Your DNA is not the same as that of any other person unless you are an identical twin.

1. What is heredity? What is DNA?

____

____

____

____

____

Genetics and Fetal Development *(pages 499–500)*

Sperm and egg cells each have 23 chromosomes. A zygote has 46 after the egg and sperm unite. The zygote carries the traits of each parent. The zygote divides many times. Each new cell will have one set of the 46 chromosomes.

Some genes are dominant. Some genes are recessive. The traits of dominant genes usually appear when they are present. A person who gets one brown eye gene and one blue eye gene will have brown eyes. A person with blue eyes must have two genes for blue eyes.

Human X and Y chromosomes determine the gender of a child. Each cell in a female has two X chromosomes. Each cell in a male has one X and one Y chromosome. The sperm determines the gender of the fetus. Eggs have only an X chromosome. Sperm have either an X or a Y chromosome.

2. How do X and Y chromosomes determine the gender of a person?

____

____

____

____

Genetic Disorders *(pages 500–502)*

Genetic disorders are *disorders caused by a defect in genes*. Here are some of the types.

- **Sickle-cell anemia.** Red blood cells have a sickle shape and clump together. It may cause pain, weakness, and kidney disease.
- **Tay-Sachs disease.** This destroys the nerves. It causes blindness, paralysis, and death.
- **Cystic fibrosis.** Mucus clogs many organs, such as the lungs and liver. It may cause serious respiratory problems.
- **Down syndrome.** This causes mental retardation, short height, round face, and more.
- **Hemophilia.** This is the failure of blood to clot.

Doctors can treat some genetic disorders if they are able to find them early. Here are two of the types of prenatal tests.

- **Amniocentesis** is *a process in which a doctor inserts a syringe through a pregnant female's abdominal wall. It goes into the amniotic fluid that surrounds the developing fetus*. Doctors check the fluid for genetic defects.
- **Chorionic villi sampling (CVS)** is *a process in which a doctor removes a small piece of membrane from the chorion. This is a layer of tissue that develops into the placenta.*

Genetic counselors can give advice about the chances of having a child with a genetically related disease. They can also help families find treatment.

3. What are two of the ways to test for genetic disorders?

____

____

____

____

USE WITH CHAPTER 19, PAGES 498–503.

Genetic Research to Cure Disease *(pages 502–503)*

Scientists work to understand and treat genetic disorders.

- **Gene therapy** is *the process of inserting normal genes into human cells to correct genetic disorders.*
- **Genetic engineering** is *the practice of placing fragments of DNA from one organism into another. It is not common practice.*

Doctors now use many genetic medicines to help treat burns and ulcers. They also use genetic medicines for growth defects and for ovarian and breast cancers.

4. What are some of the types of genetic treatments?

____

____

____

____

____

USE WITH CHAPTER 19, PAGES 504–507.

Prenatal Development and Birth: Infancy and Childhood

Vocabulary

developmental tasks	Events that need to happen in order for a person to continue growing toward becoming a healthy, mature adult *(page 504)*
autonomy	The confidence that a person can control his or her own body, impulses, and environment *(page 505)*
scoliosis	An abnormal lateral, or side-to-side, curvature of the spine *(page 507)*

Drawing from Experience

Do you have any younger siblings? What types of toys do they play with? How do young children learn how to act? Why is it important to be a good role model? Think about these questions as you read Lesson 4.

In the last lesson, you learned about heredity. In this lesson, you will learn about the stages of childhood.

Name Class Date

Organizing Your Thoughts

Use the chart below to help you take notes as you read the summaries that follow. In the first box, list the four stages of childhood. In the other box, list some of the types of childhood health screenings.

Four Stages of Childhood	Types of Childhood Health Screenings

Reading Tutor, Lesson 4 *(continued)*

USE WITH CHAPTER 19, PAGES 504–507.

Read to Learn

Read each passage carefully. Write in complete sentences to answer the following questions.

Childhood Development *(pages 504–507)*

Each person goes through eight stages of life. **Developmental tasks** are *events that need to happen in order for a person to continue growing into a healthy, mature adult.* Here are the first four stages of life.

Stage 1: Infancy: Birth–1 year. This is a period of fast growth in a person's life. The baby's weight triples. A baby learns to eat solid food, sit, crawl, and walk. An infant depends on others to meet his or her needs. He or she learns to trust.

Stage 2: Early Childhood: 1–3 years. The child learns to talk, climb, push, and pull. He or she learns to dress and feed him- or herself. The child learns **autonomy.** This is *the confidence that a person can control his or her own body, impulses, and environment.*

Stage 3: Middle Childhood: 4–6 years. The child learns to interact with others. The child models adult behavior. He or she asks lots of questions. The child develops responsibility and takes initiative. He or she creates his or her own play.

Stage 4: Late Childhood: 7–12 years. School becomes an important part of the child's life. The child learns to get along with peers and learns skills. He or she develops a conscience. The child develops an interest in performing activities.

1. What are the first four stages of life?

____

____

____

____

Health Screenings in Childhood *(page 507)*

Immunizations and health screenings can prevent many health problems.

- **Vision.** One in every 1,000 children has low vision or is blind. A doctor should give vision tests to newborns. Vision screenings should take place periodically throughout childhood.
- **Hearing.** Two to three of every 1,000 children have a hearing impairment. This often affects a child's language development. Schools often give screenings.

Reading Tutor, Lesson 4 *(continued)*

USE WITH CHAPTER 19, PAGES 504–507.

- **Scoliosis** is *an abnormal lateral, or side-to-side, curve of the spine*. It may begin in childhood and show up in the teen years. Many schools check for this disorder.

2. What are some of the health screenings that are performed during childhood?

Adolescence and the Life Cycle: Adolescence–Understanding Growth and Change

Vocabulary

adolescence	The period from childhood to adulthood *(page 514)*
puberty	The time when a person begins to develop certain traits of adults of his or her own gender *(page 514)*
hormones	Chemical substances that are produced in glands and help regulate many of your body's functions *(page 514)*
sex characteristics	The traits related to a person's gender *(page 515)*
gametes	Reproductive cells *(page 515)*
cognition	The ability to reason and think out abstract solutions *(page 516)*

Drawing from Experience

What is puberty? Have you grown taller lately? Do you ever feel happy and then sad? Do any of your friends have acne? How do you deal with the changes in your life? Think about these questions as you read Lesson 1.

In the last chapter, you learned about prenatal care and birth. In this lesson, you will learn about adolescence.

Reading Tutor, Lesson 1 *(continued)*

USE WITH CHAPTER 20, PAGES 514–510.

Organizing Your Thoughts

Use the chart below to help you take notes as you read the summaries that follow. In the first box, list some of the changes that occur during puberty. In the other box, list some of the developmental tasks of adolescence.

Changes During Puberty	Tasks of Adolescence

Reading Tutor, Lesson 1 *(continued)*

USE WITH CHAPTER 20, PAGES 514–510.

Read to Learn

Read each passage carefully. Write in complete sentences to answer the following questions.

Puberty *(pages 514–517)*

The period from childhood to adulthood is a**dolescence**. **Puberty** is *the time when a person begins to develop traits of adults of his or her own gender*. Puberty is the start of adolescence.

Hormones are the *chemical substances that glands produce. They help regulate many of your body'***s** *functions*. They control the changes that affect teens during puberty.

Here are some of the changes that occur during adolescence.

- **Physical changes.** *The traits related to a person's gender* are **sex characteristics. Gametes** are *reproductive cells*. The male gametes are **sperm.** The female gametes are the **eggs,** or **ova.**

  Here are some of the other physical changes.

  - **In females:** The breasts develop and the hips get wider. The menstrual cycle begins.
  - **In males:** Facial hair grows and the voice deepens. The muscles develop and the hairline begins to recede.
  - **In both:** Body hair appears, all of the teeth grow in, and sweat increases.
- **Mental changes.** The brain continues to develop during adolescence.
  - **Cognition** is *the ability to reason and think about abstract solutions*. A teen is able to solve problems in more complex ways. He or she begins to think logically and be open to more points of view.
- **Emotional changes.** Teens often feel strong waves of emotion. Their feelings go up and down quickly. It is important to have the support of family and friends. This support can help a teen feel confident and secure.
- **Social changes.** Teens have a need to belong. They want their peers to accept them. They begin to expand their circle of friends. They look for friends with the same goals and values.

1. What are some of the types of physical changes that occur during puberty?

____

____

____

____

Reading Tutor, Lesson 1 *(continued)*

USE WITH CHAPTER 20, PAGES 514–510.

Developmental Tasks of Adolescence *(pages 517–519)*

Certain tasks are part of the change between adolescence and being an adult.

- **Establish emotional and psychological independence.** You want to do things on your own, but you still want the security of your family support. Open discussion can help you accept family rules. It can help you learn the skills to be on your own.
- **Develop a personal sense of identity.** Your identity begins when you are a child. You learn from your parents. You begin to develop a sense of who you are as a separate person.
- **Adopt a personal value system.** Your parents gave you a set of rules to follow as a child. As a teen you begin to assess your own set of values.
- **Establish adult vocational goals.** You begin to think about what career you might want to have.
- **Develop control over your behavior.** You make choices about risky actions that may harm your health. Your values and your long-term goals affect your choices.

2. What are some of the developmental tasks that you may have as a teen?

____

____

____

____

____

Lesson 2 **Reading Tutor**

USE WITH CHAPTER 20, PAGES 520–523.

Adolescence and the Life Cycle: Moving Toward Adulthood

Vocabulary

physical maturity	The state at which the physical body and all its organs are fully developed *(page 520)*
emotional maturity	The state at which the mental and emotional capabilities of an individual are fully developed *(page 520)*
emotional intimacy	The ability to experience a caring, loving relationship with another person with whom you can share your innermost feelings *(page 523)*

Drawing from Experience

What is maturity? How do you know when you are mature? What are the things that make you become an adult? What are some of the stages of adulthood? Think about these questions as you read Lesson 2.

In the last lesson, you learned about changes during puberty. In this lesson, you will learn about moving into adulthood.

Reading Tutor, Lesson 2 *(continued)*

USE WITH CHAPTER 20, PAGES 520–523.

Organizing Your Thoughts

Use the chart below to help you take notes as you read the summaries that follow. In the first box, list the types of maturity. In the other box, list some of the aspects of young adulthood.

Types of Maturity	Aspects of Young Adulthood

Reading Tutor, Lesson 2 *(continued)*

USE WITH CHAPTER 20, PAGES 520–523.

Read to Learn

Read each passage carefully. Write in complete sentences to answer the following questions.

Physical and Emotional Maturity *(page 520)*

Physical maturity is *the state at which the physical body and all its organs are fully developed*. Most people reach this state by their early twenties.

Emotional maturity is *the state at which the mental and emotional capabilities of an individual are fully developed*. This means a person has a strong identity. He or she is able to give love and receive love. He or she can deal with reality. Family and friends provide love and support.

1. What are the two kinds of maturity?

___

___

___

___

___

Considering the Entire Life Cycle *(page 521)*

The life cycle has eight stages. The adult years are made of three major stages.

Stage 6: Young Adulthood – 19 to 40 years. The person tries to develop close personal relationships. He or she may want to start a family. The goal is to have intimacy.

Stage 7: Middle Adulthood – 40 to 65 years. The person looks outside of him- or herself and cares for others. The person may be a grandparent. The goal is to develop a sense of having given to society.

Stage 8: Late Adulthood – 65 years to death. The person tries to know the meaning of his or her own life. He or she wants to be happy with life choices. The goal is to be satisfied with one's life.

2. What are the stages of adulthood?

___

___

___

___

___

Reading Tutor, Lesson 2 *(continued)*

USE WITH CHAPTER 20, PAGES 520–523.

Young Adulthood *(pages 521–523)*

A person's goals change as he or she moves through young adulthood. Here are some of the ways that growth occurs.

- **Having independence.** This is part of a quest for **self-actualization.** It means being mature and able to take care of yourself.
- **Making job choices.** You think about what you would like to do as an adult. You have ideas about a career or job. The amount of education you need for a job may affect your choices.
- **Establishing close relationships. Emotional intimacy** is the *ability to have a caring, loving relationship with another person. You are able to share your inner feelings with this person.* Some people have several romantic relationships during this time. This may lead to marriage.
- **Giving to society.** You may develop your political views and your religious views. You may vote in elections. You may take part in community projects. This helps you to have self-esteem.

3. What are some of the aspects of growth during young adulthood?

USE WITH CHAPTER 20, PAGES 524–528.

Adolescence and the Life Cycle: Marriage and Parenting

Vocabulary

commitment	A promise or a pledge *(page 524)*
marital adjustment	How well a person adjusts to marriage and to his or her spouse *(page 525)*
adoption	The legal process of taking a child of other parents as one's own *(page 527)*
self-directed	Able to make correct decisions about behavior when adults are not present to enforce rules *(page 528)*
unconditional love	Love without limitation or qualification *(page 528)*

Drawing from Experience

Do you know any teens or young adults who are married? What factors are necessary for a good marriage? What kind of responsibility does a parent have to his or her child? Think about these questions as you read Lesson 3.

In the last lesson, you learned about maturity. In this lesson, you will learn about marriage and being a parent.

Reading Tutor, Lesson 3 *(continued)*

USE WITH CHAPTER 20, PAGES 524–528.

Organizing Your Thoughts

Use the chart below to help you take notes as you read the summaries that follow. In the first box, list some of the steps to having a good marriage. In the other box, list some of the responsibilities of being a parent.

Steps to a Good Marriage	Responsibilities of Parenthood

Reading Tutor, Lesson 3 *(continued)*

USE WITH CHAPTER 20, PAGES 524–528.

Read to Learn

Read each passage carefully. Write in complete sentences to answer the following questions.

Marriage *(pages 524–526)*

Marriage is a long-term commitment. A **commitment** is *a promise or a pledge.* Most people get married because they fall in love. They feel ready to enter into a lasting, intimate relationship.

Marital adjustment is *how well a person adjusts to marriage and to his or her spouse.* The success of a marriage relies on these factors.

- **Good communication.** Couples need to be able to share their feelings with each other. They need to be able to tell each other their needs and concerns.
- **Emotional maturity.** Couples need to be able to understand each partner's needs. They must be willing to compromise. They need to think about what is good for the relationship.
- **Similar values and interests.** Couples need to be able to share beliefs about good health, religion, culture, family, and friends. These shared beliefs will help them spend more time together.

Here are some issues that may cause problems in a marriage.

- The couple differs in spending and saving habits.
- They have different ideas about loyalty to family or friends.
- They have a lack of communication.
- They have a lack of intimacy.
- One person feels jealousy. There is infidelity or lack of attention.
- They do not agree about having children or finding child care.
- One or both are abusive.

Couples may seek counseling to help resolve serious marital problems.

1. What are some of the factors of a good marriage?

Reading Tutor, Lesson 3 *(continued)*

USE WITH CHAPTER 20, PAGES 524–528.

Teen Marriages *(page 526)*

Maturity is a very important factor in the success of a marriage. Many teens are still trying to figure out what they want to do with their lives. About 60 percent of teen marriages end in divorce.

Teens who marry may feel overwhelmed. They realize that the marriage may get in the way of their education or career goals. They may have financial stress. They may realize the amount of work needed to make the marriage succeed.

2. Why do 60 percent of teen marriages end in divorce?

Responsibilities of Parenthood *(pages 527–528)*

Many couples decide to start a family after they are married. Some couples choose to adopt. **Adoption** is *the legal process of taking a child of other parents as one's own*. Some couples also make a choice to bring foster children into their home.

Here are some of the ways that parents provide for their children.

- **Provide guidance.** Parents teach children to be responsible. They encourage and praise them. Parents teach children to make their own decisions. They are role models.
- **Instill values.** Parents pass on their value system to their children. They give them beliefs to guide the way they live. Values help children become happy and mature adults.

- **Set limits.** Parents set limits. They make rules. They teach their children to be **self-directed.** This means the child is *able to make the right decision about how to act when adults are not there.*
  - Parents should follow these tips when they must discipline their children.
  - Act quickly. Children need to know the results of their actions.
  - Separate the behavior from the child. The child is not a bad person.
  - Be consistent with the rules. Give the child praise for positive behavior.
- **Give unconditional love.** This is *love without limits or qualifications.* Parents need to show love to their children at all times. This love will help a child grow and thrive.

3. What are some of the ways that parents provide for their children?

____

____

____

____

____

____

____

Name Class Date

Lesson 4 — Reading Tutor

USE WITH CHAPTER 20, PAGES 529–533.

Adolescence and the Life Cycle: Health Through the Life Span

Vocabulary

transitions	Critical changes that occur at all stages of life *(page 529)*
empty-nest syndrome	Feelings of sadness or loneliness that accompany children's leaving home and entering adulthood *(page 531)*
integrity	A firm adherence to a moral code *(page 532)*

Drawing from Experience

Do you know any older adults? How do they keep a healthy lifestyle? What can you do now to help you have a healthy life when you are older? Think about these questions as you read Lesson 4.

In the last lesson, you learned about marriage and parenting. In this lesson, you will learn about the life span.

Reading Tutor, Lesson 4 *(continued)*

USE WITH CHAPTER 20, PAGES 529–533.

Organizing Your Thoughts

Use the chart below to help you take notes as you read the summaries that follow. In the first box, list some of the transitions in middle adulthood. In the other box, list some of the ways older adults stay healthy in late adulthood.

Middle Adulthood	Late Adulthood

Reading Tutor, Lesson 4 *(continued)*

USE WITH CHAPTER 20, PAGES 529–533.

Read to Learn

Read each passage carefully. Write in complete sentences to answer the following questions.

Middle Adulthood *(pages 529–531)*

Middle adulthood covers the years from 40 to 65. These years have many **transitions.** These are *critical changes that occur at all stages of life.* It is a time of family, graduations, having a first grandchild, a satisfactory career, and friends. It is more fulfilling when people are in good health.

Here are some of the types of transitions that occur during middle life.

- **Physical.** The skin loses elasticity and the body's organs slow. Females have menopause around ages 45 to 55. This is when the menstrual cycle stops. Hormone changes may cause hot flashes.

  The health habits you have when you are young will affect the way you feel as you grow older. Here are some of the ways to practice healthy behavior.

  - **Eyes.** The eyes have more difficulty focusing as you age. Eat leafy green vegetables and avoid the use of tobacco. Wear sunglasses.
  - **Ears.** Loud sounds take a toll on your hearing. Avoid loud noises. Use earplugs.
  - **Muscles and joints.** Arthritis affects half of those people over 65. Keep a healthy weight.
  - **Brain.** Your brain needs exercise, too! Read and keep learning.
  - **Mouth.** Teeth and gums may decay. Brush and floss. See a dentist every six months.
  - **Heart.** Lack of physical activity and a high-fat diet are risk factors for heart disease. Do aerobic activity and eat low-fat foods.
  - **Skin.** Skin may wrinkle, spot, and become dry. Use sunscreen. Cover up.

- **Mental.** Mental activities make the brain stronger. Solve puzzles, read, and play board games. Learn new hobbies. Use the computer.
- **Emotional.** Many people have had life's great joys. They have children, personal achievements, and some sorrows. The midlife crisis may result when people have concerns about whether they met their goals. Keep your health triangle balanced. Always set goals.

- **Social.** Many adults of this age may have to deal with the death of a parent. The **empty-nest syndrome** is the *feeling of sadness when children leave home and enter adulthood.* People who keep healthy relationships with family and friends have an easier time dealing with these changes. Make new friends. Develop good social skills.

1. What are some of the types of transitions that occur during middle life?

____

____

____

____

____

Late Adulthood *(pages 532–533)*

Late adulthood occurs after age 65. People look at life with a sense of fulfillment. Living a life of **integrity** means *a firm adherence to a moral code.* People who live this way are more likely to feel satisfied with their life. They can look back without regret.

Most adults live longer and can enjoy many years of late adulthood. Many look forward to retirement. Others work and still others volunteer. Those who are mentally and physically active will enjoy life more.

The Social Security system provides benefits to older adults. The government offers Medicare to adults over 65 and Medicaid to people with low income. It is important for older adults to have a financial plan. This can cover their expenses and control their retirement funds.

2. What are some of the factors about late adulthood?

____

____

____

____

____

Name Class Date

CHAPTER 21
Lesson 1

Reading Tutor

USE WITH CHAPTER 21, PAGES 540–545.

Tobacco: The Effects of Tobacco Use

Vocabulary

addictive drug	A substance that causes physiological or psychological dependence *(page 540)*
nicotine	The addictive drug found in tobacco leaves *(page 541)*
stimulant	A drug that increases the action of the central nervous system, the heart, and other organs *(page 541)*
carcinogen	A cancer-causing substance *(page 541)*
tar	A thick, sticky, dark fluid produced when tobacco burns *(page 541)*
carbon monoxide	A colorless, odorless, and poisonous gas *(page 541)*
smokeless tobacco	Tobacco that is sniffed through the nose, held in the mouth, or chewed *(page 542)*
leukoplakia	Thickened, white, leathery-looking spots on the inside of the mouth that can develop into oral cancer *(page 542)*

Drawing from Experience

Do you know anyone who smokes? How does tobacco affect the body? What is an addiction? Do you know how the use of tobacco harms the body? Think about these questions as you read Lesson 1.

In the last chapter, you learned about the life cycle. In this lesson, you will learn about the effects of tobacco use.

Reading Tutor, Lesson 1 *(continued)*

USE WITH CHAPTER 21, PAGES 540–545.

Organizing Your Thoughts

Use the chart below to help you take notes as you read the summaries that follow. In the first box, list some of the harmful effects of different forms of tobacco. In the other box, list some of the ways that tobacco affects the body.

Harmful Effects of Tobacco Products	How Tobacco Affects the Body

Reading Tutor, Lesson 1 *(continued)*

USE WITH CHAPTER 21, PAGES 540–545.

Read to Learn

Read each passage carefully. Write in complete sentences to answer the following questions.

Tobacco Use—A Serious Health Risk *(pages 540–541)*

Nicotine is *the addictive drug found in tobacco leaves.* An **addictive drug** is *a substance that causes physiological or psychological dependence.* A nicotine addict will need more and more tobacco to satisfy his or her craving for nicotine.

Nicotine is also a **stimulant.** This is *a drug that increases the action of the central nervous system, the heart, and other organs.* It may lead to heart disease and stroke.

1. What is nicotine?

____

____

____

____

____

Cigarette Smoke—A Toxic Mixture *(page 541)*

The smoke from burning tobacco is a **carcinogen.** This means it is *a cancer-causing substance.* Here are two other harmful compounds in tobacco smoke.

- **Tar** is *a thick, sticky, dark fluid produced when tobacco burns.* It destroys lung tissue. It may cause lung disease and cancer.
- **Carbon monoxide** is *a colorless, odorless, and poisonous gas.* It may cause high blood pressure and heart disease.

2. What are two of the harmful compounds in tobacco smoke?

____

____

____

____

____

Harmful Effects of Pipes and Cigars *(page 541)*

A cigar can have as much nicotine as a pack of cigarettes. It also has more tar and carbon monoxide. Pipe and cigar smokers are at greater risk for lip, mouth, and throat cancer.

3. What are some of the harmful effects of pipes and cigars?

Harmful Effects of Smokeless Tobacco *(page 542)*

Smokeless tobacco is *tobacco that a person sniffs through the nose, holds in the mouth, or chews.* It has two to three times the amount of nicotine that is in a cigarette. It may cause many types of cancer.

This kind of tobacco may also cause **leukoplakia.** These are *thick, white, leathery-looking spots on the inside of the mouth. They can develop into oral cancer.*

4. What are some of the harmful effects of smokeless tobacco?

How Tobacco Affects the Body *(pages 542–545)*

The chemicals in tobacco can cause harm to many body systems. Here are some of the short-term effects.

- **Changes in brain chemistry.** The body craves more nicotine. The user may get a headache or feel nervous as soon as 30 minutes after his or her last use of tobacco.
- **Increased respiration and heart rate.** Breathing during physical activity gets hard.
- **Dulled taste buds and reduced appetite.** Food does not taste as good.
- **Bad breath and smelly hair, clothes, and skin.** People may not want to be near the user.

Reading Tutor, Lesson 1 *(continued)*

USE WITH CHAPTER 21, PAGES 540–545.

Here are some of the long-term effects of tobacco use.

- **Chronic bronchitis.** Tobacco use can destroy the cilia in the bronchi. This leads to chronic coughing and mucus.
- **Emphysema.** This slowly destroys the tiny air sacs in the lungs. It becomes harder and harder to breathe over time.
- **Lung cancer.** Cancer cells may grow in the lungs when tobacco destroys the cilia.
- **Coronary heart disease and stroke.** Nicotine constricts the blood vessels. It cuts down on blood flow. It may lead to hardened arteries.

5. What are some of the short-term effects of tobacco use?

____

____

____

____

____

Other Consequences *(page 545)*

The use of tobacco has some other consequences for teens.

- **Legal.** It is not legal to sell tobacco to anyone under the age of 18. A school may suspend students for smoking.
- **Social.** Many people do not like the smell of smoke. They may exclude users from social events.
- **Financial.** Tobacco products are very costly. Smoking also results in more medical costs.

6. What are some of the other consequences of tobacco use?

____

____

____

____

____

USE WITH CHAPTER 21, PAGES 546–550.

Tobacco: Choosing to Live Tobacco Free

Vocabulary

nicotine withdrawal	The process that occurs in the body when nicotine, an addictive drug, is no longer used *(page 548)*
nicotine substitute	A product that delivers small amounts of nicotine into the user's system while he or she is trying to give up the tobacco habit *(page 549)*

Drawing from Experience

Do any of your friends use tobacco? Why do some teens smoke? What are some of the benefits of a smoke-free life? Have you ever tried to help a friend stop using tobacco? Think about these questions as you read Lesson 2.

In the last lesson, you learned about the effects of tobacco use. In this lesson, you will learn about the benefits of a tobacco-free lifestyle.

Reading Tutor, Lesson 2 *(continued)*

USE WITH CHAPTER 21, PAGES 546–550.

Organizing Your Thoughts

Use the chart below to help you take notes as you read the summaries that follow. In the first box, list some ways to prevent the use of tobacco. In the next box, list some reasons to give up tobacco. In the last box, list some tips for quitting.

Ways to Prevent Tobacco Use	Reasons to Stop Use	Tips for Quitting

Reading Tutor, Lesson 2 *(continued)*

USE WITH CHAPTER 21, PAGES 546–550.

Read to Learn

Read each passage carefully. Write in complete sentences to answer the following questions.

Reduced Tobacco Use Among Teens (page 546)

Many teens are choosing not to start smoking. Here are some of the reasons.

- **Antismoking campaigns.** Tobacco companies must fund ads to keep teens from smoking.
- **Cost.** Tobacco use is very expensive. Teens want to spend their money on other things.
- **Society.** Laws limit smoking in public places. Teens are used to having smoke-free air.
- **Family.** Many parents do not want their children to smoke.

1. What are some of the reasons that teens are choosing not to use tobacco?

____

____

____

____

____

Benefits of Living Tobacco Free *(page 547)*

Here are some of the benefits of living tobacco free.

- It lowers the risk of lung cancer and other diseases.
- It improves physical fitness. It gives you more energy.
- It helps you feel free of addiction.
- It makes you look and feel better. It makes you smell better.

2. What are some of the benefits of living tobacco free?

____

____

____

____

____

Reading Tutor, Lesson 2 *(continued)*

USE WITH CHAPTER 21, PAGES 546–550.

Strategies for Preventing Tobacco Use *(page 547)*

Here are some of the ways to live tobacco free.

- **Choose friends who do not use tobacco.** Be around people who share your values.
- **Avoid situations where tobacco products may be used.** Lower your risk of feeling pressure to use tobacco.
- **Practice and use refusal skills.** Plan what you will say if someone offers you tobacco. Be assertive.

3. What are some of the ways to live tobacco free?

____

____

____

____

____

Why Some Teens Use Tobacco *(page 548)*

Some teens do not resist the pressure. They begin to smoke. Here are some reasons why.

- They think it will help them lose weight. A lack of physical activity may actually make them gain weight.
- They think it will help them deal with stress. Stress may actually get worse with addiction.
- They think it will make them look mature.
- Peer pressure. They smoke to be like a friend who smokes.
- Media influence. They think smoking looks "cool."

4. What are some of the reasons why some teens choose to smoke?

____

____

____

____

____

Reading Tutor, Lesson 2 *(continued)*

USE WITH CHAPTER 21, PAGES 546–550.

Reasons to Give Up Tobacco Use *(page 548)*

Here are some of the reasons why teens decide to quit smoking.

- They begin to have health problems like asthma.
- They have the will and desire to stop.
- They find out how expensive it is.
- They see that tobacco use can lead to other risk behaviors such as the use of alcohol.
- They find it hard to buy tobacco products because they are not 18 years old.
- They do not want to hurt family and friends with secondhand smoke.

5. What are some of the reasons why teens decide to quit smoking?

____

____

____

____

Stopping the Addiction Cycle *(pages 548–550)*

Many people who decide to quit smoking will suffer from **nicotine withdrawal.** This is *the process that occurs in the body when nicotine is no longer used.* Some people try a **nicotine substitute.** This is *a product that delivers small amounts of nicotine into the user's body while he or she tries to quit smoking.*

Here are some tips to help someone quit using tobacco.

- **Prepare for the day.** Set a goal date for quitting.
- **Get support.** Support from family and friends will help you succeed.
- **Get professional help.** A doctor or a support group can help.
- **Replace tobacco with healthy alternatives.** Try sugarless gum or carrots.
- **Change your daily habits.** Avoid other tobacco users. Change daily routines.
- **Engage in healthy behavior.** Be active, eat a healthy diet, deal with stress, and abstain from alcohol and other drugs.

6. What are some of the tips to help a person give up tobacco?

____

____

____

____

Name Class Date

Lesson 3

Reading Tutor

USE WITH CHAPTER 21, PAGES 551–555.

Tobacco: Promoting a Smoke-Free Environment

Vocabulary

environmental tobacco smoke (ETS)	Air that has been contaminated by tobacco smoke *(page 551)*
mainstream smoke	The smoke exhaled from the lungs of a smoker *(page 551)*
sidestream smoke	The smoke from the burning end of a cigarette, pipe, or cigar *(page 551)*

Drawing from Experience

Have you ever noticed that there are smoking and nonsmoking areas in public places? Has cigarette smoke ever bothered you while you were in a public place? How can teens help make public places smoke free? Think about these questions as you read Lesson 3.

In the last lesson, you learned about choosing to be tobacco free. In this lesson, you will learn about a smoke-free society.

Name Class Date

Reading Tutor, Lesson 3 *(continued)*

USE WITH CHAPTER 21, PAGES 551–555.

Organizing Your Thoughts

Use the chart below to help you take notes as you read the summaries that follow. In the first box, list some of the effects of smoke on nonsmokers. In the other box, list some of the ways to reduce your risks and have a smoke-free society.

Effects of Smoke on Nonsmokers	Ways to Reduce Risks/ Have a Smoke-Free Society

Reading Tutor, Lesson 3 *(continued)*

USE WITH CHAPTER 21, PAGES 551–555.

Read to Learn

Read each passage carefully. Write in complete sentences to answer the following questions.

Risks for Smokers and Nonsmokers *(page 551)*

Environmental tobacco smoke (ETS), or secondhand smoke, is *air that tobacco smoke has contaminated*. There are two types of ETS.

Mainstream smoke is *the smoke exhaled from the lungs of a smoker*. **Sidestream smoke** is *the smoke from the burning end of a cigarette, pipe, or cigar*.

1. What is secondhand smoke?

____

____

____

____

____

Effects of Smoke on Nonsmokers *(page 552)*

ETS causes watery eyes, headaches, and coughing. It makes asthma worse. It may lead to lung cancer over time.

Smoking during pregnancy may affect the growth of the unborn baby. It may cause low birth weight and other childhood problems.

Here are some of the other ways that smoke can affect young children.

- Children of smokers have more sore throats, ear infections, and respiratory problems.
- Children who live with smokers have more risk of getting lung cancer.
- Parents are role models. Children of smokers are more likely to smoke.

2. What are some of the ways that smoke can affect young children?

____

____

____

____

____

Reducing Your Risks ***(page 553)***

Here are some of the ways to protect yourself from ETS.

- Ask visitors not to smoke while they are in your home.
- Open windows. Let in fresh air if someone in your family smokes.
- Use air cleaners to get rid of smoke contamination.
- Meet in a different place if a friend lives in a home where someone smokes.
- Sit in a nonsmoking area in public places.

3. What are some of the ways to protect yourself from ETS?

____

____

____

____

____

Toward a Smoke-Free Society ***(pages 554–555)***

Here are some of the ways that society is working toward a smoke-free society.

- Many states do not allow smoking in the workplace or in public buildings.
- Some states do not allow smoking in public places.
- Cities strictly enforce the laws that ban tobacco sales to minors.
- Some states have sued tobacco companies. They use the awards to pay for antismoking programs.
- *Healthy People 2010* is a national program. One of its goals is to reduce the number of people who smoke.
- You can work in your school or community to help stop tobacco use.

4. What are some of the ways that society is working to have a smoke-free society?

____

____

____

____

____

USE WITH CHAPTER 22, PAGES 562–567.

Alcohol: Choosing to Be Alcohol Free

Vocabulary

ethanol	The type of alcohol in alcoholic beverages *(page 562)*
fermentation	The chemical action of yeast on sugars *(page 562)*
depressant	A drug that tends to slow the central nervous system *(page 563)*
intoxication	The state in which the body is poisoned by alcohol or another substance and the person's physical and mental control is significantly reduced *(page 563)*
alcohol abuse	The excessive use of alcohol *(page 565)*

Drawing from Experience

Why do some teens drink alcohol? What are some of the risks of using alcohol? How can you stay alcohol free? Think about these questions as you read Lesson 1.

In the last chapter, you learned about the use of tobacco. In this lesson, you will learn how to be alcohol free.

Reading Tutor, Lesson 1 *(continued)*

USE WITH CHAPTER 22, PAGES 562–567.

Organizing Your Thoughts

Use the chart below to help you take notes as you read the summaries that follow. In the first box, list some of the facts about alcohol and the factors that influence alcohol use. In the other box, list some of the ways to avoid alcohol and be alcohol free.

Facts About Alcohol/Influences	Ways to Avoid Alcohol/Be Alcohol Free

Reading Tutor, Lesson 1 *(continued)*

USE WITH CHAPTER 22, PAGES 562–567.

Read to Learn

Read each passage carefully. Write in complete sentences to answer the following questions.

The Facts About Alcohol *(pages 562–563)*

Ethanol is *the type of alcohol in alcoholic beverages.* It is an addictive drug. It is the end result of the **fermentation** of fruits, vegetables, or grains. This is *the chemical action of yeast on sugars.*

Alcohol is a **depressant.** It is *a drug that slows the central nervous system.* It affects a person's motor skills, clear thinking, and good judgment.

Alcohol can cause a person to become intoxicated. **Intoxication** is *the state in which alcohol poisons the body and reduces the person's physical and mental control.*

1. What is a depressant? What does it mean to be intoxicated?

____

____

____

____

____

____

Factors That Influence Alcohol Use *(pages 563–565)*

Some teens make the choice to drink alcohol. Here are some of the reasons why.

- **Peer pressure.** The desire for a teen to fit in is strong. Find friends who also avoid alcohol.
- **Family.** Teens whose parents drink alcohol may want to try it. Parents who avoid alcohol are more likely to have teens who do the same.
- **Media messages.** Many messages in the movies and on TV make alcohol look exciting.
- **Ad techniques.** Ads show handsome and popular people having fun drinking. They suggest that you will also have fun if you drink.

2. What are some of the factors that may influence the use of alcohol?

____

____

____

____

____

Avoid Alcohol: Avoid Unsafe Situations *(pages 565–566)*

The use of alcohol can be very harmful. Alcohol-related car wrecks are the leading cause of teen death. Here are some other situations to avoid.

- **Alcohol and the law.** It is not legal for anyone who is under 21 years old to buy, hold, or drink alcohol. Teens may risk arrest. They risk harm to their reputation.
- **Alcohol, violence, and sexual activity.** Alcohol use impairs a teen's good judgment. Teens who drink are more likely to be involved in violent crimes. They are also more likely to be sexually active at an earlier age.
- **Alcohol abuse.** This is *the excessive use of alcohol.* Teens who live with a person who abuses alcohol are at risk for neglect and abuse. It may lead a teen to try alcohol to escape.
- **Alcohol and school activities.** Most schools have a zero-tolerance policy for alcohol use. Teens may lose the chance to qualify for a team or a scholarship.

3. What are some of the alcohol-related situations that a teen should avoid?

____

____

____

____

____

Reading Tutor, Lesson 1 *(continued)*

USE WITH CHAPTER 22, PAGES 562–567.

Being Alcohol Free *(pages 566–567)*

Many teens choose to be alcohol free. Here are some of the benefits of this choice.

- **You can keep your body healthy.** Avoiding alcohol protects the body organs from damage. It lowers the chance of injury.
- **You can make responsible choices.** Having a clear head helps you protect your health.
- **You can avoid risky behavior.** You lessen the risk of sexual activity or drunk driving.
- **You can avoid illegal actions.** You can avoid arrest and legal problems.

Plan ahead. Know what to say if someone tries to pressure you to drink alcohol. Be assertive and refuse to drink. Call for a ride home. Avoid places where alcohol will be an issue.

4. What are some of the benefits of choosing to be alcohol free?

Lesson 2

Reading Tutor

USE WITH CHAPTER 22, PAGES 568–573.

Alcohol: Harmful Effects of Alcohol Use

Vocabulary

metabolism	The process by which the body breaks down substances and gets energy from food *(page 569)*
blood alcohol concentration (BAC)	The amount of alcohol in a person's blood expressed as a percentage *(page 570)*
binge drinking	Drinking five or more alcoholic drinks at one sitting *(page 571)*
alcohol poisoning	A severe and potentially fatal physical reaction to an alcohol overdose *(page 571)*

Drawing from Experience

Why does alcohol affect some teens more than it does others? Why is it so dangerous to drink and drive? What can you do if someone gets sick from using alcohol? Think about these questions as you read Lesson 2.

In the last lesson, you learned how to be alcohol free. In this lesson, you will learn about the harmful effects of alcohol use.

Reading Tutor, Lesson 2 *(continued)*

USE WITH CHAPTER 22, PAGES 568–573.

Organizing Your Thoughts

Use the chart below to help you take notes as you read the summaries that follow. In the first box, list some of the short-term effects of alcohol on the body. In the other box, list some of the other risks and dangers of using alcohol.

Short-Term Effects of Alcohol on the Body	Other Risks and Dangers of Alcohol Use

Read to Learn

Read each passage carefully. Write in complete sentences to answer the following questions.

Short-Term Effects of Drinking *(page 568)*

The short-term effects of alcohol differ with each person.

- **Body size and gender.** A small person or a female will feel the effect faster.
- **Food.** Food in the stomach slows down the effects.
- **Amount and rate of intake.** A person will get drunk if he or she drinks alcohol faster than the liver can break it down. Alcohol poisoning can occur if alcohol levels get too high.

Alcohol has many physical effects on the body. These effects grow as the person drinks more.

- The **brain** is less able to control the body. Alcohol impairs **judgment.**
- **Heart** rate and blood pressure rise. The **blood vessels** expand and lower body heat.
- **Stomach** acid increases. This may cause nausea and vomiting.
- Alcohol use can cause scarring of the **liver.**
- Alcohol use can cause the **kidneys** to increase urine output. This can lead to dehydration.
- **Breathing** may slow or stop.

1. What are some of the short-term effects of drinking on the body?

____

____

____

____

____

Alcohol and Drug Interactions *(pages 569–570)*

Mixing alcohol and drugs may harm your body or even cause death. **Metabolism** is *the process by which the body breaks down substances*. Taking alcohol with medicine or other drugs may cause a **multiplier effect.** This is when a drug has a greater or different effect than if you took it alone.

Here are some of the types of alcohol-drug effects on the body.

- Alcohol may slow down the time it takes the body to absorb a drug. This causes a risk of more side effects.

- Alcohol may cause the medicine to break down faster than normal. This can make it less effective.
- Alcohol may cause the body to turn the medicine into chemicals that can harm the liver or other organs. Some types of common pain medicine and alcohol can cause severe liver damage.
- Alcohol can increase the effect of some drugs. Combining cold medicine and alcohol can cause you to be dizzy and sleepy. This is risky if a person is driving.

2. What are some of the types of alcohol-drug effects on the body?

____

____

____

____

Driving Under the Influence *(pages 570–571)*

Driving while intoxicated (DWI) or driving under the influence (DUI) is the leading cause of death among teens. **Blood alcohol concentration (BAC)** is *the amount of alcohol in a person's blood, as a percentage*. Most states define being drunk as 0.1 or 0.08 percent BAC.

Here are some of the results of drinking on the body.

- It slows your reflexes. It lowers your ability to judge distance and speed.
- It increases risk-taking behavior.
- It lowers your ability to pay attention. It makes you forgetful.

Here are some of the consequences of DWI.

- It can cause harm to the driver and others.
- It can cause injury, property damage, and death. It can cause you to live with regret.
- It can cause arrest and jail time and a heavy fine.
- It can cause you to lose your driver's license. It can cause your insurance rates to go up.

3. What are some of the results of DWI?

____

____

____

____

Reading Tutor, Lesson 2 *(continued)*

USE WITH CHAPTER 22, PAGES 568–573.

Binge Drinking *(page 571)*

Binge drinking is *drinking five or more alcoholic drinks at one sitting*. Rapid binge drinking is very dangerous because it is possible to drink a fatal dose of alcohol. Binge drinking can also cause alcohol poisoning.

4. What is binge drinking?

____

____

____

____

____

Alcohol Poisoning *(pages 571–573)*

Alcohol poisoning is *a severe and possibly fatal reaction to an alcohol overdose*. Call 911 if you think someone is in this condition. Here are some of the signs.

- Mental confusion—stupor, coma, vomiting, or seizures
- Slow breathing—10 seconds between breaths or fewer than eight breaths a minute
- Irregular heartbeat. Low body heat. Pale or bluish skin
- Severe dehydration from vomiting

5. What are some of the signs of alcohol poisoning?

____

____

____

____

____

Lesson 3

Reading Tutor

USE WITH CHAPTER 22, PAGES 574–579.

Alcohol: Alcohol, the Individual, and Society

Vocabulary

fetal alcohol syndrome (FAS)	A group of alcohol-related birth defects that includes both physical and mental problems *(page 576)*
alcoholism	A disease in which a person has a physical or psychological dependence on drinks that contain alcohol *(page 576)*
alcoholic	An addict who is dependent on alcohol *(page 576)*
recovery	The process of learning to live an alcohol-free life *(page 578)*
detoxification	A process in which the body adjusts to functioning without alcohol *(page 578)*
sobriety	Living without alcohol *(page 578)*

Drawing from Experience

Do you know anyone who has a problem with alcohol? How can drinking affect an unborn baby? Where can you go to get help for a person with a drinking problem? Think about these questions as you read Lesson 3.

In the last lesson, you learned about the short-term effects of drinking. In this lesson, you will learn about the long-term effects of drinking.

Reading Tutor, Lesson 3 *(continued)*

USE WITH CHAPTER 22, PAGES 574–579.

Organizing Your Thoughts

Use the chart below to help you take notes as you read the summaries that follow. In the first box, list some of the long-term effects of alcohol on the body. In the next, list some of the signs of alcoholism.

Long-Term Effects of Alcohol on the Body	Signs of Alcoholism

Reading Tutor, Lesson 3 *(continued)*

USE WITH CHAPTER 22, PAGES 574–579.

Read to Learn

Read each passage carefully. Write in complete sentences to answer the following questions.

Long-Term Effects of Alcohol on the Body *(pages 574–575)*

Alcohol affects many of the major organs in the body. Long-term drinking can cause death. Here are some of the long-term effects of alcohol abuse.

- **Addiction.** The person is not able to stop drinking.
- **Loss of brain functions.** The person loses verbal and visual skills and memory.
- **Brain damage.** Drinking can destroy brain cells. It can also cause the brain to shrink.
- **Heart disease.** Drinking may cause an enlarged heart. High blood pressure can cause heart disease.
- **Fatty liver.** Fat builds up in the liver. This blocks the flow of blood to liver cells. Cells die.
- **Alcoholic hepatitis.** This is an infection of the liver.
- **Cirrhosis.** Liver tissue turns into scar tissue. This may lead to liver failure and death.
- **Digestive problems.** Drinking hurts the lining of the stomach. This may lead to ulcers and cancers.
- **Swollen pancreas.** The lining of the pancreas swells. This blocks the intestine. It can lead to death.

1. What are some of the long-term effects of alcohol on the body?

Alcohol During Pregnancy *(pages 575–576)*

Alcohol passes from a mother to her fetus. This can cause major problems for the fetus. **Fetal alcohol syndrome (FAS)** is *a group of alcohol-related birth defects that includes physical and mental problems.*

FAS is the leading known cause of mental retardation. An FAS baby is born with a deformed head, face, hands, or feet. FAS babies have slow growth and learning problems. No amount of alcohol is safe for a pregnant female to drink. Even small amounts can harm a fetus.

2. What is fetal alcohol syndrome (FAS)?

____

____

____

____

____

____

Alcoholism *(pages 576–578)*

Alcoholism is *a disease in which a person has a physical or psychological dependence on drinks that contain alcohol.* An **alcoholic** is *an addict who is dependent on alcohol.* An alcoholic may have some of these signs.

- **Craving.** The person has a strong need for alcohol.
- **Loss of control.** The person cannot limit his or her drinking.
- **Physical dependence.** The person may have withdrawal if he or she stops drinking.
- **Tolerance.** The person needs to drink more and more to feel the effect of alcohol.
- **Health, family, and legal problems.** The person may get hurt a lot. He or she may have received drunk driving tickets from the police. The person may have trouble at home.
- **Genetic link.** Children of alcoholics are more likely to drink.

There are three stages to alcoholism.

- **Stage 1—Abuse.** A person may begin to use alcohol to relax. Then he or she begins to drink regularly. The person may start to lie or make excuses about drinking.
- **Stage 2—Dependence.** The person cannot stop drinking. He or she is dependent on the drug. The person begins to have problems at work or school and home.
- **Stage 3—Addiction.** Drinking is the most important thing in the person's life. He or she is addicted to the drug. His or her life is out of control.

Reading Tutor, Lesson 3 *(continued)*

USE WITH CHAPTER 22, PAGES 574–579.

3. What are the three stages of alcoholism?

Effects on Family and Society *(page 578)*

Alcohol use is a major factor in many accidents and crimes. Here are some of the effects that drinking has on society.

- Alcohol use is a major factor in car crashes, falls, drowning, and house fires.
- About 40 percent of violent crimes are alcohol related.
- About two-thirds of domestic violence victims say that alcohol was a factor in the crime.
- Almost half of all homicide victims have alcohol in their blood.
- People who live with alcoholics may be **codependents.** They do not take care of their own needs. They may put their own health at risk.

4. What are some of the effects that drinking has on family and society?

Reading Tutor, Lesson 3 *(continued)*

USE WITH CHAPTER 22, PAGES 574–579.

Treatment for Alcohol Abuse *(pages 578–579)*

You cannot cure alcoholism, but you can treat it. **Recovery** is *the process of learning to live an alcohol-free life*. One of the steps of recovery is **detoxification**, *a process in which the body adjusts to functioning without alcohol.* **Sobriety** is *living without alcohol*. Here are some of the places to get help.

- **Al-Anon/Alateen** help families and friends deal with the effects of living with an alcoholic.
- **Alcoholics Anonymous** gives help for alcohol users of all ages.
- **National Association for Children of Alcoholics** gives help to children of alcoholics.
- **National Clearinghouse for Alcohol & Drug Information** gives information about all drugs.
- **National Drug & Treatment Referral Routing Service** gives information about treatment.

5. Where are some of the places you can go to get help for alcohol abuse?

____

____

____

____

____

____

Name Class Date

CHAPTER 23
Lesson 1

Reading Tutor

USE WITH CHAPTER 23, PAGES 586–591.

Medicines and Drugs: The Role of Medicines

Vocabulary

medicines	Drugs that are used to treat or prevent diseases or other conditions *(page 586)*
drugs	Substances other than food that change the structure or function of the body or mind *(page 586)*
vaccine	A preparation of dead or weakened pathogens that are introduced into the body to stimulate an immune response *(page 587)*
analgesics	Pain relievers *(page 588)*
side effects	Reactions to medicine other than the one intended *(page 589)*
additive interaction	Medicines working together in a positive way *(page 589)*
synergistic effect	An interaction of two or more medicines that results in a greater effect than when the medicines are taken alone *(page 589)*
antagonistic interaction	Occurs when the effect of one medicine is canceled or reduced when taken with another medicine *(page 589)*

Drawing from Experience

Have you ever needed to take medicine? Why is it important to take the correct dose? What questions should you ask your doctor about medicine? Think about these questions as you read Lesson 1.

In the last chapter, you learned about alcohol. In this lesson, you will learn about the role of medicines.

Reading Tutor, Lesson 1 *(continued)*

USE WITH CHAPTER 23, PAGES 586–591.

Organizing Your Thoughts

Use the chart below to help you take notes as you read the summaries that follow. In the first box, list some of the types of medicine. In the next box, list some of the effects of medicine on the body. In the lower box, list some of the ways that people misuse medicine.

Types of Medicine	Effects of Medicine on the Body	Medicine Misuse

Reading Tutor, Lesson 1 *(continued)*

USE WITH CHAPTER 23, PAGES 586–591.

Read to Learn

Read each passage carefully. Write in complete sentences to answer the following questions.

Classification of Medicines *(pages 586–588)*

Medicines are *drugs that we use to treat or prevent disease or other disorders.* **Drugs** are *substances other than food that change the structure or function of the body or mind.* Here are the four main types of medicine.

- **Medicines to prevent disease.** There are two types.
  - A **vaccine** is *a medicine we put into the body to start an immune response. It is made of weakened or dead germs.* Your body will make antibodies to fight the germs.
  - **Antitoxins** are made of blood fluids. They have antibodies and act more quickly than vaccines. Animals make this in their immune system. We use it to fight toxins.
- **Medicines to fight pathogens**
  - Antibiotics work to kill bacteria in the body. They do not work on viruses.
  - Antivirals work on viruses. They hold back the virus but do not kill it.
- **To relieve pain**
  - **Analgesics** are *pain relievers.* They are the most common type of medicine. They can be mild like an aspirin or strong like morphine. Children use acetaminophen instead of aspirin.
- **Medicines to promote health**
  - Allergy drugs relieve the sneezing, the watery eyes, and the runny nose of an allergy.
  - Body-regulating drugs help control certain systems. Insulin treats diabetes. Inhalers treat asthma. Heart medicine treats high blood pressure or heart disease.
  - Antidepressant and antipsychotic drugs treat mood disorders, depression, and schizophrenia.
  - Cancer treatment helps stop the growth of cancer cells.

1. What are the four main types of medicine?

____

____

____

____

Medicines and the Body *(page 589)*

Side effects are *reactions to medicine other than the one the doctor intended.* Mixing more than one type of medicine may also cause reactions.

- An **additive interaction** is *when medicines work with each other in a positive way.*
- A **synergistic effect** is *an interaction of two or more medicines. It results in a greater effect than when you take each drug alone.*
- An **antagonistic interaction** *occurs when the effect of one medicine lessens or does not work when you take it with another drug.*
- **Tolerance** is when the body gets used to the effect of a medicine. You need more and more for the drug to work.
- **Withdrawal** is when a person stops using a medicine that he or she is dependent on.

2. What are some of the effects of medicine on the body?

____

____

____

____

____

____

Medicine Safety *(pages 590–591)*

The Food and Drug Administration (FDA) decides how medicine will be sold to the public.

- **Prescription.** You cannot use this type of medicine without the written approval of a doctor. The label must tell you certain information about the drug.
- **Over-the-counter (OTC).** You can buy this type of medicine in the store without a doctor's order.

Using drugs in the wrong way can be a health risk. Here are some of the types of medicine misuse.

- Not following the instructions for use of a drug.
- Giving your prescription to others. Taking someone else's medicine.
- Taking too much or too little of a drug. Taking medicine for more or less time than you should.

Reading Tutor, Lesson 1 *(continued)*

USE WITH CHAPTER 23, PAGES 586–591.

- Stopping use of a drug without letting your doctor know.
- Mixing medicines.

3. What are some of the ways that people misuse medicine?

Medicines and Drugs: Drug Use—A High-Risk Behavior

Vocabulary

substance abuse	Any unnecessary or improper use of chemical substances for nonmedical purposes *(page 592)*
illegal drugs	Chemical substances that people of any age may not lawfully manufacture, possess, buy, or sell *(page 592)*
illicit drug use	The use or sale of any substance that is illegal or otherwise not permitted *(page 592)*
overdose	A strong, sometimes fatal reaction to taking a large amount of a drug *(page 594)*
psychological dependence	A condition in which a person believes that a drug is needed in order to feel good or to function normally *(page 595)*
physiological dependence	A condition in which the user has a chemical need for a drug *(page 595)*
addiction	A physiological or psychological dependence on a drug *(page 595)*

Drawing from Experience

Do you know anyone who takes drugs? Why do some teens use drugs? Why is using drugs a risk to your health? What other risks might occur if you use drugs? Think about these questions as you read Lesson 2.

In the last lesson, you learned about medicine. In this lesson, you will learn about drug use.

Reading Tutor, Lesson 2 *(continued)*

USE WITH CHAPTER 23, PAGES 592–597.

Organizing Your Thoughts

Use the chart below to help you take notes as you read the summaries that follow. In the first box, list some of the factors that influence drug use. In the other box, list some of the health risks and other consequences of drug use.

Factors That Influence Drug Abuse	Health Risks/Other Results of Drug Use

Reading Tutor, Lesson 2 *(continued)*

USE WITH CHAPTER 23, PAGES 592–597.

Read to Learn

Read each passage carefully. Write in complete sentences to answer the following questions.

What Is Substance Abuse? *(pages 592–594)*

Substance abuse is *any improper use of chemical substances for nonmedical purposes.* **Illegal drugs** are *chemical substances that people of any age may not lawfully make, possess, buy, or sell.* **Illicit drug use** is *the use or sale of any substance that is not legal.*

Here are some of the factors that may influence a teen's choices about drug abuse.

- **Peer pressure** is the urging of friends or groups to do something. Find friends who can say no to drugs.
- **Family members** can help teens stay away from drugs.
- **Role models** are people you can look up to and admire.
- **Media messages** may give you the wrong impression about drug use.
- **Perceptions** are not always what is real. Most teens do not use drugs.

1. What are some of the factors that may influence drug abuse?

____

____

____

____

The Health Risks of Drug Use *(pages 594–595)*

Drug abuse affects all sides of the health triangle.

- **Physical health.** A great danger of drug use is overdose. An **overdose** is *a strong, sometimes fatal reaction to taking a large amount of a drug.*
- **Mental/emotional health.** Drugs affect the brain. Drug users lose control of their behavior.
- **Social health.** Drug use can affect relationships with family and friends. A school may expel a teen who uses drugs. Drug use may have legal consequences.

Here are some of the consequences of drug use.

- **Tolerance** is the need to use more and more of a drug to get the same effect.
- **Psychological dependence** is *a condition in which a person believes that he or she needs a drug in order to feel good or to function normally.*

Reading Tutor, Lesson 2 *(continued)*

- **Physiological dependence** is *a condition in which the user has a chemical need for a drug*. A person may feel very ill when he or she stops taking the drug.
- **Addiction** is *a physiological or psychological dependence on a drug*. A person who becomes addicted needs help to stop taking the drug.

2. What are some of the health risks of drug use?

____

____

____

____

Other Consequences of Drug Use *(pages 596–597)*

Drug use is a risk to your health. Here are some of the other consequences of drug use.

- **To the individual.** Drugs affect all parts of the health triangle. Drug users are also at risk for sexual activity and unplanned pregnancy or STDs. Drug users may be at risk for arrest and legal fines. They may be suspended from school or spend time in jail.
- **For family and friends.** The drug user's choice to use drugs affects everyone in his or her life. Drug users may not have time for friends. Family members may try to get help for the drug user.
- **For babies and children.** A pregnant female passes the drugs to her fetus. Babies may be born with birth defects. A mother passes the drugs to her nursing child. Children of drug users may not get the care they need from their addicted parents.
- **To society.** Drug use places burdens on society. It causes more crime, more car wrecks, and more injuries. Medical costs and legal costs add to the burden.

3. What are some of the other consequences of drug use?

____

____

____

____

USE WITH CHAPTER 23, PAGES 598–602.

Medicines and Drugs: Marijuana, Inhalants, and Steroids

Vocabulary

marijuana	A plant whose leaves, buds, and flowers are usually smoked for their intoxicating effects *(page 598)*
paranoia	Irrational suspiciousness or distrust of others *(page 600)*
inhalants	Substances whose fumes are sniffed and inhaled to achieve a mind-altering effect *(page 600)*
anabolic-androgenic steroids	Synthetic substances similar to the male hormone testosterone *(page 601)*

Drawing from Experience

Why do some teens use marijuana? How can you avoid marijuana use? How can steroids hurt an athlete? Think about these questions as you read Lesson 3.

In the last lesson, you learned about drug use. In this lesson, you will learn about marijuana, steroids, and inhalants.

Reading Tutor, Lesson 3 *(continued)*

USE WITH CHAPTER 23, PAGES 598–602.

Organizing Your Thoughts

Use the chart below to help you take notes as you read the summaries that follow. In the first box, list some of the risks of marijuana use. In the next box, list some of the risks of using inhalants. In the last box, list some of the risks of using steroids.

Marijuana Risks	Inhalant Risks	Steroid Risks

Reading Tutor, Lesson 3 *(continued)*

USE WITH CHAPTER 23, PAGES 598–602.

Read to Learn

Read each passage carefully. Write in complete sentences to answer the following questions.

Marijuana *(pages 598–600)*

Marijuana is *a hemp plant. People smoke the leaves, buds, and flowers for their intoxicating effects.* It is an illegal drug. Other names for it are grass, weed, and pot. Here are some of the risks of using this drug.

- **Risk of addiction.** Marijuana raises the levels of dopamine in the brain. This gives the user a sense of well-being. When this wears off, the person will feel let down or "crash." Here are some other physical effects.
  - Loss of short-term memory, reaction time, and concentration
  - Bloodshot eyes and dry mouth
  - Coughing. Heart and lung damage. Risk of lung cancer
  - Increase in appetite. Weight gain
  - Risk of stillbirth and birth defects
- **Risk to mental/emotional health.** Users may feel anxiety and **paranoia.** This is an *irrational distrust of others*. Short-term memory loss may affect schoolwork. Users may have trouble thinking and problem solving.
- **Risk to growth and development.** There is a risk of infertility in females. There is a lower sperm count in males. Females may grow facial hair. It lowers testosterone levels in males and raises it in females.
- **Risks of driving under the influence.** This is as dangerous as driving under the influence of alcohol. Marijuana causes trouble with vision and judgment. It slows the user's reflexes. There may also be serious legal issues.

1. What are some of the risks of using marijuana?

____

____

____

____

____

____

Reading Tutor, Lesson 3 *(continued)*

USE WITH CHAPTER 23, PAGES 598–602.

Inhalants *(pages 600–601)*

Inhalants are *substances with fumes. Some people sniff and inhale them to get a mind-altering effect.* The fumes go straight to the brain. They damage and kill brain cells. Some of the types of inhalants are glue, spray paint, gas, and varnish. They are very dangerous. Many are poisons.

Most inhalants damage the central nervous system. The user may have a glassy stare, slurred speech, and lack of judgment. The user may also have a sudden heart attack and die.

2. What are some of the risks of inhalants?

Anabolic-Androgenic Steroids *(pages 601–602)*

Anabolic-androgenic steroids are *synthetic substances. They are similar to the male hormone testosterone. Anabolic* means "muscle building." *Androgenic* means "more male traits." Steroids can cause mood swings, lack of judgment, and paranoia.

Steroid use is dangerous and illegal unless a doctor prescribes it. It does add to muscle strength, but it has many bad side effects. Athletes who fail a steroid drug test will not qualify for an event. There may also be jail time and fines.

3. What are some of the risks of taking steroids?

Name Class Date

Lesson 4 **Reading Tutor**

USE WITH CHAPTER 23, PAGES 603–610.

Medicines and Drugs: Psychoactive Drugs

Vocabulary

psychoactive drugs	Chemicals that affect the central nervous system and alter activity in the brain *(page 603)*
stimulants	Drugs that increase the action of the central nervous system, the heart, and other organs *(page 605)*
euphoria	A feeling of intense well-being or elation *(page 605)*
depressants	Drugs that tend to slow the central nervous system *(page 606)*
narcotics	Specific drugs derived from the opium plant that are obtainable only by prescription and are used to relieve pain *(page 608)*
hallucinogens	Drugs that alter moods, thoughts, and sense perceptions including vision, hearing, smell, and touch *(page 609)*
designer drugs	Synthetic substances meant to imitate the effects of hallucinogens and other dangerous drugs *(page 610)*

Drawing from Experience

How can drugs affect your success in school? What are the health risks for teens who use drugs? How can you stay away from drugs? Think about these questions as you read Lesson 4.

In the last lesson, you learned about marijuana and steroids. In this lesson, you will learn about psychoactive drugs.

Reading Tutor, Lesson 4 *(continued)*

USE WITH CHAPTER 23, PAGES 603–610.

Organizing Your Thoughts

Use the chart below to help you take notes as you read the summaries that follow. In the first oval, list some of the health risks of stimulants. In the next oval, list the health risks of depressants. Next, list the health risks of narcotics. In the next, list the health risks of hallucinogens. In the last oval, list the health risks of ecstasy and designer drugs.

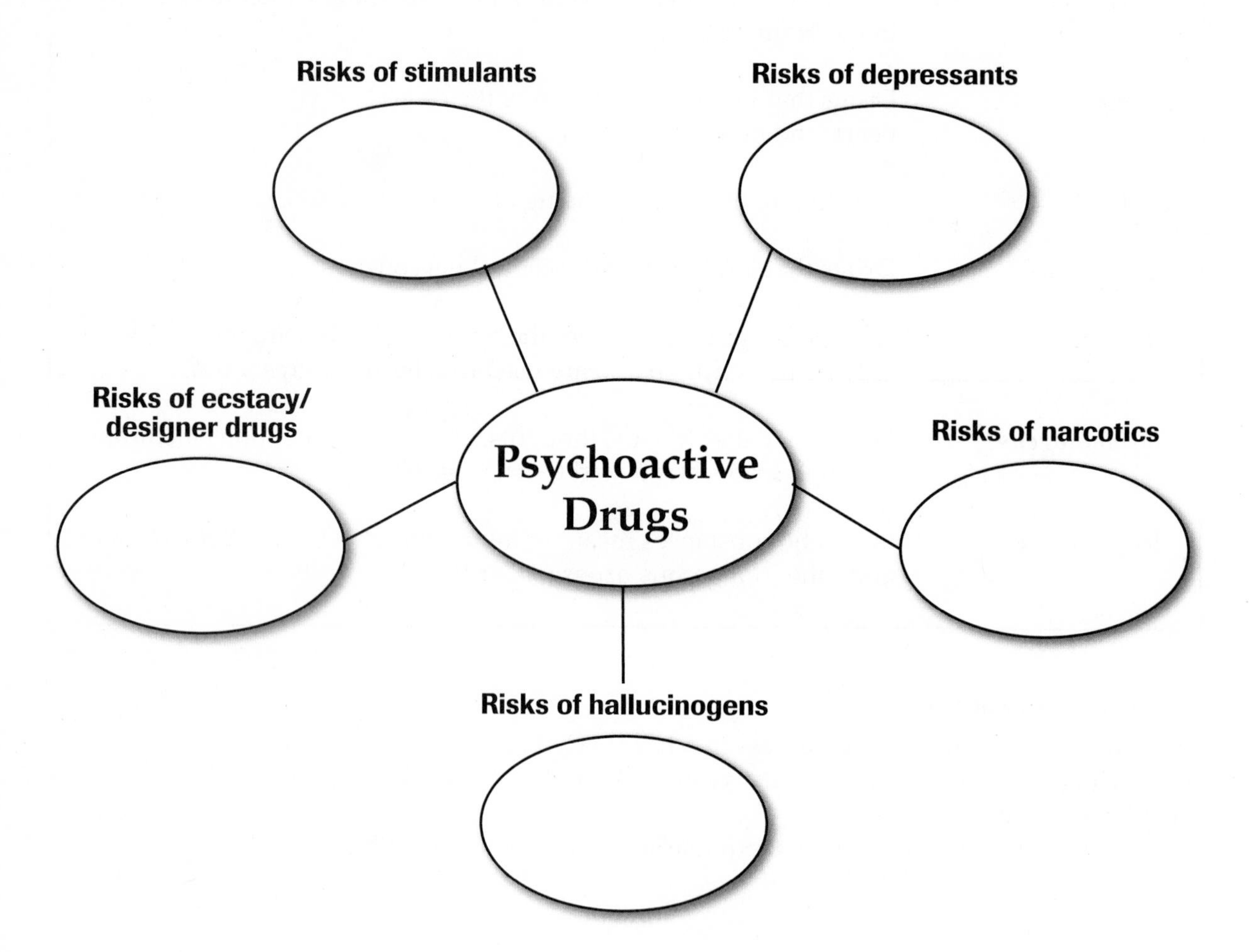

Reading Tutor, Lesson 4 *(continued)*

USE WITH CHAPTER 23, PAGES 603–610.

Read to Learn

Read each passage carefully. Write in complete sentences to answer the following questions.

Classification of Psychoactive Drugs *(pages 603–604)*

Psychoactive drugs are *chemicals that affect the central nervous system. They alter activity in the brain.*

There are four main groups of these drugs. They are stimulants, depressants, narcotics, and hallucinogens. A doctor may prescribe some of these, but all of them are dangerous.

1. What are psychoactive drugs?

___

___

___

___

___

___

___

Health Risks of Stimulants *(pages 605–606)*

Stimulants are *drugs that speed up the central nervous system.* Two of these are nicotine and the caffeine in coffee and cola. Here are some other types.

- **Cocaine** is powerful and highly addictive. It causes **euphoria**, or *a feeling of intense well-being or elation.* It causes depression, paranoia, dependence, and damage to nose tissue.
- **Crack** is more dangerous than cocaine. It is called crack cocaine, rock, or freebase. It is extremely addictive. Rapid heart rate and blood pressure can cause death.
- **Amphetamines** can be in prescribed medicine. Some people use them illegally to stay awake or lose weight. They can cause heart trouble and paranoia.
- **Methamphetamine** may be in medicine for some diseases. Some people use it illegally as a club drug. It can cause depression, paranoia, damage to the CNS, and death.

Reading Tutor, Lesson 4 *(continued)*

USE WITH CHAPTER 23, PAGES 603–610.

2. What are some of the health risks of stimulants?

____

____

____

____

____

____

____

Health Risks of Depressants *(pages 606–608)*

Depressants are *drugs that tend to slow down the CNS*. They relax tensions. They relieve worry. The most common type is alcohol. Here are some other depressants.

- **Barbiturates** can result in mood swings, sleeping more than usual, and coma. They are not usually in medicine. Some people use them illegally to get high.
- **Tranquilizers** reduce muscular activity and attention span. Doctors prescribe them to take away worry, muscle spasms, sleeplessness, and nerves. They are very addictive.
- **Rohypnol** is a very strong club drug. It is the date rape drug. A person may slip a pill into a drink. The victim wakes up later with no memory of what happened.
- **GHB** is also a club drug. It is also a date rape drug. A person can easily overdose on this.

3. What are some of the health risks of depressants?

____

____

____

____

____

____

Narcotics *(page 608)*

Narcotics are *specific drugs that come from the opium plant. A doctor may prescribe them to relieve pain*. Some of these are morphine, OxyContin, and codeine. They are very addictive.

- **Heroin** is a highly addictive drug. It is a form of morphine that a person can inject, snort, or smoke. Users must use more and more to get the same effect. Withdrawal is painful.

4. What are some of the health risks of narcotics?

____

____

____

____

____

____

Hallucinogens *(page 609)*

Hallucinogens are *drugs that alter moods, thoughts, and senses including vision, hearing, smell, and touch*. These drugs have no medical use.

- **PCP** is a very harmful drug. It causes added strength and no sense of pain. Users die from overdose and destructive actions. Flashbacks can occur at any time.
- **LSD** is a very strong drug. It affects the brain and distorts reality. Flashbacks bring back scary emotions long after the drug use is over.
- **Ketamine** is a drug for animals. Some people use it as a club drug. It may cause death from lung failure.

5. What are some of the health risks of hallucinogens?

____

____

____

____

____

____

USE WITH CHAPTER 23, PAGES 603–610.

Ecstasy and Other Dangerous Drugs *(page 610)*

Designer drugs are *synthetic substances meant to copy the effects of hallucinogens and other dangerous drugs*. They vary greatly in strength.

- **Ecstasy or MDMA** is a stimulant and a hallucinogen. It may cause euphoria and then confusion, paranoia, and long-term brain damage. Overdoses are common.

6. What are some of the health risks of ecstasy and designer drugs?

Lesson 5

Reading Tutor

USE WITH CHAPTER 23, PAGES 611–615.

Medicines and Drugs: Living Drug Free

Vocabulary

drug-free school zones	An area within 1,000 feet of a school and designated by signs, within which people caught selling drugs receive especially severe penalties *(page 612)*
drug watches	Organized community efforts by neighborhood residents to patrol, monitor, report, and otherwise try to stop drug deals and drug abuse *(page 612)*

Drawing from Experience

Have you ever had to use your refusal skills? How did you feel? What can you do to help curb drug abuse in your school? Where can you go to get help for a friend who is using drugs? Think about these questions as you read Lesson 5.

In the last lesson, you learned about the risks of psychoactive drugs. In this lesson, you will learn about living drug free.

Reading Tutor, Lesson 5 *(continued)*

USE WITH CHAPTER 23, PAGES 611–615.

Organizing Your Thoughts

Use the chart below to help you take notes as you read the summaries that follow. In the first box, list some of the ways to stay drug free and curb drug abuse. In the other box, list some of the ways to become drug free and get help.

Ways to Stay Drug Free/Curb Drug Abuse	Ways to Become Drug Free and Get Help

Reading Tutor, Lesson 5 *(continued)*

USE WITH CHAPTER 23, PAGES 611–615.

Read to Learn

Read each passage carefully. Write in complete sentences to answer the following questions.

Resisting Pressure to Use Drugs *(pages 611–612)*

Peer pressure is strong during the teen years. You may feel a lot of pressure to take drugs or drink alcohol. Keep in mind that most students are not taking drugs. Here are some ways to resist.

- Make a firm decision to be drug free.
- Avoid places where you know there will be drugs.
- Practice your refusal skills.
- Stand up for what you believe in.

1. What are some of the ways to resist pressure to use drugs?

___

___

___

___

___

Efforts to Curb Drug Abuse *(pages 612–613)*

Schools and communities work with each other to be drug free. **Drug-free school zones** are *areas within 1,000 feet of schools and designated by signs. People caught selling drugs within these areas receive very severe penalties.* Schools have zero-tolerance policies and expel students who use drugs.

Drug watches are *organized community efforts by neighborhood residents to patrol, monitor, report, and otherwise try to stop drug deals and drug abuse.* Teens can get involved in school or community programs. They can choose friends who also value a drug-free life.

2. What is a drug-free school zone? What is a drug watch?

___

___

___

___

___

Reading Tutor, Lesson 5 *(continued)*

USE WITH CHAPTER 23, PAGES 611–615.

Becoming Drug Free *(page 613)*

Some teens may already be in trouble with drugs. Here are some of the warning signs of drug use.

- Gets high or drunk often
- Lies about the drugs he or she is using
- Stops taking part in things he or she usually likes to do
- Changes eating or sleeping habits
- Has trouble concentrating
- Takes risks or takes part in unsafe behaviors
- Gets in trouble at school or with the police
- Has red-rimmed eyes and a runny nose but is not sick

Here are some steps to guide you to offer help to someone who is using alcohol or drugs.

- Find sources of help in the community such as drug counselors, treatment centers, or support groups.
- Talk to the person when he or she is sober. Let him or her know about your concern.
- Listen to the person's response. He or she may be angry or deny there is a problem.
- Discuss the sources of help you have found. Offer to go with the person.

3. What are some of the warning signs of drug use?

____

____

____

____

____

____

Getting Help *(pages 614–615)*

There is treatment for drug abuse. There are treatment centers, support groups, and counseling centers in most communities. Teens can also talk to a parent, a teacher, a school counselor, or other trusted adult.

Reading Tutor, Lesson 5 *(continued)*

USE WITH CHAPTER 23, PAGES 611–615.

Some drug users need to go to a treatment center for help. Here are some of the types of drug treatment centers.

- **Outpatient drug-free treatment.** These have counseling but do not offer medicine.
- **Short-term treatment.** These have medication and outpatient therapy. They may also include residential stays.
- **Maintenance therapy.** This is usually for heroin addicts. It includes medication.
- **Therapeutic communities.** These are homes for people with a long history of drug abuse. They have programs that last from 6 to 12 months.

Some drug users do not need a treatment center. They may need to have drug counseling. Many go to support-group meetings. These are groups of people who share a problem and help each other cope. They can give long-term support to help the user recover and stay drug free.

4. What are some of the types of help available for drug abusers?

____

____

____

____

____

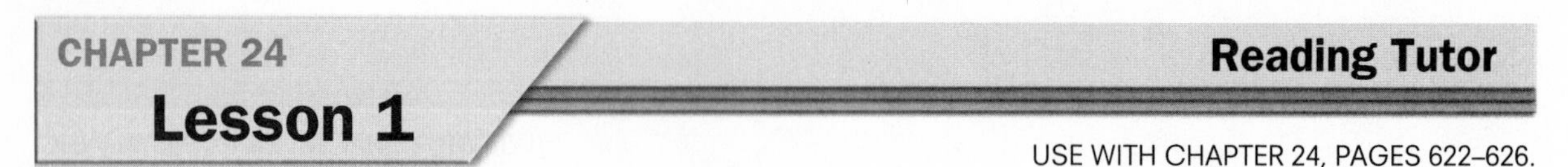

USE WITH CHAPTER 24, PAGES 622–626.

Communicable Diseases: What Are Communicable Diseases?

Vocabulary

communicable disease	A disease that is spread from one living thing to another or through the environment *(page 622)*
pathogen	An organism that causes disease *(page 622)*
infection	A condition that occurs when pathogens enter the body, multiply, and damage body cells *(page 622)*
viruses	Forms of genetic material that invade living cells to reproduce *(page 623)*
bacteria	Single-celled microorganisms *(page 623)*
toxin	A substance that kills cells or interferes with their functions *(page 623)*
vector	An organism, such as a tick, that carries and transmits pathogens to humans or other animals *(page 625)*

Drawing from Experience

Have you ever had a cold? How did the germ get into your body? Do you wash your hands before you eat? Do you share cups or forks or makeup with your friends? Do you cover your mouth when you sneeze? Think about these questions as you read Lesson 1.

In the last chapter, you learned about drugs. In this lesson, you will learn about disease that spreads from person to person.

Reading Tutor, Lesson 1 *(continued)*

USE WITH CHAPTER 24, PAGES 622–626.

Organizing Your Thoughts

Use the chart below to help you take notes as you read the summaries that follow. In the first box, list some of the causes of disease. In the next box, list some of the ways disease spreads. In the last box, list some of the ways to prevent the spread of disease.

Causes of Disease	Ways Disease Spreads	Preventing the Spread of Disease

Reading Tutor, Lesson 1 *(continued)*

USE WITH CHAPTER 24, PAGES 622–626.

Read to Learn

Read each passage carefully. Write in complete sentences to answer the following questions.

Causes of Communicable Diseases *(pages 622–624)*

A **communicable disease** is *a disease that spreads from one living thing to another or through the environment. An organism that causes disease* is a **pathogen** or a germ. An **infection** is *a condition that occurs when pathogens enter the body, multiply, and damage body cells.* A disease will result if the body is not able to fight off the infection.

Here are some of the types of pathogens or germs.

- **Viruses** are *pieces of genetic material covered by a protein coat. They need living cells to reproduce.* They invade all forms of life. They cause the common cold, the flu, measles, AIDS, and more. Antibiotics do not work on viruses.
- **Bacteria** are *single-celled microorganisms.* They live almost anywhere on earth. Most are harmless. Bacteria cause foodborne illness, strep throat, and more. Some bacteria make a **toxin.** This is *a substance that kills cells or interferes with the way they work.* A doctor can treat most bacterial disease with antibiotics.
- **Fungi** are plantlike organisms such as mold or yeast. Some types of fungi cause athlete's foot, ringworm, and yeast infections.
- **Protozoans** are single-celled organisms that are larger than bacteria. Most do not harm the body. Some may cause malaria, dysentery, and sleeping sickness.
- **Rickettsias** are pathogens that look like bacteria. They enter another life form like viruses do. They often enter humans through insect bites. They cause typhus and Rocky Mountain spotted fever.

1. What are some of the types of pathogens that cause diseases?

How Communicable Diseases Are Transmitted *(pages 624–625)*

Here are some of the ways that diseases spread from person to person.

- **Direct contact.** Many pathogens spread by direct contact with an infected person or animal. This includes touching, biting, kissing, and sexual contact. Sneezing can spray drops into someone's eyes, nose, or mouth.
- **Indirect contact.** Some diseases can spread without being close to an infected person.
  - **Contaminated objects.** You may contaminate an object if you sneeze on a table. Someone may touch the table and pick up the pathogen.
  - **Vectors.** A **vector** is *an organism, such as a tick, that carries and transmits pathogens to humans or other animals*. Common ones are flies, mosquitoes, and ticks.
  - **Water and food.** Careless handling of food causes illness and food poisoning. Human or animal feces may contaminate a water supply.
  - **Airborne.** Pathogens from a sneeze may float in the air for a long time. You do not need to be near an infected person to inhale the germs. Some of these diseases are chicken pox, tuberculosis, and the flu.

2. What are some of the ways that disease spreads from person to person?

____

____

____

____

____

____

____

Preventing the Spread of Disease *(pages 625–626)*

Here are some of the ways that you can prevent the spread of disease.

- **Wash hands.** This is the best way to stop the spread of germs. Wash your hands before you prepare food, before you eat, and after you use the bathroom.
- **Handle food properly. Foodborne illness** may occur if you do not handle food properly. Always wash your hands. Use paper towels to keep surfaces clean. Keep raw meat away from other food. Cook food to the right temperature. Chill leftover food right after you eat.

Reading Tutor, Lesson 1 *(continued)*

USE WITH CHAPTER 24, PAGES 622–626.

- **Other prevention.** Here are some ways to help you reduce your risk of spreading disease.
  - Eat a balanced diet. Be active. Avoid the use of tobacco, alcohol, and other drugs.
  - Avoid sharing utensils, makeup, combs, and other personal items.
  - Make and store food safely.
  - Stay away from people who are ill.
  - Take care of yourself when you are ill. Cover your mouth. Wash your hands.
  - Be sure you have all of your vaccinations.
  - Practice abstinence from sexual activity.
  - Learn to deal with stress.

3. What are some of the ways that you can prevent the spread of disease?

USE WITH CHAPTER 24, PAGES 627–634.

Communicable Diseases: Preventing Communicable Diseases

Vocabulary

immune system	A network of cells, tissues, organs, and chemicals that fights pathogens *(page 627)*
inflammatory response	A reaction to tissue damage caused by injury or infection *(page 628)*
phagocyte	A white blood cell that attacks invading pathogens *(page 629)*
antigen	A substance that is capable of triggering an immune response *(page 630)*
immunity	The state of being protected against a particular disease *(page 630)*
lymphocyte	A specialized white blood cell that coordinates and performs many of the functions of specific immunity *(page 630)*
antibody	A protein that acts against a specific antigen *(page 631)*
vaccine	A preparation of dead or weakened pathogens that are introduced into the body to stimulate an immune response *(page 631)*

Drawing from Experience

Have you ever had a cut on your arm or leg? Did the cut get red and swollen? Are all of your vaccinations up to date? What do you know about your immune system? Think about these questions as you read Lesson 2.

In the last lesson, you learned about the causes of diseases that spread from person to person. In this lesson, you will learn about stopping the diseases that spread from person to person.

Reading Tutor, Lesson 2 *(continued)*

USE WITH CHAPTER 24, PAGES 627–634.

Organizing Your Thoughts

Use the chart below to help you take notes as you read the summaries that follow. In the first box, list the elements of the body's first line of defense. In the next box, list the steps of the inflammatory response. In the last box, list the steps of the specific response.

First Line of Defense	The Inflammatory Response	The Specific Response

Read to Learn

Read each passage carefully. Write in complete sentences to answer the following questions.

Physical and Chemical Barriers *(pages 627–628)*

Your **immune system** is *a network of cells, tissues, organs, and chemicals that fights off pathogens*. Physical and chemical barriers work with each other as your body's first line of defense against invading germs. Here are some of the elements.

- The **skin** is the first line of defense against most pathogens.
- **Tears and saliva** have enzymes that destroy many germs.
- **Mucous membranes** line your mouth, nose, and bronchial tubes. The cells make mucus. Mucus is a sticky white substance that traps germs.
- **Cilia** are the hairlike projections that line parts of the respiratory system. They sweep mucus and germs to the throat where the body can cough them out.
- **Gastric juice** in the stomach kills many germs that enter the body through the nose or mouth.

1. What are some of the elements of the body's first line of defense?

____

____

____

____

____

____

The Immune System *(pages 628–629)*

The immune system has two major defense responses. One is general and works against all germs. The other is specific and works against certain pathogens.

The **inflammatory response** is *a reaction to tissue damage caused by injury or infection*. It stops further harm and stops the invading germs. Here is how it works.

- Blood vessels near the site of the injury expand.
- Fluid and cells from the blood leak into the area.
- This causes swelling and pain.

- A **phagocyte** is *a white blood cell that attacks invading pathogens*. It kills them with chemicals.
- Pus collects at the site as a response to bacteria.
- Tissue repair begins after the pathogens die. A scab forms.
- The specific response activates to keep this same infection from happening again.

2. What happens during the inflammatory response?

____

____

____

____

____

Specific Defenses *(pages 630–631)*

Specific defenses react to invading germs as a result of the body's ability to recognize and destroy them. Here are the steps of this immune response.

- Pathogens invade the body.
- Macrophages cover the pathogen. A **macrophage** is a type of phagocyte or white blood cell.
- Macrophages eat the pathogen. T cells recognize antigens of the pathogen as an invader. An **antigen** is *a substance that triggers an immune response*. It is on the surface of the pathogen.
- T cells bind to the antigens.
- B cells bind to antigens and helper T cells.
- B cells divide to make plasma cells.
- Plasma cells release antibodies into the blood.
- Antibodies bind to antigens to help other cells find and kill the pathogens.

The immune response results in **immunity.** This is *the state of protection against a particular disease*. A **lymphocyte** is *a white blood cell that coordinates and does many of the functions of specific immunity*. There are two types.

- **T cells**
  - **Helper T cells** trigger production of B cells and killer T cells.
  - **Killer T cells** attack and kill infected body cells. They do not attack the germs themselves.
  - **Suppressor T cells** manage the actions of the other T cells. They turn off the T cells when the infection is over.

- **B cells** make antibodies. An **antibody** is *a protein that acts against a specific antigen.*

3. What are the two types of lymphocytes? What are the types of T cells?

The Role of Memory Lymphocytes *(pages 631–632)*

Some T cells and B cells become **memory cells**. Memory cells will recognize a former invader and stop it. This means that the memory cells will remember if you had the measles. The antibodies will attack it right away if it enters your body again. You will not get sick.

- **Active immunity** is the immunity you develop to protect you from diseases. You may also get active immunity from a **vaccine.** This is *a mixture of dead or weakened germs that is put into the body to start an immune response.*
- **Passive immunity** is receiving antibodies from another person or animal. It only lasts for a few weeks or months.

4. What are the two types of immunity?

Care of the Immune System *(pages 632–633)*

Your immune system is able to fight off germs when it is strong and healthy. Here are some of the ways to stay healthy and fight illness.

- Follow a sensible eating plan. Eat whole grains and nutrient-dense foods. Drink six to eight 8-ounce glasses of water each day.
- Get plenty of rest. Get nine hours of sleep a night.
- Get an hour of physical activity each day.
- Avoid sharing personal items such as towels.

- Avoid tobacco, alcohol, and other drugs.
- Avoid sexual contact.
- Keep your immunizations up to date.

5. What are some of the ways to keep your immune system healthy?

____

____

____

____

____

____

____

Vaccines to Aid the Body's Defenses *(page 633)*

Here are the four types of vaccines.

- **Live-virus vaccines** are a weak form of a pathogen. It is grown in a lab. Some of these are for measles or mumps.
- **Killed-virus vaccines** are dead germs. Some of these are for the flu or polio shots.
- **Toxoids** are dead toxins from germs. Some of these are for tetanus and diphtheria.
- **New and second-generation vaccines** are the future. Scientists are developing them.

6. What are the four types of vaccines?

____

____

____

____

____

____

____

Reading Tutor, Lesson 2 *(continued)*

USE WITH CHAPTER 24, PAGES 627–634.

Immunization for All *(page 634)*

Vaccines help everyone. You cannot spread a disease if you have immunity to it. Make sure you have up-to-date immunizations. Some of them require booster shots or more than one dose over time. Here are some of the vaccines that you should have.

- Tetanus
- Diphtheria
- Measles, mumps, and rubella
- Hepatitis B
- Chicken pox

7. What are some of the vaccines that you should have?

____

____

____

____

____

____

Name Class Date

Lesson 3

Reading Tutor

USE WITH CHAPTER 24, PAGES 635–641.

Communicable Diseases: Common Communicable Diseases

Vocabulary

pneumonia	An inflammation of the lungs commonly caused by a bacterial or viral infection *(page 636)*
jaundice	A yellowing of the skin and eyes *(page 638)*
emerging infection	A communicable disease whose incidence in humans has increased within the past two decades or threatens to increase in the near future *(page 640)*

Drawing from Experience

Have you ever had the flu? What is the difference between a cold and the flu? How can you prevent disease from spreading to others? How can you protect yourself from disease? Think about these questions as you read Lesson 3.

In the last lesson, you learned about preventing disease. In this lesson, you will learn about common diseases.

Reading Tutor, Lesson 3 *(continued)*

USE WITH CHAPTER 24, PAGES 635–641.

Organizing Your Thoughts

Use the chart below to help you take notes as you read the summaries that follow. In the first box, list some of the types of respiratory infections. In the other box, list some of the types of hepatitis and other diseases.

Respiratory Infections	Hepatitis and Other Diseases

Reading Tutor, Lesson 3 *(continued)*

USE WITH CHAPTER 24, PAGES 635–641.

Read to Learn

Read each passage carefully. Write in complete sentences to answer the following questions.

Respiratory Infections *(pages 635–637)*

You can reduce your risk of most respiratory illnesses. Avoid close contact with people who are sick. Wash your hands often. Avoid smoking. Here are some of the most common types of respiratory illnesses.

- **Common cold.** This is a viral infection. It may cause a runny nose, sneezing, and sore throat. There is no cure. One treatment is the use of **analgesic** or pain medicine. No one under 20 years of age should use aspirin.
- **Influenza or flu.** This is a viral infection. It may cause high fever, fatigue, headache, muscle aches, and cough. You can treat this with antiviral drugs. You can help prevent it by getting a flu shot every year.
- **Pneumonia** is *an infection of the lungs caused by a bacterial or viral infection.* You can help prevent it. The air sacs fill with pus and other liquid. It is a serious disease and a major cause of death. It can be viral or bacterial. Older people are more at risk.
- **Strep throat** is a bacterial infection. It spreads by direct contact. It may cause a sore throat, fever, and large lymph nodes in the neck. You can treat it with antibiotics.
- **Tuberculosis** or TB is a bacterial disease that attacks the lungs. TB spreads through the air. It causes fatigue, coughing, fever, night sweats, and weight loss. You can treat it by taking antibiotics.

1. What are some of the most common types of respiratory infections?

____

____

____

____

____

Hepatitis *(pages 637–638)*

Hepatitis is pain and swelling in the liver. Drugs or alcohol or germs may cause it. There are three types of hepatitis.

- **Hepatitis A** spreads through contact with the feces of an infected person. Infected persons who do not wash their hands properly spread the virus. It may cause fever, nausea, vomiting, and **jaundice.** This is *a yellowing of the skin and eyes*. There is a vaccine for hepatitis A.

- **Hepatitis B** is more serious than hepatitis A. It is often spread through sexual contact or sharing needles. Most people do not have symptoms. It can cause severe liver damage. It also causes most cases of liver cancer. There is a vaccine for hepatitis B.
- **Hepatitis C** is the most common type of hepatitis. It is often spread through sharing needles. It causes liver disease, liver cancer, or liver failure. Most people do not know they have it until years later. There is no cure.

2. What is hepatitis? What are the three kinds of hepatitis?

____

____

____

____

____

Other Diseases *(page 639)*

Here are some of the other types of disease that are common among teens.

- **Mononucleosis** is a virus that spreads by direct contact and by kissing. It may cause fever, sore throat, fatigue, and swollen lymph nodes. You treat it with rest.
- **Measles** is a virus that spreads by coughing or talking. It is very contagious. It can cause high fever, cough, runny nose, and a bumpy red rash. There is a vaccine.
- **Encephalitis** is a virus that mosquitoes carry. It swells the brain. It may cause headache, fever, confusion, paralysis, and more. You can treat some kinds with antiviral medicine.
- **Meningitis** is a virus or bacteria that swells the membranes that cover the brain. It may cause fever, severe headache, nausea, and a stiff neck. You treat it with antiviral or antibiotic medicine. There is a vaccine.

3. What are some of the other types of disease that are common among teens?

____

____

____

____

____

Emerging Infections *(pages 639–641)*

An **emerging infection** is *a communicable disease whose incidence in humans has grown within the past two decades or may grow in the near future.* Here are some of the factors involved in the development of these infections.

- **Transport across borders.** Infected people or animals can travel from area to area. They bring the pathogens to new places where they were not a problem. The West Nile virus was in Asia and Africa and now it is spreading to the United States.
- **Population movement.** Lyme disease is more common now. This is because people have moved into more wooded areas where ticks live. This may cause rash, fatigue, fever, and more. You treat it with antibiotics.
- **Resistance to antibiotics.** Some germs have become resistant to one or more types of antibiotic. Some of these are the germs that cause TB, gonorrhea, and one kind of pneumonia.
- **Changes in food technology.** Mass distribution of food lets infected food reach more people more quickly. *E. coli* has made thousands of people sick.
- **Agents of bioterrorism.** It is easy for people to travel. A contagious disease like smallpox can spread very fast from place to place.

4. What are some of the factors involved in the development of the new emerging infections?

Sexually Transmitted Infections and HIV/AIDS: The Risks of STIs

Vocabulary

sexually transmitted diseases (STDs)	Infectious diseases spread from person to person through sexual contact *(page 648)*
sexually transmitted infections (STIs)	Infectious diseases spread from person to person through sexual contact *(page 648)*
epidemics	Occurrences of diseases in which many people in the same place at the same time are affected *(page 648)*
abstinence	The deliberate decision to avoid harmful behaviors, including sexual activity before marriage and the use of tobacco, alcohol, and other drugs *(page 651)*

Drawing from Experience

What do you know about STDs? What are the results of having an STD? How can you keep yourself safe from STDs? Think about these questions as you read Lesson 1.

In the last chapter, you learned about common diseases. In this lesson, you will learn about the risks of STDs.

Reading Tutor, Lesson 1 *(continued)*

USE WITH CHAPTER 25, PAGES 648–651.

Organizing Your Thoughts

Use the chart below to help you take notes as you read the summaries that follow. In the first box, list some of the high-risk actions that can cause you to get an STD. In the other box, list some of the results of getting an STD.

High-Risk Behaviors and STDs	Consequences of STDs

Reading Tutor, Lesson 1 *(continued)*

USE WITH CHAPTER 25, PAGES 648–651.

Read to Learn

Read each passage carefully. Write in complete sentences to answer the following questions.

STDs: The Hidden Epidemic *(pages 648–649)*

Sexually transmitted diseases (STDs) or **sexually transmitted infections (STIs)** are *infectious diseases that spread from person to person through sexual contact.*

An **epidemic** is *when a disease occurs that affects many people in the same place at the same time.* We are now facing an epidemic of STDs. Here are some of the reasons why.

- Many people with STDs do not know they are infected. They pass the STDs on to other people.
- Some people who have an STD may not report it to the health department. They may feel embarrassed. Contacts of the person who has an STD may spread the disease to others.

Teens are at risk for STDs. Here are some of the high-risk behaviors teens may engage in.

- **Being sexually active with more than one person.** Most teens do not know much about a partner's past behavior. They do not know if he or she has an STD.
- **Engaging in unprotected sex.** Barrier protection does not always work. Abstinence from sexual activity is the only method that is a 100 percent sure way to avoid STDs.
- **Choosing high-risk partners.** These may be people who have a history of being sexually active. These may be people who inject illegal drugs.
- **Using alcohol and other drugs.** Using alcohol or drugs can make you forget your values. Many teens who engage in sex have been drinking or taking drugs.

1. What are some of the high-risk behaviors that may lead to STDs?

Reading Tutor, Lesson 1 *(continued)*

USE WITH CHAPTER 25, PAGES 648–651.

The Consequences of STDs *(pages 650–651)*

Most teens are not fully aware of the dangers of STDs. They may alter a person's life forever. Here are some of the results.

- **Some STDs do not have a cure.** Antibiotics do not work on some STDs. The viruses that cause herpes and AIDS stay in the body for life.
- **Some STDs cause cancer.** Hepatitis B can cause liver cancer.
- **Some STDs affect the ability to reproduce.** Females can develop pelvic inflammatory disease (PID). This harms female organs and may cause sterility.
- **Some STDs can pass from an infected female to her child before, during, or after birth.** STDs can harm the bones, nerves, and brain of a fetus. Babies may be blind or get pneumonia. Some may die.

Abstinence is *the decision to avoid harmful behaviors. It covers sexual activity before marriage and the use of tobacco, alcohol, and other drugs.* Use your refusal skills to stay away from situations that may put you at risk.

2. What are some of the consequences of getting an STD?

Name Class Date

Lesson 2

Reading Tutor

USE WITH CHAPTER 25, PAGES 652–657.

Sexually Transmitted Infections and HIV/AIDS: Common STIs

Vocabulary

human papillomavirus (HPV)	A virus that can cause genital warts or asymptomatic infection *(page 652)*
chlamydia	A bacterial infection that affects the reproductive organs of both males and females *(page 654)*
genital herpes	An STD caused by the herpes simplex virus (HSV) *(page 654)*
gonorrhea	A bacterial STD that usually affects mucous membranes *(page 655)*
trichomoniasis	An STD caused by a microscopic protozoan that results in infections of the vagina, urethra, and bladder *(page 655)*
syphilis	An STD that attacks many parts of the body and is caused by a small bacterium called a spirochete *(page 655)*

Drawing from Experience

What do you know about the different types of STDs? How can this information help you avoid getting an STD? Why is it vital for people with STDs to get treatment? Think about these questions as you read Lesson 2.

In the last lesson, you learned about the risks of STDs. In this lesson, you will learn about common STDs.

Reading Tutor, Lesson 2 *(continued)*

USE WITH CHAPTER 25, PAGES 652–657.

Organizing Your Thoughts

Use the chart below to help you take notes as you read the summaries that follow. In the first oval, list some of the traits of HPV. In the next, list the traits of chlamydia. In the next, list the traits of genital herpes. In the next, list the traits of gonorrhea. In the next, list the traits of trichomoniasis. In the last oval, list the traits of syphilis.

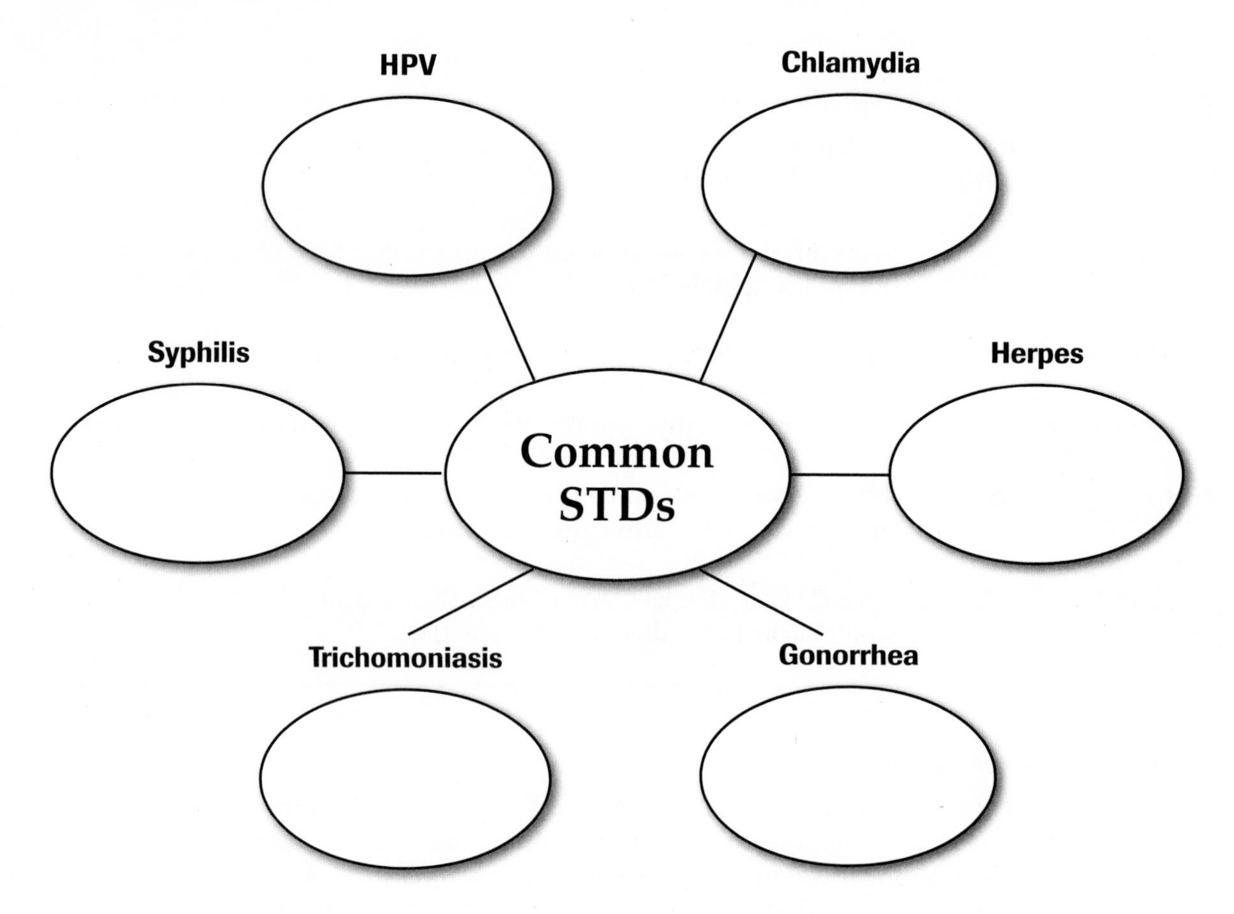

Reading Tutor, Lesson 2 *(continued)*

USE WITH CHAPTER 25, PAGES 652–657.

Read to Learn

Read each passage carefully. Write in complete sentences to answer the following questions.

Human Papillomavirus *(pages 652–653)*

Human papillomavirus or **(HPV)** is *a virus that can cause genital warts or asymptomatic infection.* It is the most common type of STD. There is no treatment.

- **Genital warts** are pink or red warts. They have tops that look like cauliflower. They appear on the genitals, vagina, or cervix one or two months after infection with HPV. They are very contagious. The warts can be treated but the infected person has the virus for the rest of his or her life. It may cause cervical cancer or cancer of the penis.

1. What are genital warts?

____

____

____

____

____

____

Chlamydia *(page 654)*

Chlamydia is *a bacterial infection that affects the reproductive organs of both males and females.* There are no visible symptoms. Some people may have discharge from the genitals and a burning while urinating. You can treat it with anitbiotics. It can lead to infertility.

2. What is chlamydia?

____

____

____

____

____

____

Reading Tutor, Lesson 2 *(continued)*

USE WITH CHAPTER 25, PAGES 652–657.

Genital Herpes *(page 654)*

Genital herpes is *an STD caused by the herpes simplex virus (HSV)*. There are two types.

- **Type 1** usually causes cold sores.
- **Type 2** usually causes genital sores.

Both types can infect the mouth and genitals. Most people who have genital herpes do not know that they have it. Some people get blisterlike sores once in a while. You can treat it with medicine, but there is no cure. It stays in the body for life.

3. What is genital herpes?

Gonorrhea *(page 655)*

Gonorrhea is *a bacterial STD that usually affects mucous membranes*. Males may have discharge from the penis and painful urination. Females may have vaginal discharge and burning when urinating. Many females do not have symptoms. You can treat it with antibiotics. It can lead to infertility.

4. What is gonorrhea?

Reading Tutor, Lesson 2 *(continued)*

USE WITH CHAPTER 25, PAGES 652–657.

Trichomoniasis *(page 655)*

Trichomoniasis is *an STD caused by a microscopic protozoan that results in infections of the vagina, urethra, and bladder*. Females may have no symptoms. They may have **vaginitis.** This is a swelling and pain in the vagina that causes discharge, odor, and itching. Males may have no symptoms. They may have itching or discharge from the penis and burning after urination.

5. What is trichomoniasis?

____

____

____

____

____

____

____

Syphilis *(page 655)*

Syphilis is *an STD that attacks many parts of the body*. It is caused by spirochete, which is a small bacterium. The first sign is a red sore or chancre. This will heal, but the infection will spread to the rest of the person's body. It can damage many internal organs. It can cause blindness and heart disease. It is vital to get early treatment.

6. What is syphilis?

____

____

____

____

____

____

____

Reading Tutor, Lesson 2 *(continued)*

USE WITH CHAPTER 25, PAGES 652–657.

Seeking Treatment *(pages 656–657)*

There are many other types of STDs, including hepatitis and pubic lice. Anyone who thinks that he or she may have an STD must go to the doctor right away. The doctor will keep your visit confidential. The doctor can give you the treatment you need. Early treatment can prevent some of the severe, long-term health problems.

A person who has an STD also has a social obligation to stop the spread of the disease. The person must contact anyone he or she had sexual contact with. It might save a person's life.

7. Why is it so important to see a doctor right away if you think you have an STD?

Lesson 3 **Reading Tutor**

USE WITH CHAPTER 25, PAGES 658–661.

Sexually Transmitted Infections and HIV/AIDS: HIV and AIDS

Vocabulary

acquired immune deficiency syndrome (AIDS)	A disease in which the immune system of the patient is weakened *(page 658)*
human immuno-deficiency virus (HIV)	A virus that attacks the immune system *(page 658)*
opportunistic infection	An infection that occurs in an individual who does not have a healthy immune system *(page 659)*

Drawing from Experience

What do you know about HIV? What do you know about AIDS? Why is it important to know about HIV and AIDS? Think about these questions as you read Lesson 3.

In the last lesson, you learned about common STDs. In this lesson, you will learn about HIV and AIDS.

Reading Tutor, Lesson 3 *(continued)*

USE WITH CHAPTER 25, PAGES 658–661.

Organizing Your Thoughts

Use the chart below to help you take notes as you read the summaries that follow. In the first box, list the ways that HIV attacks cells and affects the human body. In the other box, list some of the ways that HIV spreads to other people.

How HIV Affects the Body	How HIV Spreads to Others

Reading Tutor, Lesson 3 *(continued)*

USE WITH CHAPTER 25, PAGES 658–661.

Read to Learn

Read each passage carefully. Write in complete sentences to answer the following questions.

Teens at Risk *(pages 658–659)*

Acquired immune deficiency syndrome (AIDS) is *a disease in which the immune system of the patient weakens.* **Human immunodeficiency virus** or **(HIV)** is *a virus that attacks the immune system.* HIV is the virus that causes AIDS.

Teens have one of the fastest-growing rates of HIV infection. Many young adults who are dying from AIDS got the infection when they were in their teens. You can prevent HIV by choosing to abstain from sexual activity and from injecting drugs.

1. What is HIV? What is AIDS?

___

___

___

___

___

HIV and the Human Body *(pages 659–660)*

HIV invades T cells and other cells in the immune system when it enters the body. Here is how HIV attacks the cells.

1. HIV attaches to the cell surface.
2. The virus core enters the cell and goes to the nucleus.
3. The virus takes over the cell and makes a copy of itself.
4. The new virus collects on the surface of the cell.
5. The new virus breaks away from the host cell and destroys it.
6. The new virus infects other cells and the process repeats itself.

The immune system gets weaker as the number of viruses increases and the number of T cells goes down. The body is at risk for infection. An **opportunistic infection** is *an infection that occurs in an individual who does not have a healthy immune system.* AIDS is the advanced stage of HIV infection.

Reading Tutor, Lesson 3 *(continued)*

USE WITH CHAPTER 25, PAGES 658–661.

2. What are the steps that HIV takes when it attacks the cells in the body?

___

___

___

___

___

How HIV Is Transmitted *(pages 660–661)*

HIV lives inside cells and body fluids. Here are some ways that HIV does NOT pass to other people.

1. HIV does not survive well in the air.
2. HIV does not survive on surfaces like toilet seats or telephones.
3. HIV does not spread to other people in food.
4. HIV does not spread to others by touching.

HIV can only pass from an infected person through blood, semen, vaginal secretions, and breast milk. You can avoid HIV by abstaining from sexual intercourse and avoiding drug use.

- **Sexual intercourse.** HIV can enter a partner's blood through tiny cuts in the body. The risk of HIV is greater when a person is sexually active with more than one person. Having an STD that causes sores will increase the risk of HIV.
- **Sharing needles.** A person who injects drugs contaminates the needle with his or her own blood. HIV will be on the needle if the person has the HIV virus. Anyone who uses the same needle will inject HIV into his or her body.
- **Mother to baby.** A pregnant female can pass HIV to her baby. HIV can pass through the umbilical cord or during birth. The baby can also get HIV through the mother's breast milk.

3. What are the ways that a person can pass HIV to others?

___

___

___

___

___

USE WITH CHAPTER 25, PAGES 662–667.

Sexually Transmitted Infections and HIV/AIDS: Treatment for HIV and AIDS

Vocabulary

asymptomatic stage	A period of time during which a person infected with HIV has no symptoms *(page 662)*
symptomatic stage	The stage in which a person infected with HIV has symptoms as a result of a severe drop in immune cells *(page 663)*
EIA test	A test that screens for the presence of HIV antibodies in the blood *(page 663)*
Western blot test	The most common confirmation test for HIV in the United States *(page 664)*
pandemic	A global outbreak of infectious diseases *(page 665)*

Drawing from Experience

How does a person know if he or she has HIV? What kind of treatment is available for HIV? What can you do if a friend thinks he or she has HIV or AIDS? Think about these questions as you read Lesson 4.

In the last lesson, you learned about HIV and AIDS. In this lesson, you will learn about treatment for HIV and AIDS.

Name Class Date

Reading Tutor, Lesson 4 *(continued)*

USE WITH CHAPTER 25, PAGES 662–667.

Organizing Your Thoughts

Use the chart below to help you take notes as you read the summaries that follow. In the first box, list the stages of HIV infection. In the next box, list the ways to detect HIV in the body. In the last box, list some of the ways to prevent the spread of HIV.

Stages of HIV Infection	Ways to Detect HIV	Ways to Prevent HIV Infection

Reading Tutor, Lesson 4 *(continued)*

USE WITH CHAPTER 25, PAGES 662–667.

Read to Learn

Read each passage carefully. Write in complete sentences to answer the following questions.

Stages of HIV Infection *(pages 662–663)*

Some people have symptoms three to six weeks after being infected with HIV. They may include fever, rash, headache, body aches, and swollen glands. The person may mistake them for the flu. There are two stages of HIV infection that follow.

- The **asymptomatic stage** is *a period of time during which a person infected with HIV has no symptoms.* The person may not show signs of illness for six months to ten years. The viruses keep growing. The person can still give the virus to others.
- The **symptomatic stage** is *the stage in which a person infected with HIV has symptoms as a result of a severe drop in immune cells.* The person may have swollen glands, weight loss, and yeast infections.
- **AIDS** is the final stage of HIV. The signs are a low count of helper T cells and one or more opportunistic infections. HIV also attacks the brain cells and causes difficulty thinking.

1. What are the stages of HIV?

____

____

____

____

____

Detecting HIV *(pages 663–664)*

A person who thinks he or she may have HIV should seek testing right away. Most states have laws to protect confidentiality of the test results.

- The **EIA test** is *a test that screens for the presence of HIV antibodies in the blood.* There are two reasons that it may not be accurate.
  1. **Developing antibodies takes time.** It may be weeks or months before the antibodies develop. The EIA could show a negative result during that time even though the person does have HIV.
  2. **Certain health conditions.** Hepatitis or pregnancy might cause the EIA to give a positive reading. The person does not really have HIV.
- The **Western blot test** is *the most common confirmation test for HIV in the United States.* This test is 100 percent accurate. The person is HIV-positive if this test shows HIV.

Reading Tutor, Lesson 4 *(continued)*

USE WITH CHAPTER 25, PAGES 662–667.

2. What are the types of tests that can detect HIV in the body?

______

______

______

______

______

______

Research and Treatment *(pages 664–665)*

Several types of medication are available for HIV. They can extend life and ease symptoms.

They cannot cure HIV/AIDS. Many treatments have side effects. The drugs are very costly. Here are some of the facts about research and treatment for HIV/AIDS.

- Doctors first noticed HIV/AIDS symptoms in 1981. They named it AIDS in 1982.
- Scientists found the AIDS-causing virus and named it HIV in 1986. They developed the first treatment.
- The red ribbon became the symbol of AIDS.
- New drugs became available in 1989. Combination drug therapy became available in 1992.
- Drug treatment first reduced the risk of transmission of HIV from mother to baby in 1994.
- Scientists developed an AIDS vaccine. The first trial run was in 1998.

In 2002 HIV was the fourth leading cause of death in the world. About 40 million people around the world have HIV/AIDS. Most new cases and deaths are in Africa.

3. What are some of the facts about HIV and AIDS research and treatment?

______

______

______

______

______

______

Reading Tutor, Lesson 4 *(continued)*

USE WITH CHAPTER 25, PAGES 662–667.

HIV/AIDS—A Continuing Problem *(pages 665–667)*

HIV/AIDS is still a fatal disease with no cure. HIV is **pandemic.** It is *a global outbreak of infectious disease*. The number of people with HIV is growing.

It is important to know as much as possible about AIDS. Knowing what causes it can help people avoid passing the disease on to others. You can find information through the media and on the Internet. The state and local health departments are good sources.

You may feel pressure to engage in sexual activity when you are a teen. Your actions today can affect the rest of your life. Here are some ways to help avoid pressure.

- Avoid events where drug use or pressure to engage in sexual activity may occur. Leave a party if things get out of control.
- Practice your refusal skills. Be firm. Use body language.
- Choose your friends with care. Avoid dating someone who you know is sexually active. Avoid drug users.

4. What are some of the ways to avoid the pressure to engage in sexual activity?

Name Class Date

CHAPTER 26 **Reading Tutor**

Lesson 1

USE WITH CHAPTER 26, PAGES 674–680.

Noncommunicable Diseases and Disabilities: Cardiovascular Diseases

Vocabulary

noncommunicable disease	A disease that is not transmitted by another person, by a vector, or from the environment *(page 674)*
cardiovascular disease (CVD)	A disease that affects the heart or blood vessels *(page 674)*
hypertension	High blood pressure *(page 675)*
atherosclerosis	The process in which plaque accumulates on artery walls *(page 675)*
angina pectoris	Chest pain that results when the heart doesn't get enough oxygen *(page 677)*
arrhythmias	Irregular heartbeats *(page 677)*

Drawing from Experience

Do you know what your blood pressure is? Do you have a healthy weight? How can you protect yourself from future heart disease? Think about these questions as you read Lesson 1.

In the last chapter, you learned about STDs and HIV/AIDS. In this lesson, you will learn about heart diseases.

Reading Tutor, Lesson 1 *(continued)*

USE WITH CHAPTER 26, PAGES 674–680.

Organizing Your Thoughts

Use the charts below to help you take notes as you read the summaries that follow. In the first box, define cardiovascular disease (CVD). In the next box, list some of the types of CVD. In the last box, list some of the risk factors for CVDs.

Cardiovascular Disease	Types of CVD	Risk Factors for CVDs

Reading Tutor, Lesson 1 *(continued)*

USE WITH CHAPTER 26, PAGES 674–680.

Read to Learn

Read each passage carefully. Write in complete sentences to answer the following questions.

Cardiovascular Diseases *(pages 674–675)*

A **noncommunicable disease** is *a disease that is not transmitted through another person, a vector, or the environment.* A **cardiovascular disease (CVD)** is *a disease that affects the heart or blood vessels.* CVDs are responsible for 40 percent of all deaths in the United States.

1. What is a noncommunicable disease?

____

____

____

____

____

____

____

Types of Cardiovascular Disease *(pages 675–680)*

The heart, blood, and blood vessels are the main parts of the circulatory system. Here are some of the types of disorders that affect this system.

- **Hypertension** is *high blood pressure.* It will harm the heart and blood vessels if it continues over time. You can lower it with medication, a healthy weight, physical activity, and good nutrition. Get your pressure checked often.
- **Atherosclerosis** is *the process in which plaque gathers on artery walls.* Eating a lot of foods that are high in fats and cholesterol adds to the buildup. A blood clot may form in the artery. This can cause a heart attack or stroke if it blocks the artery. Eat low-fat and low-cholesterol foods.
- **Diseases of the heart** occur when the heart does not get enough oxygen. Here are some of the ways to diagnose heart trouble.
  - An **EKG** helps to detect the nature of a heart attack and shows heart function.
  - **MRI** images help identify heart damage and heart defects.
  - **Radionuclide imaging** helps assess the heart's blood supply and heart function.
  - **Angiography** is a process in which a thin tube goes through the blood vessels to the heart to look for a blockage.

Reading Tutor, Lesson 1 *(continued)*

USE WITH CHAPTER 26, PAGES 674–680.

Here are some of the types of treatment options for heart disease.

- **Coronary bypass** is when doctors insert a leg vein as a detour around a blocked artery.
- **Angioplasty** is when doctors open up a blocked artery with an inflated balloon.
- **Medications** can help by lowering blood pressure and by slowing blood clotting.
- **Pacemakers** can help the heart have a regular heartbeat.

Here are some of the types of diseases of the heart.

- **Angina pectoris** is *chest pain that results when the heart does not get enough oxygen*. You can treat it with medicine.
- **Arrhythmias** are *irregular heartbeats*. You can treat them with a pacemaker. Ventricular fibrillation is a very rapid irregular heartbeat that can cause a heart attack and death.
- **Heart attack** is damage to the heart muscle. A reduced or blocked blood supply causes it. It can cause intense chest pain or gradual signs like indigestion. It is often fatal.
- **Congestive heart failure** is when the heart gradually gets weak. It can no longer pump blood. You can treat it with medicine and a healthy lifestyle.
- **Stroke** is when a blocked artery stops the flow of blood to the brain. It can affect different parts of the body. A cerebral hemorrhage is when a blood vessel in the brain bursts.

You can develop good health habits as a teen. They will help you avoid CVD later in life. Here are some of the risk factors for CVDs that you can control.

- **Avoid the use of tobacco.** Also avoid secondhand smoke.
- **Have your blood pressure checked.**
- **Eat less high-fat foods.**
- **Be physically active.**
- **Keep a healthy weight.**
- **Lower stress.**
- **Avoid the use of alcohol and other drugs.**

Reading Tutor, Lesson 1 *(continued)*

USE WITH CHAPTER 26, PAGES 674–680.

Here are some of the risk factors for CVDs that you cannot control.

- **Heredity.** Teens whose parents have CVD may be at greater risk for getting CVD.
- **Gender.** Men have a greater risk for CVD than women do.
- **Age.** People are more likely to get CVD as they get older.

2. What are some of the risk factors for CVDs that you can control?

Lesson 2 | Reading Tutor

USE WITH CHAPTER 26, PAGES 681–687.

Noncommunicable Diseases and Disabilities: Cancer

Vocabulary

cancer	Uncontrollable growth of abnormal cells *(page 681)*
tumor	An abnormal mass of tissue that has no natural role in the body *(page 681)*
benign	Noncancerous *(page 681)*
malignant	Cancerous *(page 681)*
metastasis	Spread of cancer from the point where it originated to other parts of the body *(page 681)*
carcinogen	A cancer-causing substance *(page 682)*
biopsy	The removal of a small piece of tissue for examination *(page 686)*
remission	A period of time when symptoms disappear *(page 687)*

Drawing from Experience

What do you know about cancer? Do you know anyone who has had cancer? How can you reduce your risk of getting cancer? Think about these questions as you read Lesson 2.

In the last lesson, you learned about heart disease. In this lesson, you will learn about cancer.

Name Class Date

Reading Tutor, Lesson 2 *(continued)*

USE WITH CHAPTER 26, PAGES 681–687.

Organizing Your Thoughts

Use the chart below to help you take notes as you read the summaries that follow. In the first box, list the some of the risk factors for cancer. In the next box, list some of the ways to reduce your risk of cancer. In the last box, list some of the ways to detect and treat cancer.

Risk Factors for Cancer	Ways to Reduce Cancer Risk	Detect and Treat Cancer

Reading Tutor, Lesson 2 *(continued)*

USE WITH CHAPTER 26, PAGES 681–687.

Read to Learn

Read each passage carefully. Write in complete sentences to answer the following questions.

How Cancer Harms the Body *(pages 681–682)*

Cancer is the *uncontrollable growth of abnormal cells*. A **tumor** is *an abnormal mass of tissue that has no natural role in the body*. There are two types.

- A **benign** tumor is *noncancerous*. It grows slowly and does not spread.
- A **malignant** tumor is *cancerous*. **Metastasis** is *when cancer spreads from the point where it started to other parts of the body*. Cancer cells divide and form new tumors.

1. What are the two types of tumors?

____

____

____

____

____

____

Types of Cancer *(page 682)*

Cancer can form in almost any part of the body. Here are some of the types of cancer and risk factors for each.

- **Skin cancer** is the most common type. Exposure to the sun or tanning beds is the main cause.
- **Breast cancer** is the second leading cause of cancer death in women. Obesity and alcohol use are risks.
- **Prostate cancer** occurs mostly in men over age 55. A high-fat diet is a risk factor.
- **Lung cancer** is the leading cause of cancer death. Smoking is the main cause.
- **Colon** or **rectal cancer** is the second leading cause of cancer death. The risk rises as you get older.
- **Mouth cancer** occurs mostly in people over 40. The use of chewing tobacco is one of the main causes.
- **Cervical cancer** occurs in women who have a history of HPV infection.
- **Testicular cancer** is most common in men ages 15 to 34. An undescended testicle is a risk factor.

Reading Tutor, Lesson 2 *(continued)*

USE WITH CHAPTER 26, PAGES 681–687.

We classify some cancers by the tissues that they affect. Here are some different types.

- **Lymphomas** are cancers of the immune system.
- **Leukemias** are cancers of the blood-forming organs.
- **Carcinomas** are cancers of the glands and body linings.
- **Sarcomas** are cancers of the connective tissues. This includes bones, ligaments, and muscles.

2. What are some types of cancers, based on the tissues they affect?

Risk Factors for Cancer *(pages 682–684)*

Five to ten percent of cancers are hereditary. A **carcinogen** is *a cancer-causing substance* that may be a factor. Lifestyle choices may also be a factor. Here are some of the risk factors for cancer.

- **Tobacco** use is the major cause of cancer death. Smoking causes lung cancer. It can also cause bladder, pancreas, or kidney cancer. Avoid all forms of tobacco and secondhand smoke.
- **STDs** such as HPV and hepatitis B can cause cervical and liver cancer. Abstain from sexual activity and from injecting drugs.
- **Dietary factors** cause about 30 percent of all cancer deaths. Eating plenty of low-fat and high-fiber foods lower the risk of colon, breast, and prostate cancers.
- **Ultraviolet (UV) radiation** is the main cause of skin cancer. Limit your time in the sun. Don't use tanning beds. Use a sunscreen. Pay attention to the seven warning signs of cancer. The first letters, when combined, spell the word CAUTION.
  1. **C**hange in bowel habits
  2. **A** sore that does not heal
  3. **U**nusual bleeding or discharge
  4. **T**hickening or a lump in the breast or elsewhere

5. **I**ndigestion or difficulty swallowing
6. **O**bvious change in a wart or mole
7. **N**agging cough or hoarseness

3. What are the seven warning signs of cancer?

Reducing Your Risk *(page 685)*

You can reduce your risk of cancer by practicing these healthful behaviors.

- **Abstain from sexual activity.** This can reduce the risk of STDs.
- **Be physically active.**
- **Maintain a healthy weight.**
- **Eat nutritious foods.** Eat fruits and vegetables every day. They act against carcinogens.
- **Eat a low-fat and high-fiber diet.**
- **Protect your skin from UV rays.**
- **Avoid tobacco and alcohol.** Tobacco is the single major cause of cancer death in the United States.
- **Look for the warning signs of cancer.** Do regular self-exams.

4. What are some of the ways to reduce your risk of cancer?

Reading Tutor, Lesson 2 *(continued)*

USE WITH CHAPTER 26, PAGES 681–687.

Detecting and Treating Cancer *(pages 686–687)*

Early detection is a critical factor in treating cancer. Here are some of the ways to detect cancer.

- **Self-exams** can help you find breast, testicular, and skin cancers.
- **Medical screenings** can result in early detection for about half of all new cancer cases.
- A **biopsy** is *the removal of a small piece of tissue for examination* to see if cancer is present.

Here are some of the types of treatment for cancer.

- **Surgery** removes the cancer mass from the body.
- **Radiation therapy** aims rays at the cancer cells and kills or shrinks them.
- **Chemotherapy** uses chemicals to destroy cancer cells.
- **Immunotherapy** helps a person's immune system find specific cancers and destroy them.
- **Hormone therapy** is the use of medicines that interfere with the production of hormones. This can kill cancer cells or slow their growth.

Remission is *a period of time when symptoms disappear* and cancer is under control. It can recur.

5. What are some of the types of treatment for cancer?

USE WITH CHAPTER 26, PAGES 688–694.

Noncommunicable Diseases and Disabilities: Allergies, Asthma, Diabetes, and Arthritis

Vocabulary

allergy	A specific reaction of the immune system to a foreign and frequently harmless substance *(page 688)*
histamines	Chemicals that can stimulate mucus and fluid production in an area *(page 689)*
asthma	An inflammatory condition in which the small airways in the lungs become narrowed, causing difficulty in breathing *(page 690)*
diabetes	A chronic disease that affects the way body cells convert food into energy *(page 691)*
autoimmune disease	A condition in which the immune system mistakenly attacks itself, targeting the cells, tissues, and organs of a person's own body *(page 691)*
arthritis	A group of more than 100 different diseases that cause pain and loss of movement in the joints *(page 693)*
osteoarthritis	A disease of the joints in which cartilage breaks down *(page 693)*
rheumatoid arthritis	A disease characterized by the debilitating destruction of the joints due to inflammation *(page 694)*

Drawing from Experience

Do you ever sneeze when you walk outside? Do you have trouble breathing when the air is cold? Do you know anyone who has arthritis? Think about these questions as you read Lesson 3.

In the last lesson, you learned about cancer. In this lesson, you will learn about allergies, asthma, diabetes, and arthritis.

Name Class Date

Reading Tutor, Lesson 3 *(continued)*

USE WITH CHAPTER 26, PAGES 688–694.

Organizing Your Thoughts

Use the chart below to help you take notes as you read the summaries that follow. In the first box, list some of the facts about allergies. In the next box, list some of the facts about asthma.

Allergies	Asthma

In the next box, list some facts about diabetes. In the last box, list some facts about arthritis.

Diabetes	Arthritis

Reading Tutor, Lesson 3 *(continued)*

USE WITH CHAPTER 26, PAGES 688–694.

Read to Learn

Read each passage carefully. Write in complete sentences to answer the following questions.

Allergies *(pages 688–690)*

An **allergy** is *a specific reaction of the immune system to a foreign and frequently harmless substance.* **Allergens** are things that cause allergies. Some of these are pollen, foods, dust, mold, insect venom, medicine, and others.

Histamines are *chemicals that can start mucus and fluid production in an area.* They cause sneezing, itchy eyes, and a runny nose. Some people get hives, or raised itchy bumps. A severe reaction might cause difficulty breathing or swallowing.

Three kinds of tests can tell if you have an allergy. A blood test, a food elimination diet, or a skin test. Here are three of the ways to treat an allergy.

- The best treatment is to avoid the allergen.
- **Antihistamines** are medicines that can help.
- **Immunotherapy** is a series of shots to help stop the body from reacting to the allergen.

1. What are three of the ways to treat an allergy?

____

____

____

____

____

____

Asthma *(page 690)*

Asthma is *a condition in which the small airways in the lungs become narrow, causing difficulty in breathing*. The bronchial tubes are sensitive to certain **triggers.** These may be air pollution, pet dander, smoke, mold, pollen, or dust.

Asthma can cause wheezing or severe breathing difficulty. It can be life threatening. Here are some of the ways to keep it under control.

- **Monitor the condition.** Look for signs such as shortness of breath, chest pain, coughing, or sneezing. Treat the signs quickly to keep an attack from getting worse.
- **Manage the environment.** Take away the asthma triggers. Avoid tobacco smoke and take away any dusty rugs or carpet. Wash your bedding often.

- **Deal with stress.** Stress can trigger asthma. Relax. Use your stress-management skills.
- **Take medication. Bronchodilators** are medicines that you take with an inhaler. They relax and widen the breathing passages.

2. What are some of the ways to keep asthma under control?

____

____

____

____

Diabetes *(pages 691–693)*

Diabetes is *a disease that affects the way body cells change food into energy*. There is no cure. It may cause blindness, kidney failure, heart disease, and stroke. It may lead to amputations.

Type 1 diabetes makes up about 5 to 10 percent of all cases.

- The body does not make insulin and glucose builds up in the blood.
- Over time it can cause harm to the eyes, the kidneys, the nerves, and the heart.
- It is an **autoimmune disease.** This is *a condition in which the immune system attacks itself.*
- People with type 1 diabetes must take a dose of insulin each day.

Type 2 diabetes makes up 90 to 95 percent of all cases.

- It usually occurs after age 40. Some younger adults and children also get this disease.
- The body is not able to make enough insulin or to use insulin properly.
- The buildup of glucose causes the same symptoms as type 1 diabetes.
- It can be the result of obesity or an inactive lifestyle.
- You can treat it by managing your weight, by being active, and with some medication.

3. What are the two types of diabetes?

____

____

____

____

Reading Tutor, Lesson 3 *(continued)*

USE WITH CHAPTER 26, PAGES 688–694.

Arthritis *(pages 693–694)*

Arthritis is *a group of more than 100 different diseases that cause pain and loss of movement in the joints*. It is the number one cause of disability. There are two types.

Osteoarthritis is *a disease of the joints in which cartilage breaks down*. It is most common in women and people over the age of 45. It can occur in any joint but mainly affects the knees and hips.

Here are some of the ways to reduce the risk.

- **Control weight.** This puts less stress on the joints.
- **Prevent sports injuries.** Warm up before you exercise. Use the right safety gear.
- **Avoid getting Lyme disease.** Use insect repellent and wear long sleeves in wooded areas.

Rheumatoid arthritis is *a disease that causes destruction of the joints due to inflammation*.

- It is the result of an autoimmune disease. There is no cure.
- The signs are joint pain, swelling, and stiffness. The joints may become deformed.
- Early diagnosis and treatment can control the effects.
- Exercise, rest, and therapy can help you deal with the disease.

4. What are the two types of arthritis?

____

____

____

____

____

Name Class Date

Lesson 4

Reading Tutor

USE WITH CHAPTER 26, PAGES 695–699.

Noncommunicable Diseases and Disabilities: Physical and Mental Challenges

Vocabulary

disability	Any physical or mental impairment that limits normal activities, including seeing, hearing, walking, or speaking *(page 695)*
profound deafness	A hearing loss so severe that a person affected cannot benefit from mechanical amplification, such as a hearing aid *(page 696)*
mental retardation	The below-average intellectual ability present from birth or early childhood and associated with difficulties in learning and social adaptation *(page 697)*
Americans with Disabilities Act	A law prohibiting discrimination against people with physical or mental disabilities in the workplace, transportation, public accommodations, and telecommunications *(page 699)*

Drawing from Experience

Do you know anyone who has a disability? Do you know anyone who uses sign language? What would life be like if you could not see or hear? Do you treat people with disabilities the same as you treat everyone else? Think about these questions as you read Lesson 4.

In the last lesson, you learned about allergies and some other noncommunicable diseases. In this lesson, you will learn about physical and mental disability.

Reading Tutor, Lesson 4 *(continued)*

USE WITH CHAPTER 26, PAGES 695–699.

Organizing Your Thoughts

Use the chart below to help you take notes as you read the summaries that follow. In the first box, list some of the kinds of physical and mental challenges. In the other box, list some of the ways to accommodate people with special needs.

Physical and Mental Challenges	Ways to Accommodate Special Needs

Reading Tutor, Lesson 4 *(continued)*

USE WITH CHAPTER 26, PAGES 695–699.

Read to Learn

Read each passage carefully. Write in complete sentences to answer the following questions.

Physical Challenges *(pages 695–697)*

A **disability** is *any physical or mental impairment that limits normal activities. This can be seeing, hearing, walking, or speaking*. Here are some of the common types of physical challenges.

- **Sight impairment** can mean vision impaired or blind. Many people treat vision problems by wearing glasses or contacts. Here are some of the causes of blindness.
  - **Diabetes** is the main reason that many adults go blind.
  - **Macular degeneration** is when the retina in the eye breaks down. It is the leading cause of blindness in adults over the age of 55.
  - **Glaucoma** is a disease that destroys the optic nerve of the eye.
  - **Cataracts** are a clouding of the lens of the eye.

Eye exams and early diagnosis are vital to help stop blindness.

- **Hearing impairment** can range from minor to severe. **Profound deafness** is *a severe hearing loss. The person cannot get help from a hearing aid*. Here are some of the causes of hearing impairment.
  - Heredity, injury, or disease
  - Obstructions that prevent sound waves from getting to the inner ear. The blockage may be ear wax or bone growth. It may affect only one ear. Having surgery may help.
  - Nerve damage from old age
  - Nerve damage from repeated exposure to loud sounds. Some types might be loud stereos, traffic, video games, machines, or a loud concert.
- **Motor impairment** occurs when an injury to the brain or a disorder of the nervous system affects the body's range of motion and balance. Here are some of the ways to treat it.
  - **Physical therapy** can keep joints flexible and muscles stretched. This can help the person move around.
  - **Prosthetics** are artificial limbs to help people who have had a limb removed.
  - **Motorized wheelchairs** let many people get around without help.
  - **Computers** with mouth sticks or head sticks can help people who cannot use their hands or arms.

1. What are some of the types of physical challenges?

____

____

____

____

____

____

____

Mental Challenges *(page 697)*

Mental retardation is *below-average intellectual ability. It is present from birth or early childhood. It causes learning and social problems.* Here are some of the causes.

- **A head injury or disease**
- **Genetic disorders** such as Down syndrome, PKU, Tay-Sachs, and Fragile X syndrome
- **Fetal alcohol syndrome (FAS)** which occurs when a pregnant female drinks alcohol
- **Rubella** that passes to the fetus from the mother
- **Not getting enough oxygen at birth**

2. What are some of the causes of mental retardation?

____

____

____

____

____

____

____

Reading Tutor, Lesson 4 *(continued)*

USE WITH CHAPTER 26, PAGES 695–699.

Accommodating Differences *(pages 698–699)*

People with special needs also have many of the same needs and interests as everyone else. Here are some of the ways to accommodate people who have special needs.

- We need to make sure that there is wheelchair access to public buses and trains and buildings. This lets people with special needs take part in public events.
- We need to judge others on the basis of merit. We must not base our beliefs on a stereotype.
- If they are able, people with special needs must have the same chances as people who do not have disabilities.

The **Americans with Disabilities Act** is *a law that does not allow discrimination against people with disabilities. This includes at work and in transportation, public places, and telecommunications*. Here are some of the parts of the law.

- Employers with 15 or more workers must give qualified persons with disabilities an equal opportunity to the same benefits as others.
- State and local agencies must follow building standards. This applies when they build new buildings or alter old buildings. They must provide access in older buildings.
- Phone companies must have telecommunications relay services (TRS). This lets callers with hearing and speech disabilities use the phone.

The Workforce Investment Act of 1998 makes sure that anything a public agency posts to a Web site must be accessible to people with special needs.

3. What are some of the steps we can take to accommodate people with special needs?

Injury Prevention and Safe Behaviors: Safety at Home and at Work

Vocabulary

unintentional injury	An injury resulting from an unexpected event, or accident *(page 706)*
accident chain	A sequence of events that leads to an unintentional injury *(page 706)*
smoke alarm	An alarm that is triggered by the presence of smoke *(page 708)*
fire extinguisher	A portable device that puts out small fires by ejecting fire-extinguishing chemicals *(page 708)*
Occupational Safety and Health Administration (OSHA)	The agency in the federal government that is responsible for promoting safe and healthful conditions in the workplace *(page 713)*

Drawing from Experience

Have you ever tripped over something that you did not put away? Do you have a fire safety plan at home? Have you ever been hurt at work? What can you do to make your home or workplace safe? Think about these things as you read Lesson 1.

In the last chapter, you learned about noncommunicable diseases and disabilities. In this lesson, you will learn about safety at home and at work.

Reading Tutor, Lesson 1 *(continued)*

USE WITH CHAPTER 27, PAGES 706–713.

Organizing Your Thoughts

Use the chart below to help you take notes as you read the summaries that follow. In the first oval, list some ways to prevent fires. In the next, list some ways to prevent falls. Next, list some ways to prevent electrical shock. Next, list some ways to prevent poisoning. Next, list some facts about gun safety. In the next, list some facts about computer safety. In the last oval, list some of the ways to stay safe at work.

Reading Tutor, Lesson 1 *(continued)*

USE WITH CHAPTER 27, PAGES 706–713.

Read to Learn

Read each passage carefully. Write in complete sentences to answer the following questions.

Unintentional Injuries *(pages 706–707)*

An **unintentional injury** is *an injury resulting from an unexpected event, or accident*. An **accident chain** is *a sequence of events that leads to an unintentional injury*. Here are the steps of the accident chain.

Step 1. The situation. You sleep in. You have to rush to get ready for school.

Step 2. The unsafe habit. You often leave your books on the stairs.

Step 3. The unsafe action. You are not looking where you are going when you race down the stairs.

Step 4. The accident. You trip over your books and fall down the stairs.

Step 5. The result. You sprain your wrist when you fall. You are also late for school.

1. What are the steps of the accident chain?

____

____

____

____

____

____

Safety at Home *(pages 707–712)*

Preventing fires. Here are some of the ways to avoid fire injuries.

- Never leave a candle burning when you leave a room.
- Store matches and lighters out of the reach of children.
- Make sure no one falls asleep while smoking.
- Keep your stove and oven clean.
- Fix or replace frayed electric cords.
- Have the right fire safety equipment.
  - A **smoke alarm** is *an alarm that the presence of smoke will trigger.*
  - A **fire extinguisher** is *a portable device that puts out small fires by emitting fire-extinguishing chemicals.*

Reading Tutor, Lesson 1 *(continued)*

USE WITH CHAPTER 27, PAGES 706–713.

Preventing falls. Here are some of the ways to avoid the risk of injuries from falls.

- Keep the stairs well lit. Make sure the stairs are in good repair and free of clutter.
- Keep the floor clean. Mop up spills right away.
- Use nonskid throw rugs. Put nonskid mats under rugs.
- Make sure the bathtub and shower have safety rails and nonskid mats.
- Do not put cords across areas where people walk.
- Put safety latches on windows if there are small children in your home.
- Use a sturdy step stool when you reach for items in high places.

Preventing electrical shock. Here are some of the ways to avoid electrical shock.

- Unplug an electric appliance right away if anything seems to be wrong. Pull the plug and not the cord.
- Check cords for cracks and replace frayed cords.
- Do not put cords under carpets or rugs.
- Never use an appliance or power tools if your body or the floor is wet.
- Check outlets to make sure they that you have not overloaded them.
- Cover outlets if you have small children in your home.

Preventing poisoning. Here are some ways to prevent poisoning in your home.

- Keep medicine in a childproof container. Store them out of the reach of children.
- Store household chemicals in the original container. Do not store in drink containers.
- Never mix household chemicals. Ammonia and bleach give off toxic gas when mixed.
- Use products that give off fumes in a well-ventilated area.
- Make sure there is good ventilation when you use fuel-burning appliances.

Firearm safety. Here are some of the ways to reduce the risk of injury from guns.

- Never point a gun at anyone for any reason.
- Treat all guns as if you had loaded them. Leave the area and call an adult if you find a gun.
- Store guns unloaded and in a locked cabinet. Store the ammunition in a separate locked place.

Computer and video game safety. Here are some of the ways to use your computer safely.

- Take a ten-minute break every hour.
- Give your eyes a break by looking up and focusing on things that are far away.
- Use indirect lighting to avoid glare.
- Chairs, monitors, desks, and other work surfaces should be adjustable.
- Adjust your chair so your feet are on the floor.
- Your forearms, wrists, and hands should be straight when you use the mouse or keyboard.

2. What are the main areas of home safety?

____

____

____

____

____

____

____

Safety on the Job *(page 713)*

Many teens have jobs. The Department of Labor does not let teens under 18 do certain jobs. Some of these are roofing, construction work, or driving a forklift.

The **Occupational Safety and Health Administration (OSHA)** is *the agency in the federal government that promotes safe and healthy conditions in the workplace.*

3. What is OSHA?

____

____

____

____

____

____

____

Name Class Date

Lesson 2

Reading Tutor

USE WITH CHAPTER 27, PAGES 714–718.

Injury Prevention and Safe Behaviors: Recreation and Water Safety

Vocabulary

heat exhaustion	An overheating of the body that results in cold, clammy skin and symptoms of shock *(page 715)*
hypothermia	A condition in which body temperature becomes dangerously low *(page 715)*

Drawing from Experience

Do you know how to swim? Do you ever go camping, skiing, or boating? What kinds of things do you like to do outdoors? What things do you need to do to stay safe when you are outdoors? Think about these things as you read Lesson 2.

In the last lesson, you learned about safety in the home and at work. In this lesson, you will learn about outdoors and water safety.

Reading Tutor, Lesson 2 *(continued)*

USE WITH CHAPTER 27, PAGES 714–718.

Organizing Your Thoughts

Use the chart below to help you take notes as you read the summaries that follow. In the first oval, list the ways to stay safe while camping and hiking. In the next, list the ways to stay safe during winter sports. In the next, list the ways to stay safe during water sports. In the last oval, list the ways to stay safe while swimming in lakes, rivers, or the ocean.

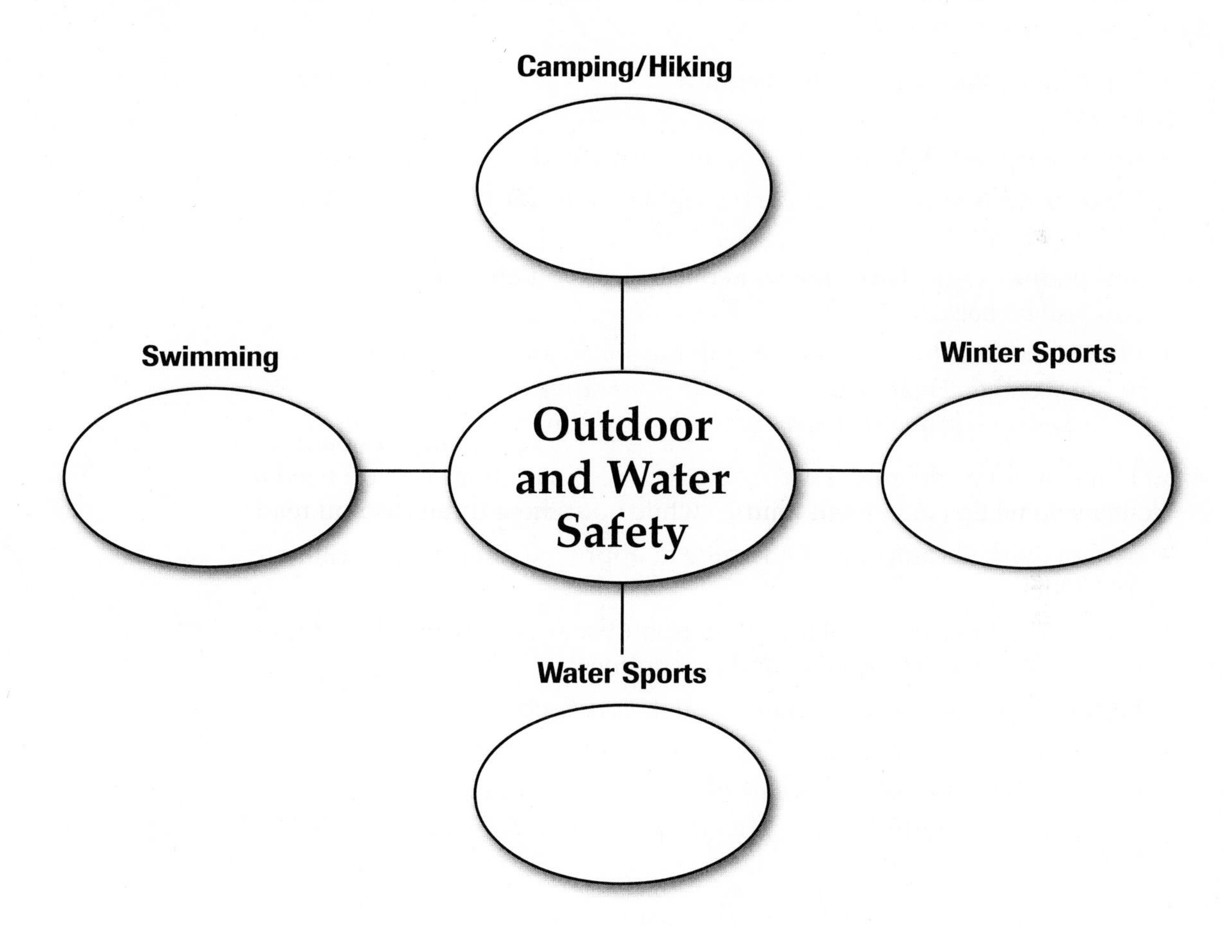

Reading Tutor, Lesson 2 *(continued)*

USE WITH CHAPTER 27, PAGES 714–718.

Read to Learn

Read each passage carefully. Write in complete sentences to answer the following questions.

Recreational Safety *(pages 714–718)*

Outdoor activities can be lots of fun. Here are some ways to stay safe during outdoor activities.

- **Know your limits.** Stay on a beginner slope if you are just learning to ski.
- **Bring supplies.** Take plenty of water with you. Plan simple meals.
- **Wear protective clothes.** Have the right clothes for the weather and insect protection.
- **Tell people your plans.** Tell someone where you are going and when you will be back.
- **Plan ahead for the weather.** Stay in the shade and drink plenty of water in hot weather. **Heat exhaustion** is *an overheating of the body that results in cold, clammy skin and symptoms of shock.* Use sunscreen to protect your skin from UV rays.

Here are some tips to prevent injuries while you are camping and hiking.

- Stay in marked campsites. Only hike in approved areas. Never camp or hike alone.
- Know about poisonous plants, insects, and snakes. Cover yourself to protect your body from ticks and mosquitoes.
- Be careful around wild animals. Do not store food in your tent.
- Be careful around campfires. Observe fire safety rules. Never cook inside a tent. Put out all fire with dirt and water.
- Never drink water from lakes, rivers, or streams. They may contain pathogens.

Here are some ways to stay safe during winter sports.

- Dress in layers. This can help prevent **hypothermia.** This is *a condition in which body heat becomes dangerously low.*
- Wear a waterproof outer layer.
- Wear a hat.
- Put on sunscreen.
- Wear the right safety gear.

Reading Tutor, Lesson 2 *(continued)*

USE WITH CHAPTER 27, PAGES 714–718.

The four major reasons that people drown are not wearing a life jacket, alcohol use, not being able to swim well, and hypothermia. Here are some ways to stay safe during water sports.

- **Swimming**
  - Learn how to swim. Always swim with a buddy.
  - Swim in marked swimming areas where a lifeguard is on duty.
  - Relax and float if you get a muscle cramp. Press and squeeze the muscle until it relaxes.
- **Diving**
  - Learn the right diving techniques. Check the water depth before you dive. It must be at least 9 feet deep.
  - Never dive in an area you are not familiar with. Never dive in shallow or dark water.
  - Make sure the area is clear of swimmers and floating objects.
- **Boating**
  - Learn how to handle a boat correctly. Know the laws about using a boat.
  - Always wear life jackets.
  - Return to shore at the first hint of bad weather.
  - Never ride in a boat with a driver who has been drinking.
  - Try one of these positions if you fall into the water.
    1. Draw your knees up to your chest. Keep your upper arms close to the sides of your body. Keep your head out of the water.
    2. Huddle close with others. Put a child or smaller person in the center of the circle.

Here are some of the ways to stay safe when you are swimming in a lake, river, or ocean.

- **Swim in supervised areas only.** Find an area that is clean.
- **Enter feet first.** Look for hidden objects, drop-offs, and water creatures.
- **Watch for marine warnings.** Look for warning flags. Check with the lifeguard. Check surf conditions in the ocean. Do not enter a "no swimming" area.
- **Be aware of what is around you.** Make sure docks or rafts are in good condition. Stay away from piers and diving platforms when in the water. Never swim under a raft or dock.
- **Plan ahead.** Make sure you have enough energy to swim back to shore. Swim parallel to the shore if you find yourself in a current or undertow.

Name Class Date

Reading Tutor, Lesson 2 *(continued)*

USE WITH CHAPTER 27, PAGES 714–718.

1. What are some of the ways to stay safe during outdoor activities?

Name Class Date

Lesson 3

Reading Tutor

USE WITH CHAPTER 27, PAGES 719–724.

Injury Prevention and Safe Behaviors: Safety on the Road

Vocabulary

vehicular safety	Obeying the rules of the road, as well as exercising common sense and good judgment *(page 719)*
graduated driver's license	A licensing program that gradually increases a new driver's driving privileges over time as experience and skill are gained *(page 720)*
road rage	A practice of endangering drivers by using a vehicle as a weapon *(page 722)*
defensive driver	A driver who is aware of potential hazards and reacts to avoid them *(page 722)*

Drawing from Experience

Do you always wear a seat belt in the car? Do you follow all driving rules? Do you wear a helmet when you ride your bike or skateboard? What are some of the other ways you can prevent road injuries? Think about these things as you read Lesson 3.

In the last lesson, you learned about recreation and water safety. In this lesson, you will learn about safety on the road.

Reading Tutor, Lesson 3 *(continued)*

USE WITH CHAPTER 27, PAGES 719–724.

Organizing Your Thoughts

Use the chart below to help you take notes as you read the summaries that follow. In the first box, list some of the rules of automobile safety. In the other box, list some of the rules of bicycle, skating, motorcycle, and ATV safety.

Automobile Safety	Safety on Wheels

Reading Tutor, Lesson 3 *(continued)*

USE WITH CHAPTER 27, PAGES 719–724.

Read to Learn

Read each passage carefully. Write in complete sentences to answer the following questions.

Automobile Safety *(pages 719–722)*

Vehicular safety is *obeying the rules of the road, as well as practicing common sense and good judgment*. This means driving within the speed limit, yielding the right of way, and obeying local traffic rules.

- **Pay attention to your vehicle.** Adjust the mirrors and seat. Buckle your safety belt.
- **Pay attention to other drivers.** Turn on your headlights at night or when the weather is poor. "Watch out for the other guy." Drive defensively.
- **Pay attention to road conditions.** Go slower when the road is icy or wet or there is traffic.
- **Pay attention to your physical state.** Do not drive when you are sleepy.
- **Pay attention to your emotional state.** Do not drive if you are angry or upset.

A **graduated driver's license** is *a licensing program. It increases a new driver's driving privileges over time as he or she gains experience and skill*. This is an attempt to reduce the number of teen deaths in car crashes. Teen drivers are more likely to speed, run red lights, and drive while drinking or using drugs.

- Here are some ways to be a more responsible driver.
- Always signal when you are about to make a turn or change lanes.
- Follow all traffic signals and signs. Follow all speed limits.
- Do not tailgate.
- Let other drivers merge safely into traffic.
- **Road rage** is *a practice of endangering drivers by using a vehicle as a weapon*. Stay away from someone who is a danger on the road. Report the person's license plate number to the police.

Safety belts save lives. Make sure everyone in your car buckles up. Take these precautions.

- Never speed, drag race, or do daredevil stunts.
- Never use alcohol or other drugs and drive a car. The results may be fatal.

USE WITH CHAPTER 27, PAGES 719–724.

- Do not eat, adjust the radio, or use your cell phone when you are driving.
- Know that you have no control over what other drivers do. A **defensive driver** is *a driver who is aware of potential hazards and reacts to avoid them.*

1. What are some of the ways to be a more responsible driver?

____

____

____

____

____

____

Safety on Wheels *(pages 723–724)*

It is important to use proper safety gear when you are biking, skateboarding, or riding a scooter, motorcycle, off-road vehicle, or moped.

- **Bicycle safety.** Here are some rules for safe cycling.
  - Always wear a helmet that fits properly.
  - Ride with traffic. Yield the right-of-way.
  - Watch for cars pulling into traffic. Watch for opening car doors.
  - Obey the same rules as drivers. Signal before you turn. Stop for red lights.
  - Use hand signals for making turns and stopping.
  - Keep both hands on the handlebars unless you are signaling.
  - Make sure your bike has a bright headlight and reflectors for night riding.
  - Wear reflective and light-colored clothes when you ride at dawn, dusk, after dark, or in the rain.
- **Skating safety.** Here are some rules for skateboarding and in-line skating.
  - Wear safety gear. Wear wrist guards, elbow and kneepads, and a helmet.
  - Watch for pedestrians. Keep your speed under control.
  - Curl up into a ball and roll if you fall.
  - Do not hold anything in your hands.

Reading Tutor, Lesson 3 *(continued)*

USE WITH CHAPTER 27, PAGES 719–724.

- **Motorcycle and ATV safety.** Here are safety rules to use when you drive motorcycles, mopeds, and all-terrain vehicles (ATVs).
  - Be aware of hazards like a car door opening or a pedestrian.
  - Wear a helmet and proper clothing. Include eye protection.
  - Be careful in wet weather.
  - Do not carry another rider unless you have a second seat and another helmet.
  - Do not grab onto objects or other vehicles when moving.
  - Do not use ATVs on paved streets. Ride four-wheeled ATVs rather than three-wheeled ones.

2. What are some of the safety rules for cycling?

____

____

____

____

____

____

Name Class Date

Lesson 4 **Reading Tutor**

USE WITH CHAPTER 27, PAGES 725–729.

Injury Prevention and Safe Behaviors: Weather Emergencies and Natural Disasters

Vocabulary

severe weather	Harsh or dangerous weather conditions *(page 725)*
emergency survival kit	A group of items that can be used for a short time until an emergency situation has stabilized *(page 726)*
hurricane	A powerful storm that originates at sea, characterized by winds of at least 74 miles per hour, heavy rains, flooding, and sometimes tornadoes *(page 727)*
flash flood	A flood with great volume and of short duration that is usually caused by heavy rainfall *(page 727)*
tornado	A whirling, funnel-shaped windstorm that drops from the sky to the ground and produces a narrow path of destruction on land *(page 728)*
blizzard	A snowstorm with winds of at least 35 miles per hour *(page 728)*
earthquake	A violent shaking movement of the earth's surface *(page 729)*

Drawing from Experience

Have you ever been in a hurricane or a flood? Have you ever felt an earthquake? What can you do to prepare for a weather emergency or a natural disaster? Think about these things as you read Lesson 4.

In the last lesson, you learned about safety on the road. In this lesson, you will learn about weather emergencies and natural disasters.

Reading Tutor, Lesson 4 *(continued)*

USE WITH CHAPTER 27, PAGES 725–729.

Organizing Your Thoughts

Use the chart below to help you take notes as you read the summaries that follow. In the first box, list some types of weather emergencies. In the other, list some types of natural disasters.

Weather Emergencies	Natural Disasters

Reading Tutor, Lesson 4 *(continued)*

USE WITH CHAPTER 27, PAGES 725–729.

Read to Learn

Read each passage carefully. Write in complete sentences to answer the following questions.

Severe Weather *(pages 725–728)*

Severe weather refers to *harsh or dangerous weather conditions*. The National Weather Service (NWS) uses the media to issue watches and warnings. A **watch** means that the weather conditions are right for a specific weather event to occur. A **warning** means that they have sighted severe weather and it is heading toward your area.

An **emergency survival kit** is *a group of items that you can use for a short time until a situation has stabilized*. Here are some of the supplies to get.

- **Water and food.** Plan on 1 gallon of water per person per day. Store cans of food and a can opener.
- **Phone, radio, lighting, and blankets.** Charge your cell phone. Keep a radio, flashlights, and extra batteries for each.
- **Other supplies.** Add extra medicine and money.

A **hurricane** is *a powerful storm that starts at sea. It has winds of at least 74 miles per hour, heavy rains, flooding, and sometimes tornadoes*. The NWS tracks hurricanes and issues warnings when they get near. Bring in items from outside and board up windows and doors for a hurricane watch. Seek shelter inland for a hurricane warning.

Floods can occur any time of year. Move your valuables and furniture to a higher area if a flood is likely to occur. Listen to the radio and prepare to evacuate. Turn off utilities before you leave. Never walk, swim, ride a bike, or drive a car through flood water. Drowning is a risk. Drink only bottled water.

A **flash flood** is *a flood with great volume and of short duration that is usually the result of heavy rainfall*. Leave low-lying areas. Do not drive through flood waters.

Severe thunderstorms can occur anywhere. They may have heavy rains, strong winds, lightening, and hail. Storm clouds tell you the storm is coming. Go to shore if you are on the water. Get inside if you are outdoors. Stay away from tall structures and trees. Do not use computers, phones, or TVs.

A **tornado** is *a funnel-shaped windstorm that drops from the sky to the ground. It makes a narrow path of destruction on land*. Here are a few safety tips.

- Seek shelter in a sturdy building if you are outside or in a car. Lie down in a ditch if you cannot get to shelter. Cover yourself with a blanket and cover your head with your hands.
- Stay away from windows if you are indoors. Go to a storm cellar, a basement, or a crawl space. Go to an interior room with no window. Cover yourself with a blanket.

Reading Tutor, Lesson 4 *(continued)*

USE WITH CHAPTER 27, PAGES 725–729.

A **blizzard** is *a snowstorm with winds of at least 35 miles per hour*. Here are some steps to take in a severe winter storm.

- **Stay inside.** The safest place to be in a storm is inside.
- **Wear protective clothes.** Wear several layers. Wear a hat, mittens, and gloves. Wear water-resistant boots.
- **Avoid getting lost.** Use landmarks to find your way. Stay where you are until help arrives.

1. What are some of the supplies to put in an emergency survival kit?

Earthquakes *(page 729)*

An **earthquake** is *a violent shaking movement of the earth's surface*. They can occur in all parts of the United States. They are most common in California. Follow these safety tips if an earthquake occurs.

Stand or crouch in a doorway if you are inside a building. Get under a sturdy piece of furniture. Cover your head with your arms or a pillow.

Stay away from buildings, trees, and power lines if you are outdoors.

Use care once the tremors stop. Stay out of damaged buildings. Check gas lines. Be ready for aftershocks.

2. What are some of the ways to keep safe if an earthquake occurs?

Name Class Date

CHAPTER 28
Lesson 1

Reading Tutor

USE WITH CHAPTER 28, PAGES 736–741.

First Aid and Emergencies: Providing First Aid

Vocabulary

first aid	The immediate, temporary care given to an ill or injured person until professional medical care can be provided *(page 736)*
universal precautions	Actions taken to prevent the spread of disease by treating all blood and other body fluids as if they contained pathogens *(page 737)*

Drawing from Experience

Do you know what to do if someone is bleeding? Do you know what to do if someone has a burn? Why is it important to learn how to give first aid? Think about these things as you read Lesson 1.

In the last chapter, you learned about injury prevention and safe behaviors. In this lesson, you will learn about first aid.

Reading Tutor, Lesson 1 *(continued)*

USE WITH CHAPTER 28, PAGES 736–741.

Organizing Your Thoughts

Use the chart below to help you take notes as you read the summaries that follow. In the first box, list some facts about first aid and responding to an emergency. In the next box, list the steps of first aid for bleeding. In the last box, list the types of burns and treatment for each.

First Aid	First Aid for Bleeding	Types of Burns/Treatment

Reading Tutor, Lesson 1 *(continued)*

USE WITH CHAPTER 28, PAGES 736–741.

Read to Learn

Read each passage carefully. Write in complete sentences to answer the following questions.

First Aid *(pages 736–737)*

First aid is *the immediate, temporary care given to an ill or injured person until professional medical care can be provided*. Your reaction to an accident can reduce the harm and might help save a life.

Universal precautions are *actions taken to prevent the spread of disease by treating all blood and other body fluids as if they contained pathogens*. This means wearing gloves when you might touch blood. It means using mouthpieces when you need to give emergency breathing. Always wash your hands before and after giving first aid.

1. What is first aid?

____

____

____

____

____

Responding to an Emergency *(page 737)*

Check, call, and care. These are the first steps to take in an emergency.

1. **Check the scene and the victim.** Look for fire, traffic, or downed electric lines. See how many victims there are. Do not move the victim if there is no immediate danger.
2. **Call for help.** Call 911. Do not hang up until they tell you to. Have someone else make the call if you can. You stay with the victim.
3. **Provide care for the victim.** Get the victim's permission to give first aid if that is possible. Take care of breathing or severe bleeding first. Tap a person on the shoulder if he or she seems unconscious. Ask if he or she is okay.

2. What are the first three steps to take in an emergency?

____

____

____

____

____

Reading Tutor, Lesson 1 *(continued)*

Types of Injuries *(pages 738–739)*

Open wounds are one type of injury. Here are several types of open wounds.

- **Abrasion.** Tiny blood vessels in the outer layer of the skin break if you scrape your skin against a hard surface. Dirt and bacteria can enter the site. Clean the wound.
- **Laceration.** This is a cut that a sharp object like a knife causes. It bleeds. A deep wound may cause heavy bleeding and damage to nerves and large blood vessels.
- **Puncture.** This is a small but deep hole. A pin, nail, fang, or other object that pierces the skin may cause it. It does not usually bleed a lot. It carries a high risk of infection such as tetanus.
- **Avulsion.** This is when tissue partly or completely separates from the body. It may hang like a flap. Heavy bleeding may occur. Pack any severed body part in ice and get help right away.

3. What are the four types of open wounds?

____

____

____

____

____

First Aid for Bleeding *(pages 739–740)*

Put on clean gloves before stopping the blood flow from an open wound if possible. Take these steps to control bleeding.

- Cover the wound with a sterile cloth. Press firmly.
- Elevate the wound above the heart if possible.
- Cover the cloth with a sterile bandage.
- Cover it with a pressure bandage if needed. Use a pressure point to control bleeding.
- Call for help or have someone else call for help.

You can use roller bandages to control bleeding. Here is how to use a roller bandage.

- Place a dressing over the wound.
- Secure the roller bandage over the dressing.
- Use overlapping turns. Cover the entire dressing.

Reading Tutor, Lesson 1 *(continued)*

USE WITH CHAPTER 28, PAGES 736–741.

- Split the end into two strips. Tie the ends tightly.
- Make sure it does not cut off circulation.

You must use pressure point bleeding control if the bleeding will not stop. You press a main artery against a bone to stop blood to the injured area. You should only do this if absolutely needed. It is serious. Get help right away.

4. What are the steps to take to control bleeding?

____

____

____

____

____

____

____

Burns *(pages 740–741)*

Heat, radiation, chemicals, and electricity can all burn the skin. There are three types of burns.

- In a **first-degree burn**, the outer layer of skin turns red. You can treat it with cold running water for ten minutes. Pat the area dry and cover with a clean bandage.
- A **second-degree burn** is when there is damage to several layers of skin. The skin has blisters. You can treat it with cold water. Elevate the burned area. Wrap it loosely in a sterile, dry dressing. Get medical help.
- A **third-degree burn** is a very serious burn. There is damage to deeper layers of skin, fat, muscle, nerves, and bone. Get medical help right away. Treat with large amounts of cold water. Cover with a dry, sterile cloth.

5. What are the three types of burns and how do you treat them?

____

____

____

____

____

____

USE WITH CHAPTER 28, PAGES 742–748.

First Aid and Emergencies: CPR and First Aid for Shock and Choking

Vocabulary

chain of survival	A sequence of actions that maximize the victim's chances of survival *(page 742)*
defibrillator	A device that delivers an electric shock to the heart to restore its normal rhythm *(page 742)*
cardiopulmonary resuscitation (CPR)	A lifesaving first-aid procedure that combines rescue breaths with chest compressions, supplying oxygen to the body until normal body functions can resume *(page 743)*
shock	A failure of the cardiovascular system to keep an adequate supply of blood circulating to the vital organs of the body *(page 747)*

Drawing from Experience

What do you know about CPR? Why is it important to check for signs of breathing? How do you know if a person is choking? What could you do to help a person who is choking? Think about these things as you read Lesson 2.

In the last lesson, you learned about first aid. In this lesson, you will learn about CPR, shock, and choking.

Reading Tutor, Lesson 2 *(continued)*

USE WITH CHAPTER 28, PAGES 742–748.

Organizing Your Thoughts

Use the chart below to help you take notes as you read the summaries that follow. In the first box, list the ABCs of adult CPR. In the next box, list some of the first-aid steps for shock. In the last box, list the first-aid steps for choking.

ABCs of Adult CPR	First Aid for Shock	First Aid for Choking

Reading Tutor, Lesson 2 *(continued)*

USE WITH CHAPTER 28, PAGES 742–748.

Read to Learn

Read each passage carefully. Write in complete sentences to answer the following questions.

Life-Threatening Emergencies *(page 742)*

The **chain of survival** is *a sequence of actions that maximize the victim's chances of survival*. You can start the first two links of the chain. Call 911 and begin CPR. Early defibrillation and transfer are steps made by medical persons when they arrive. A **defibrillator** is *a device that delivers an electric shock to the heart to restore its normal rhythm*.

1. What is the chain of survival?

___

___

___

___

___

___

___

CPR *(page 743)*

Cardiopulmonary resuscitation (CPR) is *a life-saving first-aid procedure that combines rescue breaths with chest compressions, supplying oxygen to the body until normal body functions can resume*.

2. What is CPR?

___

___

___

___

___

___

___

Reading Tutor, Lesson 2 *(continued)*

USE WITH CHAPTER 28, PAGES 742–748.

CPR for Adults *(pages 743–746)*

The steps of CPR are the ABCs. Tap victim on the shoulder and ask if he or she is okay. Start the chain of survival if a victim is not responding. Call 911 and then follow these steps.

- **Airway.** Remove anything you see in the person's mouth. Gently tilt the head back with one hand. Push down on the forehead with the other. Do not do this if you think the person may have a head or neck injury. Lift the jaw instead.
- **Breathing.** Look, listen, and feel for breathing. Look for chest movement. Listen for breathing. Feel for exhaled air on your cheek. Begin rescue breathing if there is no breathing.
  1. Keep the person's head in the right position. Pinch the nostrils shut.
  2. Place your mouth over the person's. Give two slow breaths.
- **Circulation.** Check for signs of circulation such as breathing. Begin chest compressions if there are no signs of circulation. Give one rescue breath every 5 seconds.

Here are the steps for chest compressions and CPR cycles.

1. **Position your hands.** Find a spot on the lower part of the person's breastbone between the nipples. Place the heel of one hand over that point. Lace your fingers with your other hand.
2. **Begin chest compressions and rescue breathing.** Lean over the person. Lock your elbows and press straight down quickly and firmly. Let the chest spring back up between compressions. Give two rescue breaths for every 15 compressions. Finish four cycles of CPR and then check for circulation. Turn the person on his or her side and wait for help if he or she begins to breathe.

Here are the steps to follow for the ABCs of infant and child CPR.

- **Airway.** Remove anything you see in the victim's mouth. Gently tilt head back. Lift chin with one hand and push down on the forehead with the other hand.
- **Breathing.** Look, listen, and feel for breathing. Pinch a child's nostrils shut and cover his or her mouth with yours. Seal your mouth over an infant's nose and mouth. Give two slow breaths.
- **Circulation.** Check for signs of circulation. Begin chest compressions if there is still not breathing. Give one rescue breath every 3 seconds for either a child or an infant.

Reading Tutor, Lesson 2 *(continued)*

USE WITH CHAPTER 28, PAGES 742–748.

Here are the steps for infant and child CPR cycles.

1. **Position your hands.** Keep the person's head tilted. Place the heel of your hand on the lower part of the breastbone. Put your shoulder directly over your straight arm and hand. Place two or three of your fingers on the infant's breastbone.
2. **Begin chest compressions and rescue breathing.** Compress the person's chest down. Release pressure completely between compressions. Give one rescue breath for every five compressions. Check for signs of circulation after 20 cycles. Continue until the person starts breathing or medical help comes.

3. What are the ABCs of adult CPR?

____

____

____

____

____

First Aid for Shock *(page 747)*

Shock is *a failure of the cardiovascular system to keep an adequate supply of blood circulating to the vital organs of the body*. Some signs of shock are restlessness, nausea, pale or ashen face, cool and moist skin, and rapid breathing and pulse. Here are the steps of first aid.

- Phone 911.
- Control any external bleeding.
- Elevate the legs about 12 inches. Do not do this if there is a head, back, leg injury.
- Never give the person anything to eat or drink.
- Let the person know help is on the way.

4. What are the steps of first aid for shock?

____

____

____

____

____

Reading Tutor, Lesson 2 *(continued)*

USE WITH CHAPTER 28, PAGES 742–748.

First Aid for Choking *(pages 747–748)*

Choking will occur when food or some other object blocks a person's airway. A person may clutch his or her throat with one or both hands. The person may also cough weakly or turn blue in the face. Here are the steps of first aid for choking.

- Ask the person, "Are you choking?" Then ask, "Can you speak?" The item is blocking the airway if the person cannot reply.
- Use abdominal thrust if the person is an adult or a child.
    1. Stand behind the person and place your arms around him or her.
    2. Make a fist with one hand and grasp it with your other hand.
    3. Pull inward and upward just under the ribcage.
- Use your own hand to do this if you are alone and choking. You can also use the back of a chair.
- Hold the baby facedown on your forearm if the person is an infant.
    1. Support the infant's head and neck with your hand and point the head downward.
    2. Give the infant five blows between the shoulder blades with the heel of your hand.
    3. Turn the infant over and do five chest thrusts if the object is still in the throat.
    4. Switch back and forth between five blows between the shoulders and five chest thrusts until the object comes out or the infant begins to breathe and cough.
    5. Call 911 if the object does not come out within one minute.

5. What are the steps of an abdominal thrust for adults?

First Aid and Emergencies: Responding to Common Emergencies

Vocabulary

fracture	A break in the bone *(page 750)*
unconsciousness	A condition in which a person is not alert and aware of his or her surroundings *(page 751)*
concussion	A jarring injury to the brain that affects normal brain function *(page 752)*

Drawing from Experience

Have your ever had a broken bone? Do you know what to do if someone is unconscious? Why do some people get nosebleeds? How should you treat a dog bite? Think about these questions as you read Lesson 3.

In the last lesson, you learned about CPR. In this lesson, you will learn about reacting to common injuries.

Reading Tutor, Lesson 3 *(continued)*

USE WITH CHAPTER 28, PAGES 749–754.

Organizing Your Thoughts

Use the chart below to help you take notes as you read the summaries that follow. In the first oval, list some facts about muscle, joint, and bone injuries. In the next oval, list some facts about unconsciousness. In the next, list the facts about animal bites. In the next, list the facts about nosebleeds. In the last oval, list some of the facts about objects in the eye.

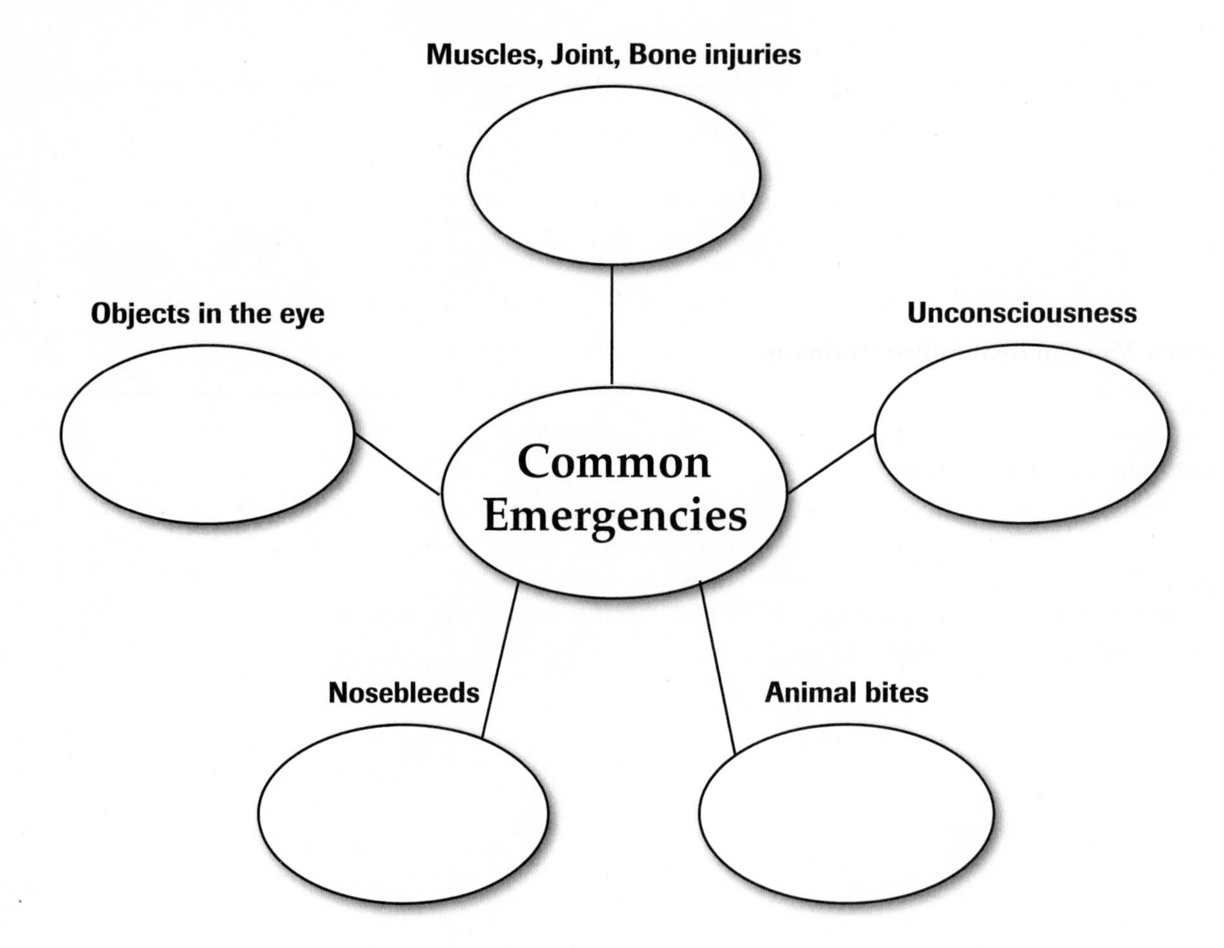

Reading Tutor, Lesson 3 *(continued)*

USE WITH CHAPTER 28, PAGES 749–754.

Read to Learn

Read each passage carefully. Write in complete sentences to answer the following questions.

Muscle, Joint, and Bone Injuries *(pages 749–750)*

A **muscle cramp** is the sudden and painful tightening of a muscle. Try these steps.

- Stretch out the muscle.
- Massage the cramped muscle.
- Apply moist heat.
- Get medical help if the cramp will not go away.

A **strain** is an injury to a muscle. The signs are pain, swelling, bruising, and a loss of movement.

A **sprain** is an injury to a ligament. They may be the result of a twisting force. You can treat minor strains and sprains with the R.I.C.E. method.

- **R**est. Help the person find a comfortable position.
- **I**ce. Ice the area for 20 minutes. Remove for 20 minutes. Ice for 20 minutes. Repeat every 3 waking hours over 3 days.
- **C**ompression. Wear an elastic wrap or firm bandage.
- **E**levation. Raise the limb above the level of the heart.

A **fracture** is *a break in the bone*. A joint may dislocate if it is under extreme stress.

- Keep the person still and call 911.
- Secure the splint to the body with a clean cloth.
- You can make a splint from rolled newspaper or heavy cardboard.
- Seek medical help right away.

1. What are the steps of the R.I.C.E. method?

____

____

____

____

____

____

____

____

Reading Tutor, Lesson 3 *(continued)*

USE WITH CHAPTER 28, PAGES 749–754.

Unconsciousness *(pages 751–752)*

Unconsciousness is a *condition in which a person is not alert and aware of his or her surroundings.* The primary goal is to keep the person from choking. Put the person in the recovery position. This is on the side with the head on a pillow.

- **Fainting** occurs when the blood supply to the head is not enough. It is usually brief. Lie down and put your head between your knees if you feel faint. Put the person on his or her back and elevate the legs if someone else feels faint. Do not put a pillow under the person's head. Loosen clothes and sponge the person's face with water. Roll the person into the recovery position if he or she begins to vomit.
- **Concussion** is *a jarring injury to the brain that affects normal brain function.* The brain can hit the inside of the skull even if there are no signs of injury. Do not move the person if you think there may be a head injury or concussion. Get medical help. Check the person's airway, breathing, and circulation.
- Have a conscious person lie down.
- Use first aid for any bleeding.
- Place the person in the recovery position on his or her side if the person is unconscious and you do not think there is a head or neck injury. Call 911.

2. What are the two types of unconsciousness? What is the recovery position?

____

____

____

____

____

____

____

____

____

Animal Bites *(page 752)*

Rabies is a serious possible result of an animal bite. There is no cure. A person can get a vaccine right away after the dog bites him or her. The person can develop immunity before the symptoms appear.

Reading Tutor, Lesson 3 *(continued)*

USE WITH CHAPTER 28, PAGES 749–754.

Report the incident to the animal control department. They will capture the animal and test it for rabies. There is also a risk of infection or tetanus. You can treat tetanus, but it is best to keep immunizations up to date. Here are some ways to give first aid for a dog bite.

- Wash the bite area with a mild soap and warm water. Remove saliva and other matter.
- Use direct pressure to stop any bleeding.
- Apply ice for 10 minutes if the wound swells.
- Cover the wound with a clean bandage.

3. What are the steps of first aid for a dog bite?

____

____

____

____

____

____

Nosebleeds *(page 753)*

A nosebleed may occur when an object hits a person in the face. It may also happen if the mucous membranes in the nose dry out. A person who keeps getting nosebleeds should see a doctor. Here are some ways to care for the person.

- Keep the person quiet. Have him or her breathe through the nose.
- Have the person sit forward. Do not tilt the head back.
- Press on the bleeding nostril with a clean cloth.
- Maintain the pressure for 15 minutes.
- Repeat this if the nose is still bleeding after 15 minutes.
- Call for medical help if the nose continues to bleed.

4. What are some of the steps to follow when a person has a nosebleed?

____

____

____

____

____

____

Reading Tutor, Lesson 3 *(continued)*

USE WITH CHAPTER 28, PAGES 749–754.

Object in the Eye *(pages 754)*

Dirt, sand, slivers of wood, metal, or other foreign objects in the eye can cause irritation and damage to the eye. Try these steps to help the person remove the object.

- Tell the person to blink several times. Tell him or her not to rub the eye.
- Wash your hands. Try to find the object. Gently pull the lower lid down while the person looks up. Hold the upper lid open and have the person look down.
- Lightly touch the object with a cotton swab or clean cloth if you find it.
- Flush the person's eye with water if you still cannot find the object.
- Tilt the person's head to the side so the affected eye is lower. Do not remove contact lenses. Gently hold the eye open while you pour a steady stream of water into the eye from the inside corner to the outside corner.
- Seek medical help if the object is still in the eye.

5. What are some of the steps you can take to help a person who has an object in his or her eye?

First Aid and Emergencies: Treatment for Poisonings

Vocabulary

poison	Any substance—solid, liquid, or gas—that causes injury, illness, or death when introduced into the body *(page 755)*
venom	A poisonous substance secreted by a snake, spider, or other creature *(page 755)*
poison control center	A 24-hour hot line that provides emergency medical advice on treating poisoning victims *(page 755)*

Drawing from Experience

Has a bee ever stung you? Have you ever gotten a rash from a poisonous plant? What do you know about poison? Do you know what to do when a poisoning occurs? Think about these questions as you read Lesson 4.

In the last lesson, you learned about common injuries. In this lesson, you will learn how to treat a poisoning.

Reading Tutor, Lesson 4 *(continued)*

USE WITH CHAPTER 28, PAGES 755–759.

Organizing Your Thoughts

Use the chart below to help you take notes as you read the summaries that follow. In the first box, list some of the ways to treat poisoning. In the next box, list some of the ways to treat poisonous bites and stings. In the last box, list some of the ways to treat poisonous plants.

First Aid for Poisoning	First Aid for Bites/Stings	First Aid for Plants

Reading Tutor, Lesson 4 *(continued)*

USE WITH CHAPTER 28, PAGES 755–759.

Read to Learn

Read each passage carefully. Write in complete sentences to answer the following questions.

Types of Poisoning *(pages 755–757)*

A **poison** is *any substance—solid, liquid, or gas—that causes injury, illness, or death when introduced into the body.* A poisoning can occur when a substance enters the body that should not be there.

A poison can be a chemical, a pesticide, or an insect bite. **Venom** is *a poisonous substance secreted by a snake, spider, or other creature.* A poison can come from contact with a poisonous plant or food, or when a person breathes poisonous gas or fumes.

A **poison control center** is *a 24-hour hot line that provides emergency medical advice on treating poison victims.* Have the phone number of the center near your phone. You may need to move quickly to prevent a death. First call 911. Then follow these first-aid tips.

- **Swallowed poisons** vary in the kind of first-aid treatment.
  - Find out what the person swallowed and call the poison control center right away.
  - Follow the instructions they give you. They may tell you to dilute the poison with milk or water. They may tell you to induce vomiting. Do NOT do this unless they tell you to.
- **Inhaled poison** is serious because of possible damage to the lungs.
  - Quickly get the person to fresh air. Do not breathe in the fumes.
  - Start rescue breathing if needed.
- **Poison on the skin** may absorb into the skin.
  - Remove the poison as quickly as possible. Remove contaminated clothes.
  - Rinse the person's skin with water for 15 minutes. Then rinse with mild soap and water. Rinse again with fresh water.
  - Have someone call 911 while you are rinsing the skin.
- **Poison in the eye** may absorb quickly.
  - Start flushing the eye with lukewarm water right away. Continue for 15 minutes.
  - Have the person blink the eye. Do not force the eye open and do not rub the eye.
  - Have someone call 911 while you are flushing the eye.

Reading Tutor, Lesson 4 *(continued)*

USE WITH CHAPTER 28, PAGES 755–759.

Here are some tips for your call to the poison center.

- Give your name, location, and phone number.
- Give the name of the substance, when the person swallowed it, and the amount. Give the brand name and a list of the ingredients if you can.
- Describe the state of the person. Give his or her age and weight.
- Follow instructions and answer any questions.

1. What are some of the types of poisoning?

____

____

____

____

First Aid for Poisonous Bites and Stings *(pages 758–759)*

A poisonous bite or sting can come from insects, spiders, ticks, scorpions, snakes, marine life, and other animals.

Snakebite. There are about 20 kinds of poisonous snakes in the United States. Some of these are rattlesnakes, copperheads, coral snakes, and water moccasins. A bite can cause severe pain, but it is not usually fatal. Here are the steps of first aid for a snakebite.

- Get the person to a hospital. Keep the person calm and lying down. The venom will go throughout the body if the person moves around.
- Keep the bitten area below the heart. Do not move a bitten limb. Keep it still.
- Call 911 or have someone else do it. Follow instructions.
- Do not apply ice or heat. Do not give the person aspirin or drugs.
- Maintain breathing. If you are the victim, walk slowly and rest once in awhile to keep the venom from spreading through your blood.

Insect bites and stings. Bees, hornets, yellow jackets, wasps, and fire ants cause painful stings. They can also produce a strong allergic reaction. A person with an allergy needs medical help right away. Here are first-aid steps for insect bites and stings.

- Move to a safe area. Try to scrape the stinger off with a firm, sharp-edged object such as a credit card or fingernail.
- Wash the area with mild soap and water. Apply a cold compress. Apply hydrocortisone cream, calamine lotion, or baking soda to the area several times a day until the pain is gone.
- Call 911 right away if the person begins to have trouble breathing or has signs of a severe reaction.

Reading Tutor, Lesson 4 *(continued)*

USE WITH CHAPTER 28, PAGES 755–759.

2. What are some of the first-aid steps for snakebite?

____

____

____

____

____

____

First Aid for Poisonous Plants *(page 759)*

Most people will develop an allergic skin reaction if they have contact with poison ivy, poison oak, or poison sumac. This may include blistering, swelling, burning, or itching at the site. The person may get a fever. Take the following steps if you come in contact with a poisonous plant.

- Recognize poisonous plants and stay away from them.
- Remove contaminated clothes.
- Flush the affected area with water. Then wash with soap and water.
- Use calamine lotion if the person gets a rash.
- Seek medical help for severe discomfort or pain.

3. What are some of the things you can do for someone who has had contact with a poisonous plant?

____

____

____

____

____

____

Name Class Date

USE WITH CHAPTER 29, PAGES 766–771.

Environmental Health: Air Quality

Vocabulary

air pollution	The contamination of the earth's atmosphere by substances that pose a health threat to living things *(page 766)*
smog	A yellow-brown haze that forms when sunlight reacts with air pollution *(page 767)*
Air Quality Index (AQI)	An index for reporting daily air quality *(page 768)*
asbestos	A fibrous mineral that has fireproof properties, once widely used as an insulator *(page 769)*
radon	An odorless, radioactive gas *(page 769)*
noise pollution	Harmful and unwanted sound of sufficient intensity to damage hearing *(page 770)*
decibel	A unit used to express the relative intensity of loudness of sound *(page 770)*

Drawing from Experience

Do you have smog in the area where you live? How does smog affect your day-to-day activities? Do you have asthma? What causes indoor air pollution? What can you do to help keep our air clean? Think about these questions as you read Lesson 1.

In the last chapter, you learned about first aid. In this lesson, you will learn about air quality.

Organizing Your Thoughts

Use the chart below to help you take notes as you read the summaries that follow. In the first box, list some of the types and factors of outdoor air pollution. In the other box, list some of the types and factors of indoor air pollution.

Outdoor Air Pollution	Indoor Air Pollution

Reading Tutor, Lesson 1 *(continued)*

USE WITH CHAPTER 29, PAGES 766–771.

Read to Learn

Read each passage carefully. Write in complete sentences to answer the following questions.

Air Pollution *(pages 766–767)*

Air pollution is *the contamination of the earth's atmosphere by substances that pose a health threat to living things*. Here are the five major air pollutants.

- **Ozone** is a gas made of three oxygen atoms. Ground-level ozone is a major part of smog. **Smog** is *a yellow-brown haze that forms when the sun reacts with air pollution*. Car exhaust, factory emissions, and gas vapors are the main sources. It can irritate the lungs and is linked to asthma and some respiratory diseases.
- **Particulate matter (PM)** is a term for dust, dirt, soot, smoke, and mold in the air. Car exhaust, factories, and gases are the source. It can trigger asthma, bronchitis, lung problems, and even death.
- **Carbon monoxide** is a colorless, odorless gas. It forms when carbon in fuel does not burn completely. Car exhaust, factory processes, gas stoves, smoke, and gas space heaters are the sources. It is poisonous. It keeps the body from getting oxygen. It can harm the CNS. It can be fatal.
- **Sulfur dioxide** is a gas made of sulfur and oxygen. It dissolves in water and forms an acid. It forms sulfates. Fuel that contains sulfur, gas taken from oil, and metals taken from ore are the sources. It adds to respiratory and heart and lung diseases.
- **Nitrogen oxides** is a term for a group of highly reactive gases. Cars and electric utilities are the main sources. These gases help form ground-level ozone. They can cause or trigger respiratory problems.

1. What are the five main air pollutants?

____

____

____

____

____

Reducing Air Pollution *(page 768)*

The **Air Quality Index** is *an index for reporting daily air quality*. It alerts people to the health concerns of polluted air. Here are some of the ways that you and your family can reduce air pollution.

- **Reduce car use.** Walk or ride your bike. Take public transportation. Join a carpool.

Reading Tutor, Lesson 1 *(continued)*

USE WITH CHAPTER 29, PAGES 766–771.

- **Conserve energy.** Turn off the lights when you are not using them. Set the air conditioner at a higher level. Put on an extra layer of clothes instead of turning up the heat.
- **Use air-friendly machinery.** Lawn mowers, chain saws, and leaf blowers emit pollutants. Use manual tools when you can.

2. What are some of the ways that you can reduce air pollution?

____

____

____

____

Indoor Air Pollution *(pages 769–770)*

Indoor air pollutants may be 2 to 5 times higher than outdoor levels.

- **Asbestos** is *a fibrous mineral that has fireproof properties.* Tiny fibers of the mineral go into the air when materials made of asbestos fall apart. It can cause lung cancer.
- Household cleaning products, stoves, furnaces, and tobacco smoke can all pollute the air. Having no source of ventilation or fresh air may also add to the problem.
- Lead exposure can cause kidney, liver, and brain damage.
- **Radon** is *an odorless, radioactive gas.* It causes lung cancer. It forms in rock and can seep into the house from below. The only way to check radon levels is to get home testing.

Indoor air pollution can cause you to have runny eyes and nose, sore throat, headaches, and more. It can cause asthma. You must identify the pollutants to help deal with indoor pollution.

- Make sure your house has enough ventilation and fresh air coming in.
- Make sure that heaters and furnaces have vents.
- There are detectors for carbon monoxide and radon.
- Get help to remove asbestos or lead.

3. What are some of the ways that you can deal with indoor air pollution?

____

____

____

____

Reading Tutor, Lesson 1 *(continued)*

USE WITH CHAPTER 29, PAGES 766–771.

Noise Pollution *(pages 770–771)*

Noise pollution is *harmful and unwanted sound of enough intensity to damage hearing*. A **decibel** is *a unit used to express the relative intensity of the loudness of sound*. Normal speaking is about 65 decibels. Noise about 85 decibels can cause a hearing loss. It may return later. A long exposure to high levels of noise can cause long-term hearing damage.

Power lawn mowers are at 90 decibels and a chain saw is 110 decibels. Amplified music is at 120 and a jet engine at takeoff is at 140.

You can reduce noise pollution by keeping the volume down on your stereo and radio. Try to avoid using the car horn. Use manual tools instead of power tools when you can.

4. What are some of the ways that you can help reduce noise pollution?

____

____

____

____

____

____

USE WITH CHAPTER 29, PAGES 772–776.

Environmental Health: Protecting Land and Water

Vocabulary

biodegradable	Able to be broken down by microorganisms in the environment *(page 772)*
landfill	An area that has been safeguarded to prevent disposed wastes from contaminating groundwater *(page 772)*
hazardous waste	A substance that is explosive, corrosive, highly reactive, or toxic to humans or other life forms *(page 773)*
deforestation	Destruction of forests *(page 774)*
urban sprawl	The spreading of city development (houses, shopping centers, businesses, and schools) onto undeveloped land *(page 774)*
wastewater	Used water that comes from homes, communities, farms, and businesses *(page 775)*

Drawing from Experience

Have you ever seen trash floating in a river? Where does the trash go that you throw into your trash can? What can you do to help keep our land and water clean? Think about these questions as you read Lesson 2.

In the last lesson, you learned about air quality. In this lesson, you will learn about land and water pollution.

Reading Tutor, Lesson 2 *(continued)*

USE WITH CHAPTER 29, PAGES 772–776.

Organizing Your Thoughts

Use the chart below to help you take notes as you read the summaries that follow. In the first box, list some of the facts about waste disposal and land pollution. In the other box, list some of the factors about water pollution.

Land Pollution	Water Pollution

Reading Tutor, Lesson 2 *(continued)*

USE WITH CHAPTER 29, PAGES 772–776.

Read to Learn

Read each passage carefully. Write in complete sentences to answer the following questions.

Waste Disposal *(pages 772–773)*

Some waste is **biodegradable.** This means that *microorganisms in the environment can break it down*. We must find other waste disposal when the materials are not biodegradable.

A **landfill** is *an area that is safeguarded to prevent disposed wastes from contaminating groundwater*. We locate them away from certain areas to protect the water that collects under the earth's surface. Landfill owners must line them with special material to stop any leakage. They must reduce odor and control rodents.

A **hazardous waste** is *a substance that is explosive, corrosive, highly reactive, or toxic to humans or other life forms*. Some of these are paints, solvents, and oils. Some others are batteries, pesticides, and some cleaning materials. You must dispose of many of these at a special disposal site.

1. What is a landfill?

____

____

____

____

____

____

Expansion and Development *(pages 773–774)*

Population growth can affect the land. We need room for new cities. This affects our wilderness areas and rain forests.

Deforestation means *destruction of forests*. Many nations in Central America, Africa, and Asia are growing. They clear rain forests for fuel and to make room for farms.

These large forests have a role in soil erosion, floods, and sediment in rivers and lakes. Clearing the forests also changes local patterns of rain. Rainfall goes down when there are no trees. The region gets hotter and drier and it may turn into a desert.

Urban sprawl is *the spread of city development (houses, shopping centers, businesses, and schools) onto open land*. Runoff from parking lots and fertilizer from lawns may ruin the drinking water. Air quality gets worse as more and more cars enter an area.

Reading Tutor, Lesson 2 *(continued)*

USE WITH CHAPTER 29, PAGES 772–776.

Cities try to find ways to reduce the use of our resources. They work to lower the air and land pollution. They try to locate schools and stores close to homes. People can walk to these places and do not need to use their cars. They include public buses and trains to lower the number of cars going back and forth to work each day.

2. What are two of the ways that population growth can affect the land?

____

____

____

____

____

Water Supplies and Pollution *(pages 774–775)*

The EPA requires water suppliers to check and test water before they send it to people's homes. There are times when pollution does get into the drinking water. The supplier shuts down and fixes the problem when this occurs.

Many of our rivers, lakes, and waters are not safe to swim in. Here are some of the sources of water pollution.

- Illegal dumping causes some of our water pollution.
- Other pollution comes from runoff. This is rainwater or snow that runs over the land and picks up pesticides, fertilizer, and other wastes. This can pollute the drinking water.
- **Wastewater** is *used water that comes from homes, towns, farms, and businesses.* It holds human and animal wastes, metals, and germs. Some of this water must cool before it goes back into the environment. The EPA regulates this process under the Clean Water Act.
- **Sediment** from land erosion can ruin water ecosystems. It can clog lakes and stream channels. It can clog harbors.
- **Oil** pollution can come from cleaning oil tankers. It can come from oil from offshore drilling rigs. It can come from people who dump motor oil in storm drains.

3. What are some of the sources of water pollution?

____

____

____

____

____

Reading Tutor, Lesson 2 *(continued)*

USE WITH CHAPTER 29, PAGES 772–776.

Reducing the Risks *(page 776)*

You and your family can take steps to keep water clean.

- Recycle materials to reduce the waste that goes into landfills.
- Throw away all materials in the right place. Do not put oils or paints in the trash. Do not pour motor oil down the drain. Take these items to the right collection site.
- Follow directions carefully when using cleaning products and fertilizers. Do not use them more than you need to.
- Reduce your use of water. Repair leaks. Find out how much water your lawn really needs.

4. What are some of the ways that you and your family can help keep water clean?

____

____

____

____

____

____

____

Name Class Date

Lesson 3

Reading Tutor

USE WITH CHAPTER 29, PAGES 777–781.

Environmental Health: Advocating for a Healthy Environment

Vocabulary

conservation	The production and preservation of the environment by managing natural resources to prevent abuse, destruction, and neglect *(page 777)*
precycling	Reducing waste before it is generated *(page 779)*
recycling	The processing of waste materials so that they can be used again in some form *(page 779)*

Drawing from Experience

So you save your aluminum cans? Do you turn out the light when you leave a room? What are some of the ways that you and your family can protect our environment? Think about these questions as you read Lesson 3.

In the last lesson, you learned about land and water pollution. In this lesson, you will learn about conservation.

Reading Tutor, Lesson 3 *(continued)*

USE WITH CHAPTER 29, PAGES 777–781.

Organizing Your Thoughts

Use the chart below to help you take notes as you read the summaries that follow. In the first box, list some of the ways to conserve resources. In the next box, list some of the ways to recycle.

Ways to Conserve	Ways to Recycle

Reading Tutor, Lesson 3 *(continued)*

USE WITH CHAPTER 29, PAGES 777–781.

Read to Learn

Read each passage carefully. Write in complete sentences to answer the following questions.

Conserving Resources *(pages 777–778)*

Conservation is *the protection and preservation of the environment by managing natural resources to prevent abuse, destruction, and neglect*. Here are some of the ways that you can conserve natural resources.

- **Heating and cooling**
  - Seal leaks around doors and windows.
  - Keep doors and windows shut.
  - Close the fireplace vents,
  - Wear an extra layer of clothes in the winter.
  - Turn the heat down when you go to bed.
  - Keep the thermostat at about 78 degrees during the summer.
  - Use a fan to keep air circulating.
- **Water conservation**
  - Wash clothes in warm or cold water instead of hot.
  - Do a full load when you wash clothes or dishes.
  - Fix leaky faucets.
  - Never let water run when you do not need it.
  - Use an efficient toilet tank to reduce water use.
- **Lighting and appliances**
  - Replace regular light bulbs with fluorescent bulbs.
  - Switch off lights when you leave a room.
  - Turn off the TV, radio, computer, and other appliances when they are not in use.
  - Use a microwave or toaster oven to cook a small amount of food.
  - Do not preheat your oven for longer than necessary.

1. What are some of the ways that you and your family can help conserve natural resources?

____

____

____

____

____

Reading Tutor, Lesson 3 *(continued)*

USE WITH CHAPTER 29, PAGES 777–781.

Precycling and Recycling *(pages 779–780)*

Precycling and recycling are two ways to reduce the amount of waste. **Precycling** is *reducing waste before you generate it*. It means buying and using products wisely. Here are some of the ways that you can precycle.

- Use cloth napkins instead of paper ones.
- Purchase products in bulk or in the biggest box you can find. This reduces packaging.
- Buy laundry detergent and fruit juice as a concentrate.
- Choose products that can be recycled. Look for the code on plastic products.
- Reuse paper or plastic shopping bags.
- Donate goods or clothes you do not need to charity.

Recycling is *the processing of waste materials so that we can use them again*. Here are some of the benefits of recycling.

- **Recycling conserves resources.** Making a can from recycled aluminum takes only 10 percent of the energy needed to make a new can from raw materials.
- **Recycling reduces the use of landfills.** It is important to reduce our amount of waste. The space in landfills is not endless.
- **Recycling protects environmental health.** Recycling uses materials that might harm the environment if we put them in landfills. Recycling leads to a healthy and clean environment.

Here are some tips for recycling and reducing waste.

- **Aluminum.** Rinse cans and crush them to save space.
- **Cardboard.** Flatten the boxes and tie them together.
- **Glass.** Rinse all glass containers. Recycle the metal lids.
- **Plastics.** Look for the code on the container. Most places will take those that are a 1, 2, or 3.
- **Newspaper.** Stack newspapers and tie the bundles with string.
- **Glossy paper.** Get your name off of mailing lists.

2. What is precycling? What are some of the benefits of recycling?

____

____

____

____

____

Reading Tutor, Lesson 3 *(continued)*

USE WITH CHAPTER 29, PAGES 777–781.

Protecting the Environment *(page 781)*

Here are some of the ways that you can involve yourself in protecting the environment.

- **Become an informed consumer.** Evaluate products. Give feedback to the companies on ways that they can help protect the environment.
- **Contact organizations that promote the conservation of resources and educate people on environmental issues.** Ask for ideas on how to conserve. You may want to join a group to find out more about current health issues.
- **Take action against local polluters.** Find local polluters and work to protect the health of your family and friends. Join with others to tell elected officials about your concerns.

3. What are some of the ways that you can work to protect your family and your environment?

____

____

____

____

____

____

CHAPTER 1

Lesson 1 Read to Learn

1. It is important to stay well because being well helps you reach and keep your goals.
2. A person can be health literate by:
   - Being a critical thinker and problem solver.
   - Being a responsible and productive citizen.
   - Being a self-directed learner.
   - Being a good communicator.

Lesson 2 Read to Learn

1. The three parts of your health triangle are:
   1) Physical health—taking care of your body.
   2) Mental/emotional health—accepting who you are.
   3) Social health—getting along with others.
2. Some of the things that have a major influence on your health are as follows:
   - Heredity
   - Environment
   - Attitude
   - Behavior
   - The media
   - Technology

Lesson 3 Read to Learn

1. Some of the types of risk behavior that can harm your health are as follows:
   - Behavior that adds to the risk of injury
   - Tobacco use
   - Alcohol and other drug use
   - Sexual activity
   - Poor eating habits
   - Lack of physical activity
2. Some of the reasons that teens should abstain from risk behaviors:
   - The use of tobacco, alcohol, and other drugs can cause addiction and serious harm to the body.
   - Risk behaviors can upset your family and friends.
   - Some risk behaviors are not legal.
   - Sexual activity can cause unplanned pregnancy and sexually transmitted diseases.

CHAPTER 2

Lesson 1 Read to Learn

1. The three kinds of skills that are a part of interpersonal communication are as follows:
   - Communication skills
   - Refusal skills
   - Conflict resolution skills
2. You can practice healthy behavior and deal with stress by eating nutritious food; wearing safety gear; getting regular checkups; avoiding tobacco, alcohol, and other drugs; expressing your feelings in healthy ways; having healthy friendships; and being physically active.
3. The two types of influences on your health are internal influences and external influences.
4. Some reliable sources of health information:
   - Parents, guardians, and other trusted adults
   - The library
   - The Internet
   - Newspapers and magazine articles
   - Government agencies, health care providers, and health care organizations
5. Advocacy is taking action to influence others to address a health concern or to support a health belief.

Lesson 2 Read to Learn

1. The six steps of the decision-making process are:
   1) State the situation.
   2) List the options.
   3) Weigh the possible outcomes.
   4) Consider values.
   5) Make a decision and act on it.
   6) Evaluate the decision.
2. The steps of an action plan that can help you reach your goals are:
   1) Set a goal and write it down.
   2) List the steps.
   3) Identify sources of help.
   4) Set a time frame.
   5) Evaluate your progress.
   6) Reward yourself.

Lesson 3 Read to Learn

1. Character is those qualities that describe how a person thinks, feels, and behaves.
2. The six primary traits of good character are:
   1) Trustworthiness
   2) Respect
   3) Responsibility
   4) Fairness
   5) Caring
   6) Citizenship
3. Some of the ways that you can develop good character include the following:
   - Standing up for your beliefs.
   - Learning from others who have good character traits. Having good role models.
   - Being a volunteer at your school or in your community.
4. Some of the ways that you can show good character:
   - Show you are reliable and trustworthy at home. Do your chores.
   - Show you have respect for teachers and fellow students. Follow school rules.
   - Show you are a good citizen by obeying laws and respecting other people.

CHAPTER 3

Lesson 1 Read to Learn

1. A health consumer is anyone who purchases or uses health products or services.
2. Some of the things to look at when you comparison shop are cost, features, quality, warranty, safety, Underwriters Laboratory (UL) logo, recommendations.
3. Some of the rights you have when you buy a product or service are the right to Safety, to choose, be informed, be heard, have problems corrected, and consumer education.
4. Some of the things to think of when you shop online are cost, convenience, and product information.

Lesson 2 Read to Learn

1. Some of the types of health services are general care from a primary care physician, specialist care, and preventive care.
2. Some of the types of health care facilities are private practices, clinics, group practices, hospitals, emergency rooms, and urgent care centers.
3. The three major types of managed care plans:
   - Health maintenance organization (HMO)
   - Preferred provider organization (PPO)
   - Point of service (POS) plans
4. Some of the other ways to provide health care are birthing centers, drug treatment centers, continuing care and assisted living facilities, hospices, and telemedicine.
5. Some of the things to do when you go see the doctor are to write down your reasons for seeing the doctor, ask questions about anything you do not understand, tell the nurse about any allergies you have, and ask the pharmacist about any type of medicine that the doctor may order for you.

Lesson 3 Read to Learn

1. If you buy an item that is defective, you can take it back to the store where you bought it, send it back to the company that made it, read the directions to be sure you are using the item correctly, decide if you want a new item or your money back, and more.
2. Some of the products and treatments that have health fraud problems are weight loss products, beauty and anti-aging products, and cures for arthritis or other ailments.

Lesson 4 Read to Learn

1. Some of the agencies that work to protect out health include the following:
   - The National Cancer Institute
   - The Environmental Protection Agency
   - The Occupational Safety and Health Administration (OSHA)
   - The U.S. Department of Agriculture
   - The Department of Health and Human Services
   - and more.
2. Teens can advocate for public health by following all health and safety laws, practicing healthy behavior, staying away from risky actions, being a part of health events such as a 10K walk, supporting groups that deal with public events; and reporting things you see that may be a harm to public health.

CHAPTER 4

Lesson 1 Read to Learn

1. Physical fitness is the ability to carry out daily tasks easily and have energy left over to respond to unexpected demands.
2. The benefits of physical activity include strong muscles and bones, good posture, a stronger heart; reduced stress, better sleep, self-confidence, and more.
3. The risks of not being active include weight gain; diabetes, osteoporosis, higher stress, and less opportunity to meet friends who have an active lifestyle.
4. Physical activity helps you keep a healthy weight because it makes your metabolic rate go up and you burn more calories.
5. You can be active for life by doing 60 minutes of physical activity every day, by walking or riding your bike; by hiking or swimming, by having a basketball game with friends, and more.

Lesson 2 Read to Learn

1. The five elements of fitness are:
   1) Cardiorespiratory endurance
   2) Muscular strength
   3) Muscular endurance
   4) Flexibility
   5) Body composition
2. You can improve your fitness with aerobic exercise, anaerobic exercise, stretching exercises, getting enough calcium, and more.

Lesson 3 Read to Learn

1. A teen can be active every day by doing moderate-intensity activities, doing aerobic activities, doing anaerobic activities, doing flexibility activities, and by limiting sedentary activities.
2. Some factors that may affect your choice of activities are cost, where you live, your level of health, time and place, personal safety, comprehensive planning, and cross training.
3. The three basic stages of each activity are:
   1) the warm-up
   2) the workout
   3) the cool-down
4. A resting heart rate is the number of times your heart beats in one minute when you are not active.

Lesson 4 Read to Learn

1. Some of the ways to prepare for physical activity are to eat nutritious foods, get lots of sleep, and avoid harmful substances.
2. You can lower your risk of injury when you are being active if you get a health screening, use the right safety gear, be aware of who and what is near you, play at your skill level, warm-up and cool-down, stay in the right area; obey the rules, and more.

Lesson 5 Read to Learn

1. Some of the health risks related to weather are overexertion, heat cramps, heatstroke, frostbite, and hypothermia.
2. The parts of the R.I.C.E. method of treatment are:
   1) Rest
   2) Ice
   3) Compression
   4) Elevation
3. Some of the major types of sports injuries are fractures and dislocations, tendonitis, and concussions.

CHAPTER 5

Lesson 1 Read to Learn

1. Good nutrition provides the body with what it needs to be well and have energy.
2. Some of the things that can influence your food choices are family, friends, and peers; cultural and ethnic background; ease and cost; and advertising.
3. Some of the long-term benefits of healthy eating habits when you are a teen include the following:
   - Keeping a healthy weight
   - Avoiding obesity and type 2 diabetes
   - Lowering risk for heart disease, stroke, some cancers, and osteoporosis

Lesson 2 Read to Learn

1. Simple carbohydrates are sugars and complex carbohydrates are starches.
2. Complete proteins have all nine essential amino acids. Incomplete proteins do not have all nine essential amino acids.
3. Saturated fatty acids are solid at room temperature. Unsaturated fatty acids are liquid at room temperature.

4. Water-soluble vitamins dissolve in water and pass into the blood. Fat-soluble vitamins are absorbed in fat and are stored in your liver and kidneys.
5. Some of the important minerals are calcium, phosphorous, magnesium, and iron.
6. Water benefits your entire body by moving other nutrients, carrying waste out of your body, helping you digest food, and maintaining your body heat.

Lesson 3 Read to Learn

1. The *Dietary Guidelines for Americans* is a set of recommendations for healthful eating and active living.
2. Two guidelines to keep you fit:
   1) Aim for a healthy weight
   2) Be physically active every day
3. The six parts of the Food Guide Pyramid:
   1) Bread, Cereal, Rice, and Pasta Group (Grains Group)
   2) Vegetable Group
   3) Fruit Group
   4) Milk, Yogurt, and Cheese group (Milk group)
   5) Meat, Poultry, Fish, Dry beans, Eggs, and Nuts Group (Meat and Beans group)
   6) Fats, Oils, and Sweets
4. Some of the ways to make healthy food choices include the following:
   - Choose a diet that is low in fat and low in cholesterol.
   - Choose drinks and food with less sugar.
   - Choose food with less salt.
5. You can make a healthy eating plan by eating breakfast, eating healthy snacks, and eating right when you eat out.

Lesson 4 Read to Learn

1. Some of the facts you will find on a product label include the following:
   - Serving size and servings per container
   - Calories and calories from fat
   - Names and amounts of nutrients
   - Percent Daily Values
2. Some of the nutrient terms you will find on a product label are light or lite; less; free; more; high, rich in, or excellent source of; and lean.
3. Two types of food sensitivity are food allergy and food intolerance.
4. Some of the things you can do to keep food safe are to clean, separate, cook, and chill.

CHAPTER 6

Lesson 1 Read to Learn

1. Your body image is the way you see your body. You can maintain a healthy weight by burning the same number of calories that you eat.
2. The Body Mass Index (BMI) is a ratio that allows you to assess your body size in relation to your height and weight.
3. Body composition is the ratio of your body fat to your lean body tissue.
4. The risks of being overweight are strain on the heart and the skeletal system, high blood pressure, and type 2 diabetes. The risks of being underweight are weakness and illness.
5. Some of the ways to manage your weight are to figure out your appropriate weight, set realistic goals, personalize your plan, put your goal and plan in writing; and evaluate your progress.

Lesson 2 Read to Learn

1. Some of the types of risky weight loss plans are fad diets, liquid diets, fasting, and diet pills.
2. Weight cycling is the repeated pattern of loss and regain of body weight.
3. The types of eating disorders:
   - Anorexia nervosa
   - Bulimia nervosa
   - Binge eating disorder

Lesson 3 Read to Learn

1. Some tips to follow for good sports nutrition:
   - Eat nutrient-dense foods.
   - Drink lots of water.
   - Follow a sensible plan if you need to lose weight.
   - Follow a balanced plan of nutrition and exercise to gain weight.
   - Eat 3 to 4 hours before you compete.
2. The four types of vegetarian eating plans:
   1) lacto-ovo vegetarianism
   2) lacto vegetarianism
   3) ovo vegetarianism
   4) vegan

3. A dietary supplement is a nonfood form of one or more nutrients.
4. Some of the nutrients a pregnant female may need to take are folate, iron, and calcium.

CHAPTER 7

Lesson 1 Read to Learn

1. Some of the traits of good mental/emotional health:
   - Positive self-esteem
   - Sense of belonging
   - Positive outlook
   - Autonomy
2. The five levels of needs:
   1) physical needs
   2) safety needs
   3) the need to love and belong
   4) the need to be valued and recognized
   5) the need to reach your potential
3. The ways you choose to meet your needs affects your mental/emotional health.
   - Having respectful friends will help meet your need for love.
   - Some teens may join a gang to meet the need to belong.
   - Some teens may have sexual activity to meet the need to feel love.
   - Finding healthy ways to meet your emotional needs with help you have good mental health.
4. Some of the things that influence your personality are heredity, environment, and behavior.
5. Some of the ways that you can promote good mental and emotional health are to avoid gangs and sexual activity, deal with your emotions and cope with stress, and meet your needs in healthy ways.

Lesson 2 Read to Learn

1. Some of the things that make up your personal identity are your name and age; your role as a son, daughter, brother, sister, or student; your interests; your likes and dislikes; your talents and abilities; your values and beliefs; and your goals.
2. Some of the assets that can help you grow up to be a healthy person are family support, empowerment, boundaries and expectations, good use of time; commitment to learning; positive values, social skills, and positive identity.
3. Some of the ways to build a healthy identity:
   - Know your strengths and weaknesses.
   - Show positive values.
   - Have a purpose to your life.
   - Form healthy relationships.
   - Give to your community.
   - Avoid unhealthy risk behaviors.
4. Some tips to build self esteem and positive outlook are to look at events realistically, accept constructive criticism, and listen to your self-talk.

Lesson 3 Read to Learn

1. Emotions or feelings are signals that tell your mind and body how to react.
2. Some of the ways to identify your emotions:
   - You are happy if you feel pleased or good or positive.
   - You are sad if you feel disappointed or feel a loss.
   - You feel love if you feel affection and concern and respect.
   - Your feel empathy if you imagine and understand how someone else feels.

Lesson 4 Read to Learn

1. Some ways to deal with your emotions in a positive way:
   - Think about your emotion and ask yourself what you are reacting to.
   - Think about the situation.
   - Think about the consequences.
   - Get rid of your negative feelings by doing physical activity.
   - Seek help from a parent or adult.
2. Some of the ways to deal with difficult emotions are to use defense mechanisms, handle your fear; deal with your guilt, manage your anger, and more.

CHAPTER 8

Lesson 1 Read to Learn

1. Stress is the reaction of the body and mind to everyday challenges and demands.
2. We react to stress in positive or negative ways by being motivated to do well, having extra energy to reach our goals, playing better in a stressful game, losing sleep, and worrying.

3. Some of the causes of stress are biological stressors, environmental stressors, thinking stressors, personal behavior stressors, or life situation stressors.
4. The three parts of the body's stress response:
   1) alarm
   2) resistance
   3) fatigue
5. Stress has physical effects such as psychosomatic response, headache, asthma, and more. Stress has mental/emotional and social effects such as difficulty paying attention, mood swings, and risk of substance abuse.
6. Some of the ways to deal with chronic stress include: engaging in physical activity; looking for support among friends and family; finding a hobby or activity that relaxes you; and avoiding the use of tobacco, alcohol, or other drugs.

Lesson 2 Read to Learn

1. Some of the things that may trigger stress are life events, physical stressors, or daily hassles.
2. Some of the ways to use refusal skills to avoid stress are walk away from a tense situation, calm down, and say no when necessary.
3. Some of the ways to deal with stress are plan ahead; get plenty of sleep; get regular physical activity; eat nutritious foods; and avoid tobacco, alcohol, and other drugs.
4. Some of the techniques that you can use to help deal with stress include redirect your energy, relax and laugh, keep a positive outlook, and seek out support.

Lesson 3 Read to Learn

1. Anxiety is the condition of feeling uneasy or worried about what may happen. Some of the symptoms of anxiety are feelings of fear or dread, sweating or trembling, and rapid heart rate or dizziness.
2. The two types of depression are reactive depression and major depression.
3. You can get help for serious anxiety and depression from a doctor, a parent or other adult, a counselor, school psychologist, or other health care professional.

Lesson 4 Read to Learn

1. Resiliency is the ability to adapt and recover from disappointment, difficulty, or crisis.
2. Some of the factors that affect teen resiliency are external factors such as family, school, community and peers. Internal factors include commitment to learn, positive values, social competency, and positive identity.
3. Some ways to build resiliency by making your protective factors strong are as follows:
   - Be a part of activities at school.
   - Commit to learn.
   - Stand up for your beliefs.
   - Be honest with yourself and others.
   - Resist negative peer pressure.

CHAPTER 9

Lesson 1 Read to Learn

1. A mental disorder is an illness of the mind that can affect the thoughts, feelings, and behaviors of a person, preventing him or her from leading a happy, healthful, and productive life.
2. Some of the types of mental disorders:
   - Anxiety disorders
   - Mood disorders
   - Eating disorders
   - Conduct disorders
   - Schizophrenia
   - Personality disorders

Lesson 2 Read to Learn

1. Some of the risk factors of suicide are a history of abuse a history of suicide tries, and a family history of emotional disorders or suicide.
2. Some of the ways that you can help prevent suicide are to start a meaningful talk, show support and ask questions, try to get the person to seek help, and get counseling for close friends of suicide victims.

Lesson 3 Read to Learn

1. Some of the reasons to seek help for mental problems are: You feel trapped with no way out; your feelings affect your sleep and eating habits; your family and friends say they are concerned; and more.

2. Some of the signs that a person may need help for mental problems: you feel sad for no reason for a long period of time, you often have angry outbursts, you have lots of fear, anger, or anxiety at the world.
3. Some of the types of mental health therapy are psychotherapy, behavior therapy, cognitive therapy, group therapy, and biomedical therapy.

Lesson 4 Read to Learn

1. Some of the types of loss: you miss a chance to play in a big game; you break up with a good friend; your pet dies; a friend or family member passes away; or you have to move and change schools.
2. The steps of the grieving process:
   1) denial or numbness
   2) emotional releases
   3) anger
   4) bargaining
   5) depression
   6) remorse
   7) acceptance
   8) hope
3. A person can do some of these things to cope with the death of a loved one: remember good things about the person; think about the good times you had; talk with others about the person.
4. To cope with disasters or crises: Spend time with others and talk about your feelings; get back to your daily routine as soon as possible; eat nutritious foods; and do something positive for your community.

CHAPTER 10

Lesson 1 Read to Learn

1. Some of the common types of relationships: family relationships, friendships, community relationships, and roles with family and friends.
2. Some of the skills and traits that you need to build healthy relationships include communication, cooperation, and compromise; mutual respect and consideration; honesty; dependability; and commitment.
3. The six main traits of good character:
   1) trustworthiness
   2) fairness
   3) respect
   4) caring
   5) responsibility
   6) citizenship

Lesson 2 Read to Learn

1. The three basic skills we need to communicate well are as follow:
   1) speaking skills
   2) listening skills
   3) body language
2. Some of the things that may block communication: image and identity issues, unrealistic expectations, lack of trust, prejudice, and gender stereotyping.
3. Constructive criticism means nonhostile comments that point out problems to help a person improve.
4. Some of the benefits of giving praise to others: It makes you feel good about yourself; it makes you feel good about the person who gave you the praise; it builds healthy relationships; and it can show others that you care about them.

Lesson 3 Read to Learn

1. Some of the common causes of conflict: power struggles, loyalty, jealousy and envy, property disputes, and territory and space.
2. Some tips for resolving conflicts: take time to calm down and think over the situation; take turns telling each side of the story; ask questions to clarify; think about possible solutions; agree on a solution; follow up to see if the solution worked.
3. Some facts about mediation: It takes place in a neutral location; it is confidential; each person tells his or her side; the mediator gives a summary; each side speaks to the other through the mediator; each side signs an agreement.

CHAPTER 11

Lesson 1 Read to Learn

1. A family is the basic unit of society.
2. Families affect the three sides of the health triangle in these ways:
   - Physical—The family provides food, clothing, and shelter to its members.

- Mental/emotional—the family cares for and supports each other.
- Social—the family teaches communication skills, values, and traditions.

3. Some of the roles of family members include:
   - Parents set limits and protect the health and safety of the children.
   - Grandparents may pass along family history.
   - Aunts or uncles may give advice.
   - Teens may watch younger children.
4. Some of the ways to make your family strong: Show care and love; show support; show trust; show commitment; be responsible; spend time together.

Lesson 2 Read to Learn

1. The two major types of change in a family are: change in the structure of the family and change in the circumstances of the family.
2. Some of the types of change in family structure include separation and divorce, remarriage, and death of a family member.
3. Some of the types of change in family circumstances include: moving, financial problems, illness and disability, and drug and alcohol abuse.
4. Some of the ways to cope with family changes: Do what you can to help; read books about the subject or talk to others who have similar problems; and use stress-management techniques.

Lesson 3 Read to Learn

1. Some of the types of family violence and abuse: Domestic violence, including emotional, physical, and sexual abuse; spousal abuse; and child abuse.
2. Some of the ways to break the cycle of violence: Tell a trusted adult; call an abuse hotline; and report the abuse to the police.
3. Some of the ways to avoid or prevent abuse: Recognize the abuse; resist the abuse; and report the abuse.

Lesson 4 Read to Learn

1. Some of the sources of help for families in need: community services, support groups, counseling, and mediation.
2. Some of the ways to keep your family healthy: Cooperate, show appreciation, be a good communicator, offer help, be empathetic, work to resolve conflict.

CHAPTER 12

Lesson 1 Read to Learn

1. Some of the types of friendship are these: a platonic friendship, a casual friendship; a close friendship, and a clique.
2. Some of the ways to build a healthy friendship include being loyal, encouraging each other, and respecting each other.

Lesson 2 Read to Learn

1. The types of peer pressure are positive peer pressure and negative peer pressure. Manipulation is an indirect, dishonest way to control others.
2. Some of the ways to resist negative peer pressure are to avoid it, be assertive, and use refusal skills.

Lesson 3 Read to Learn

1. Dating is a way to get to know a person of the opposite gender. Some of the activities you can do on a date are: go to the movies, go to a dinner or school dance, or go to sports activities.
2. Some of the facts about dating relationships include the following: Some teens choose to date only one person, limiting chances to meet others; ending dating relationships can be hard.
3. Some of the limits you set regarding dating might include putting a limit on the age of the person you date, limiting the places you go and how you will get there, limits to avoid risky situations, and being clear and firm about your decision to abstain from sexual activity.

Lesson 4 Read to Learn

1. Some tips to help you abstain are as follows: Establish your priorities, set limits on how you express your affection, share your thoughts with your partner, talk to a trusted adult, avoid high pressure situations, and do not use alcohol or other drugs.
2. Some of the reasons to practice abstinence include: legal issues, effects on physical health, effects on emotional health, and effects on social health.
3. Ways to say no to sexual activity: If your date says, "If you love me you will," you say, "If you care about me, you won't pressure me."Accept all reasonable responses.

CHAPTER 13

Lesson 1 Read to Learn

1. Some of the protective factors that can reduce a teen's risk of violence include the following:
   - Individual factors such as no history of violent behavior, getting along with others
   - Family factors such as parents monitoring a teen's behavior, or assessing peers
   - Peer/school factors such as a teen's friends avoiding high-risk behavior, a teen who has a commitment to school
   - Community factors such as a teen who helps out in the community.
2. Some of the ways that you can keep yourself and your home safe to avoid unsafe areas; walk briskly; park your car in a well-lit area; use body language and self-defense; be assertive; lock doors with a bolt; never open the door to strangers.
3. Some of the ways to make your community safe include increasing police patrol, having a Neighborhood Watch program, having after-school programs, and improving lights in parks and playgrounds.

Lesson 2 Read to Learn

1. Some of the factors that play a role in school violence are bullying, sexual harassment, and gangs.
2. Some of the ways to reduce violence in schools are to report anyone who has a gun, report acts or threats of violence, use conflict resolution skills, use refusal skills, have a zero-tolerance policy for weapons and drugs, have metal detectors, have a "closed" campus, use peer mediation.

Lesson 3 Read to Learn

1. Some of the reasons that violence occurs include the need to control others, a way of expressing anger, prejudice, and retaliation.
2. Some of the factors that may influence violence are weapons availability, the media, alcohol and other drugs, and mental/emotional issues.
3. Some of the types of violence are assault, random violence, homicide, sexual assault, and rape.
4. Here are some facts about gang violence:
   - Teens commit many crimes that are gang-related.
   - Teens may join gangs to be part of a group.
   - Most gangs are involved in violent activities.
   - Teens who join gangs are at risk for arrest, injury, or death.

Lesson 4 Read to Learn

1. Physical abuse and emotional abuse, including verbal abuse and stalking, are some of the kinds of abuse.
2. Some of the signs of dating abuse are expressions of jealousy, attempts to control a partner's behavior, use of insults, and use of guilt.
3. Some of the sources of help for a victim of abuse or rape include parents and guardians; a teacher, coach, or counselor; a clergy member; the police; a doctor; a battered women's shelter; a rape crisis center.
4. Some of the possible ways to break the cycle of violence are to have classes for parents on family life and child development; provide counseling for all victims of abuse and violence; and have treatment programs for abusers.

CHAPTER 14

Lesson 1 Read to Learn

1. The epidermis and the dermis are the main parts of the skin. Some other parts are keratin, lipids, and melanin; sebaceous glands and sebum; blood vessels, and sweat glands.
2. Some of the most common types of skin problems are acne, warts, vitiligo, boils, moles, and melanoma.
3. Dandruff and head lice are some of the common types of hair problems.
4. Keeping your nails clean and trimmed, using a nail file to smooth nails, keeping cuticles pushed back, and cutting toenails straight across are some of the ways to take care of your nails.

Lesson 2 Read to Learn

1. The main parts of the teeth are the crown, neck, and root. Some of the other parts are enamel, calcium, dentin, and pulp.
2. Some of the ways to keep your teeth and mouth healthy: Brush your teeth to remove plaque, floss your teeth, have your dentist clean your teeth, eat a well-balanced diet; and avoid sugary snacks and tobacco.

3. Halitosis, periodontal disease, and malocclusion are some of the problems of the teeth and mouth.

Lesson 3 Read to Learn

1. The lacrimal gland is the gland that secretes tears into ducts that empty into the eye. It protects your eye by moving tears across the eye as you blink.
2. The two main parts of the eye are the optic nerve and the three layers of the eyeball wall. Some of the other parts of the eye are the sclera, the cornea, the choroid, the iris, the pupil, the retina, the rods and cones, the lens, the aqueous humor, and the vitreous humor.
3. 20/20 vision means that when you stand 20 feet away from an eye chart, you can read the top 8 lines.
4. Some of the things that you can do to help keep your eyes healthy are to eat a well-balanced diet, protect your eyes, have regular eye exams, and rest your eyes.
5. Some of the types of vision problems and diseases of the eye are myopia, hyperopia, astigmatism, strabismus, conjunctivitis, detached retina, glaucoma, cataracts, and macular degeneration.

Lesson 4 Read to Learn

1. The outer ear, middle ear, and inner ear are the three main parts of the ear. Some of the other parts are the auricle, external auditory canal, and the eardrum; the auditory ossicles and the eustachian tube; the labyrinth, cochlea, vestibule, and semicircular canals.
2. The vestibule and semicircular canals are the parts of the ear that control your sense of balance.
3. Some of the ways to keep your ears healthy are keep your ears clean, wear a helmet when you play sports, wear a hat that covers the auricles and earlobes in winter, keep foreign objects out of your ears, avoid loud noise
4. Conductive hearing loss, sensorineural hearing loss, and tinnitus are some of the types of problems that occur in the ear.

CHAPTER 15

Lesson 1 Read to Learn

1. Some of the functions of the skeletal system are: it gives support to your upper body and head; it is a strong and mobile framework for muscles to act on; it protects your internal tissues and organs.
2. The axial skeleton and the appendicular skeleton are the two main types of bones. Some of the other bones are long bones, short bones, flat bones, irregular bones; cartilage, joints, ligaments, tendons.

Lesson 2 Read to Learn

1. Some of the things that you can do for your skeletal system include eating foods that have calcium, eating foods that have vitamin D, and engaging on regular physical activity.
2. Some of the types of problems of the skeletal system include fractures, osteoporosis, scoliosis, injuries to the joints, repetitive motion injury.

Lesson 3 Read to Learn

1. The involuntary and voluntary muscles are the two main types of muscles in the body.
2. Some of the types of muscles include smooth muscles, skeletal muscles, and cardiac muscle.
3. Some of the types of muscle problems include bruises, muscle strain or sprain, tendonitis, hernia, and muscular dystrophy.

Lesson 4 Read to Learn

1. The central nervous system (CNS) and the peripheral nervous system (PNS) are the two main parts of the nervous system.
2. The cell body, dendrites, and axons are the three main parts of a neuron.
3. The two main parts of the central nervous system are the spinal cord and the brain. Some of the other parts of the central nervous system are the vertebrae, the spinal meninges, the cerebrospinal fluid; the cerebrum, the cerebellum, and more.
4. The autonomic nervous system and the somatic nervous system are the two main parts of the peripheral nervous system.

Lesson 5 Read to Learn

1. You can care for your nervous system by using helmets and other safety gear, eating a well-balanced diet, checking the depth of water before you dive, and avoiding the use of alcohol and other drugs.
2. Some of the types of head or spinal cord injuries are concussion, contusion, and coma; swelling of the spinal cord, paraplegia; and quadriplegia.

3. Some of the more common types of degenerative diseases are Parkinson's disease, multiple sclerosis, and Alzheimer's disease.
4. Epilepsy and cerebral palsy are some other types of problems of the nervous system.

CHAPTER 16

Lesson 1 Read to Learn

1. Functions of the cardiovascular system include the following: Pump and circulate blood, get nutrients to all cells; deliver oxygen to the lungs; and take waste to the kidneys for removal.
2. Blood vessels, capillaries, and veins are the three main types of blood vessels.
3. B cells, T cells, killer cells, and helper cells are some of the types of lymphocytes.

Lesson 2 Read to Learn

1. Some of the healthy habits that can help you care for your body systems are eating a healthy diet, keeping a healthy weight, doing aerobic exercise, avoiding the use of tobacco, and avoiding the use of illegal drugs.
2. Some of the types of problems of the cardiovascular system are congenital heart defects, cardiovascular disease, heart murmur, varicose veins, anemia, leukemia, and hemophilia.
3. Some of the types of problems of the lymphatic system are immune deficiency, Hodgkin's disease, and tonsillitis.

Lesson 3 Read to Learn

1. External respiration and internal respiration are the two main parts of respiration.
2. Some of the parts of the lungs and respiratory system are the diaphragm, bronchi, bronchioles, cilia, trachea, larynx, and epiglottis.

Lesson 4 Read to Learn

1. Some of the healthy habits that can help you care for your respiratory system are choosing not to smoke, being physically active, washing your hands often, limiting time in areas that have heavy pollution.
2. Some of the types of respiratory system problems are bronchitis, pneumonia, pleurisy, asthma, sinusitis, tuberculosis, and emphysema.

CHAPTER 17

Lesson 1 Read to Learn

1. Digestion, absorption, and elimination are the three main functions of the digestive system.
2. Some of the parts of the digestive system include teeth, salivary glands, tongue, esophagus, stomach, pancreas, liver, gallbladder, small intestine, and large intestine.

Lesson 2 Read to Learn

1. Some of the habits that will keep your digestive system healthy include eating a well-balanced diet, washing your hands before you prepare food or eat; eating slowly and chewing your food well, drinking 8 glasses of water a day, and avoiding the use of food to deal with stress.
2. Some of the types of functional digestive problems are these: gallstones; appendicitis; gastritis; lactose intolerance; peptic ulcer; cirrhosis; and more.

Lesson 3 Read to Learn

1. The kidneys, ureters, and bladder are the main parts of the urinary system.
2. Some of the things you can do to keep your urinary system healthy are: drink 8 glasses of water a day, eat a well-balanced diet, use good hygiene, and have regular medical checkups.
3. Cystitis, urethritis, nephritis, kidney stones, and uremia are some of the types of problems that occur in the urinary system.

CHAPTER 18

Lesson 1 Read to Learn

1. Some of the types of glands that make up the endocrine system are the pituitary gland, adrenal glands, thyroid gland, parathyroid glands, testes, ovaries, hypothalamus, pineal gland, thymus gland, and pancreas.
2. Diabetes mellitus, Grave's disease, Cushing's disease, goiter, and growth disorders are some of the types of trouble that may occur in the endocrine system.

Lesson 2 Read to Learn

1. Some of the parts of the male reproductive system include the testes or testicles, scrotum, penis, semen, vas deferens, urethra, seminal vesicles, prostate gland; and the epididymis.
2. Chlamydia, gonorrhea, syphilis, and genital herpes are some of the types of STDs that affect the male reproductive system.
3. Inguinal hernia, sterility, testicular cancer, and enlarged prostate are some of the types of problems of the male reproductive system.

Lesson 3 Read to Learn

1. Some of the parts of the female reproductive system are the uterus, ovaries, fallopian tubes, vagina, endometrium, and cervix.
2. Some of the ways to care for the female reproductive system are bathing often, practicing abstinence, and doing breast self-exams.
3. Vaginitis; blocked fallopian tubes; ovarian cysts; and cervical, uterine, and ovarian cancers are some of the types of problems of the female reproductive system.

CHAPTER 19

Lesson 1 Read to Learn

1. Fertilization is the union of a male sperm cell and a female egg cell.
2. The structures that form outside the embryo are the amniotic sac, umbilical cord, and placenta.
3. Some of the major changes to the fetus during the second trimester are as follows:
   - 15–20 weeks—the fetus can blink, the body grows, eyebrows and eyelashes form.
   - 21–28 weeks—the fetus can hear, it sleeps and wakes, and its weight goes up.
4. The three stages of labor or birth are dilation; passage through the birth canal, and afterbirth.

Lesson 2 Read to Learn

1. Some of the choices a mother-to-be may have for prenatal care are an obstetrician, a certified nurse-midwife, and a birthing center.
2. Calcium, protein, iron, vitamin A, vitamin B complex, and folic acid are some of the nutrients a female may need to take while she is pregnant.
3. Some of the harmful things a mother-to-be should avoid are alcohol; tobacco; medicines and drugs; and environmental hazards such as lead, smog, and more.
4. Miscarriage, stillbirth, ectopic pregnancy, and preeclampsia are some of the problems that may occur during pregnancy.

Lesson 3 Read to Learn

1. Heredity is the passing of traits from parents to their children. DNA is the chemical unit that makes up chromosomes.
2. Each cell in a female has two X chromosomes. Each cell in a male has one X and one Y chromosome. The sperm determines the gender of the fetus. Eggs have only an X chromosome. Sperm have either and X or a Y chromosome.
3. Amniocentesis and chorionic villi sampling are two of the ways to test for genetic disorders.
4. Gene therapy and genetic engineering are some of the types of genetic treatment.

Lesson 4 Read to Learn

1. The first four stages of life are as follows:
   1) Infancy—birth to one year
   2) Early childhood—1 to 3 years
   3) Middle childhood—4 to 6 years
   4) Late childhood—7 to 12 years
2. Vision, hearing, and scoliosis screenings are some of the health screenings that are performed during childhood.

CHAPTER 20

Lesson 1 Read to Learn

1. Some of the types of physical changes that occur during puberty are as follows: In females—the breasts develop, the hips get wider, and the menstrual cycle begins; in males—facial hair grows, the voice deepens, muscles develop, and the hairline begins to recede; in both genders—body hair appears, all of the teeth grow in, and sweat increases.
2. Some of the developmental tasks that you may have as a teen include establishing emotional and psychological independence, developing a personal sense of identity, adopting a personal value system, establishing adult vocational goals, and developing control over your behavior.

Answer Key: Read to Learn

Lesson 2 Read to Learn

1. Physical maturity and emotional maturity are the two kinds of maturity.
2. The stages of adulthood are as follows:
   1) Young adulthood—19 to 40 years
   2) Middle adulthood—40 to 65 years
   3) Late adulthood—65 years to death
3. Some of the aspects of growth during young adulthood are having independence, making job choices, establishing close relationships, and giving to society.

Lesson 3 Read to Learn

1. Good communication, emotional maturity, and similar values and interests are some of the factors of a good marriage.
2. Sixty percent of teen marriages end in divorce because teens may feel overwhelmed, they may realize that marriage can get in the way of their education or career goals; they may have financial stress; they may realize the amount of work needed to make the marriage succeed.
3. Parents provide for their children by giving guidance, instilling values, setting limits, and giving unconditional love.

Lesson 4 Read to Learn

1. The types of transitions that occur during middle life are physical, mental, emotional, and social.
2. Some of the factors about late adulthood include the following: It occurs after age 65; those who live with integrity are more likely to feel satisfied with their lives; many look forward to retirement; the government offers Medicare to people over age 65.

CHAPTER 21

Lesson 1 Read to Learn

1. Nicotine is the addictive drug found in tobacco leaves.
2. Tar and carbon monoxide are two of the harmful compounds in tobacco smoke.
3. Some of the harmful effects of pipes and cigars: A cigar can have as much nicotine as a pack of cigarettes and has more tar and carbon monoxide; pipe and cigar smokers are at greater risk for lip, mouth, and throat cancer.
4. Smokeless tobacco may cause many types of cancer; it may cause leukoplakia, which are thick, white, leathery looking spots on the inside of the mouth.
5. Short-term effects of tobacco use include changes in brain chemistry; increased respiration and heart rate; dulled taste buds; bad breath and smelly hair, clothes, and skin.
6. There are also legal, social, and financial consequences of tobacco use.

Lesson 2 Read to Learn

1. Some of the reasons that teens are choosing not to use tobacco include antismoking campaigns, cost, society, and family.
2. Some of the benefits of living tobacco free are as follows: It lowers the risk of lung cancer; it improves physical fitness; it helps you feel free of addiction; and it makes you look and feel better.
3. Some of the ways to live tobacco free are to choose friends who do not use tobacco; avoid situations where tobacco products may be used, and practice and use refusal skills.
4. Some teens choose to smoke because they think it will help them lose weight, they think it will help them deal with stress, they think it will make them look mature and because of peer pressure, and media influence.
5. Teens may decide to quit smoking because they begin to have health problems, they have the desire to stop, or because of the cost.
6. Some tips to help a person give up tobacco include to prepare for the day, get support, get professional help, replace tobacco with healthy alternatives, change your daily habits, engage in healthy behavior.

Lesson 3 Read to Learn

1. Secondhand smoke is air that tobacco smoke has contaminated. It is also known as environmental tobacco smoke.
2. Smoke can affect young children in these ways: Children of smokers have more sore throats, ear infections, and respiratory problems; children who live with smokers have more risk of getting lung cancer; and children of smokers are more likely to smoke.

3. Some ways to protect yourself from ETS are to ask visitors not to smoke, open windows, use air cleaners, meet in a different place if there is smoke present, and sit in a nonsmoking area.
4. Some of the ways to have a smoke-free society include not allowing smoking in the workplace, not allowing smoking in public places, having laws that ban tobacco sales to minors, and more.

CHAPTER 22

Lesson 1 Read to Learn

1. A depressant is a drug that slows the central nervous system. Intoxication is the state in which alcohol poisons the body and reduces the person's physical and mental control.
2. Peer pressure, family, media messages, and ad techniques are some of the factors that may influence the use of alcohol.
3. Alcohol-related situations that a teen should avoid include buying or drinking alcohol; alcohol, violence, and sexual activity; alcohol abuse; and alcohol and school activities.
4. If you choose to be alcohol free, you can keep your body healthy, make responsible choices, avoid risky behavior, and avoid illegal actions.

Lesson 2 Read to Learn

1. Short-term effects of drinking on the body include the following: The brain is less able to control the body; heart and blood pressure rise, stomach acid increases, the liver may scar, kidneys increase urine output, and breathing may slow or stop.
2. Some of the types of alcohol-drug effects on the body are that alcohol may slow down the time it takes the body to absorb a drug, alcohol may cause the medicine to break down faster than normal, alcohol may cause the body to turn the medicine into chemicals that can harm the liver, and alcohol can increase the effect of some drugs.
3. DWI can cause harm to the driver and others; can cause injury, property damage, and death; can cause arrest and jail time and a heavy fine; and can cause loss of driver's license.
4. Binge drinking is drinking five or more alcoholic drinks at one sitting.
5. Some of the signs of alcohol poisoning are mental confusion, stupor, coma, vomiting, seizures, slow breathing, irregular heartbeat, and severe dehydration.

Lesson 3 Read to Learn

1. Addiction; loss of brain functions; brain damage; enlarged heart; fatty liver; cirrhosis; and more are some of the long-term effects of alcohol on the body.
2. Fetal alcohol syndrome (FAS) is a group of alcohol-related birth defects that include physical and mental problems.
3. The stages of alcoholism are as follows:
   1) Abuse
   2) Dependence
   3) Addiction
4. The effects that drinking has on family and society include the following: alcohol use is the major factor in car crashes, falls, drowning, and house fires; about 40 percent of violent crimes are alcohol related; about two-thirds of all domestic violence victims say that alcohol was a factor in the crime.
5. Al-Anon/Alateen, Alcoholics Anonymous and the National Association for Children of Alcoholics are some of the places to get help for alcohol abuse.

CHAPTER 23

Lesson 1 Read to Learn

1. The four main types of medicine are as follows:
   1) Medicines to prevent disease
   2) Medicines to fight pathogens
   3) Medicines to relieve pain
   4) Medicines to promote health
2. Some of the side effects of medicine on the body include addictive interaction, synergistic effect, antagonistic interaction, tolerance, and withdrawal.
3. People misuse medicine by not following the directions, by giving a prescription to others, by taking too much or too little of a drug, by stopping use of a drug, or by mixing medicines.

Lesson 2 Read to Learn

1. Peer pressure, family members, role models, media messages, and perceptions are some of the factors that may influence drug abuse.
2. Some of the health risks of drug use:
   - Physical health—Drug overdose is a great danger.
   - Mental health—Drugs affect the brain and drug users lose control of their behavior.
   - Social health—Drug use can affect family and friends. A school may expel a student who takes drugs.
3. Some of the other consequences of drug use are as follows:
   - To the individual—Drugs affect all parts of the health triangle.
   - For family and friends —Drug users often do not have time for family or friends.
   - For babies and children—A pregnant female passes the drugs to her fetus.
   - Costs to society—Drug use causes more crime, more car wrecks, and medical costs.

Lesson 3 Read to Learn

1. Risks of using marijuana include addiction, risks to mental health, paranoia, risk to growth and development, infertility, risks of driving under the influence, and trouble with vision and judgment.
2. Some of the risks of inhalants are destruction of brain cells, damage to the central nervous system, lack of judgment, and sudden heart attack.
3. Steroids can cause mood swings, lack of judgment, paranoia, disqualification for athletic events, and jail time or fines.

Lesson 4 Read to Learn

1. Psychoactive drugs are chemicals that affect the central nervous system and alter activity in the brain.
2. Some of the health risks of stimulants are addiction, depression, paranoia, rapid heart rate, heart trouble, damage to the CNS, and death.
3. Some of the health risks of depressants are mood swings, coma, addiction, and use as a date rape drug.
4. Some of the health risks of narcotics are addiction and painful withdrawal.
5. Some of the health risks of hallucinogens are added strength with no sense of pain, overdose, flashbacks, distortion of reality, and death.
6. Some of the health risks of ecstasy and designer drugs are: confusion, paranoia, overdose, and long-term brain damage.

Lesson 5 Read to Learn

1. Resist pressure to use drugs by making a firm decision to be drug free, avoiding places where you know there will be drugs, practicing your refusal skills, and standing up for what you believe in.
2. A drug-free school zone is an area within 1,000 feet of schools and designated by signs. People caught selling drugs in these areas receive very severe penalties. A drug watch is an organized community effort by neighborhood residents to patrol, monitor, report, and otherwise try to stop drug deals and drug abuse.
3. Some of the warning signs of drug use are getting high or drunk often, lying about the drug use changes in eating or sleeping habits, and trouble concentrating.
4. The help available to drug users includes outpatient drug-free treatment, short-term treatment, maintenance therapy, and therapeutic communities.

CHAPTER 24

Lesson 1 Read to Learn

1. Viruses, bacteria, fungi, protozoans, and rickettsias are some of the types of pathogens that cause diseases.
2. There are two main ways disease spreads from person to person, direct and indirect contact. Direct contact includes touching, kissing, biting, and sexual contact. Indirect contact includes contaminated objects, vectors, water and food, and airborne transmission.
3. You can prevent the spread of disease by washing your hands, handling food properly, eating a balanced diet, not sharing utensils, and staying away from people who are ill.

Lesson 2 Read to Learn

1. Skin, tears and saliva, mucous membranes, cilia, and gastric juices are the elements of the body's first line of defense.
2. The inflammatory response is as follows:
   - Blood vessels expand.
   - Fluid and cells leak into the area.
   - Swelling and pain occurs.
   - Phagocytes attack invading pathogens.
   - Pus collects at the site.
   - Tissue repair begins. A scab forms.
   - The specific response activates to keep this infection from happening again.
3. T cells and B cells are the two types of lymphocytes. Helper T cells, killer T cells, and suppressor T cells are the types of T cells.
4. Active immunity, such as getting a vaccine, and passive immunity, such as receiving antibodies from another person, are the two types of immunity.
5. Some of the ways to keep your immune system healthy are to follow a sensible eating plan, get plenty of rest, get an hour of physical activity each day, and avoid sharing personal items such as towels.
6. The four types of vaccines are as follows:
   1) Live-virus vaccines
   2) Killed-virus vaccines
   3) Toxoids
   4) New and second-generation vaccines
7. You should have these vaccinations: tetanus; diphtheria; measles, mumps, and rubella; hepatitis B; and chicken pox.

Lesson 3 Read to Learn

1. The common cold, influenza or the flu, pneumonia, strep throat, and tuberculosis or TB are some of the most common types of respiratory illness.
2. Hepatitis is pain and swelling of the liver. The three kinds of hepatitis are hepatitis A, hepatitis B, and hepatitis C.
3. Mononucleosis, measles, encephalitis, and meningitis are some of the other types of disease that are common among teens.
4. Reasons for new emerging infections include transport across borders, population movement, resistance to antibiotics, changes in food technology, and agents of bioterrorism.

CHAPTER 25

Lesson 1 Read to Learn

1. High-risk actions that may lead to STDs are being sexually active with more than one partner, engaging in unprotected sex, choosing high-risk partners, and using alcohol and other drugs.
2. Some of the consequences of getting an STD: Some STDs do not have a cure; some cause cancer; some affect the ability to reproduce; and some can pass from an infected female to her child before, during, and after birth.

Lesson 2 Read to Learn

1. Genital warts are pink or red warts that have cauliflower-like tops and appear on the genitals, vagina, or cervix one or two months after infection from HPV.
2. Chlamydia is a bacterial infection that affects the reproductive organs of both males and females.
3. Genital herpes is an STD caused by the herpes simplex virus (HSV).
4. Gonorrhea is a bacterial STD that usually affects mucous membranes.
5. Trichomoniasis is an STD caused by a microscopic protozoan that results in infections of the vagina, urethra, and bladder.
6. Syphilis is an STD that attacks many parts of the body and is caused by a small bacterium called a spirochete.
7. It is important to see a doctor right away if you think you have an STD because early treatment can prevent some of the severe, long-term health problems.

Lesson 3 Read to Learn

1. HIV is a virus that attacks the immune system. AIDS is a disease in which the immune system of the patient weakens.

2. HIV takes these steps when it attacks the cells in the body:
   1) HIV attaches to the cell surface.
   2) The virus core enters the cell and goes to the nucleus.
   3) The virus takes over the cell and makes a copy of itself.
   4) The new virus collects on the surface of the cell.
   5) The new virus breaks away from the host cell and destroys it.
   6) The new virus infects other cells and the process repeats itself.
3. A person can pass HIV to others by sexual intercourse, sharing needles, and mother to baby.

Lesson 4 Read to Learn

1. The stages of HIV infections are as follows:
   - The asymptomatic stage
   - The symptomatic stage
   - AIDS is the final stage.
2. The EIA test and the Western blot test are the two types of tests that can detect HIV in the body.
3. Some of the facts about HIV/AIDS: Doctors first noticed AIDS symptoms in 1981; scientists found the AIDS-causing virus and named it HIV in 1986; new drugs became available in 1989; the first trial run of the AIDS vaccine was in 1998.
4. Avoid pressure to engage in sexual activity by avoiding events where drug use or pressure to have sex may occur, practice your refusal skills, and choose friends who are not sexually active and are not drug users.

CHAPTER 26

Lesson 1 Read to Learn

1. A noncommunicable disease is a disease that is not transmitted through another person, a vector, or the environment.
2. Some of the risk factors for CVDs that you can control are the use of tobacco, getting your blood pressure checked, eating less high-fat foods, being physically active, keeping a healthy weight, lowering stress, and the use of alcohol or other drugs.

Lesson 2 Read to Learn

1. Benign tumors and malignant tumors are the two types of tumors.
2. Cancers can be classified as lymphomas, leukemias, carcinomas, and sarcomas.
3. The seven warning signs of cancer:
   1) Change in bowel habits
   2) A sore that does not heal
   3) Unusual bleeding or discharge
   4) Thickening or a lump in the breast or elsewhere
   5) Indigestion or difficulty swallowing
   6) Obvious change in a mole or wart
   7) Nagging cough or hoarseness
4. You can reduce your risk of cancer by abstaining from sexual activity, being physically active, maintaining a healthy weight, eating nutritious meals, eating a low-fat and high fiber diet.
5. Some of the types of treatment for cancer are surgery, radiation therapy, chemotherapy, immunotherapy, and hormone therapy.

Lesson 3 Read to Learn

1. Three ways to treat an allergy are avoiding the allergen, taking antihistamines, and immunotherapy.
2. Keep asthma under control by monitoring the condition, managing the environment, dealing with stress, and taking medication.
3. The two types of diabetes are type 1 and type 2 diabetes.
4. Osteoarthritis and rheumatoid arthritis are the two types of arthritis.

Lesson 4 Read to Learn

1. Sight impairment, hearing impairment, and motor impairment are some of the types of physical challenges.
2. A head injury or disease, genetic disorders such as Down syndrome, fetal alcohol syndrome, rubella, and not enough oxygen at birth are some of the causes of mental retardation.

3. People with special needs can be accommodated by making sure there is wheelchair access to public buses, trains and buildings; by judging others on the basis of merit; and by offering people with disabilities the same opportunities as those who do not have disabilities.

CHAPTER 27

Lesson 1 Read to Learn

1. The steps in the accident chain are as follows:
   Step 1) The situation
   Step 2) The unsafe habit
   Step 3) The unsafe action
   Step 4) The accident
   Step 5) The result
2. The main areas of home safety are preventing fires, preventing falls, preventing electrical shock, preventing poisoning, firearm safety, and computer and video game safety.
3. OSHA is the Occupational Safety and Health Administration. It is the agency in the federal government that promotes safety and healthy conditions in the workplace.

Lesson 2 Read to Learn

1. Some ways to stay safe during outdoor activities:
   - Know your limits.
   - Bring supplies.
   - Wear protective gear.
   - Tell people your plans.
   - Plan ahead for the weather.
   - Avoid heat exhaustion.

Lesson 3 Read to Learn

1. Some of the ways to be a more responsible driver are to always signal when you are about to make a turn or change lanes, follow all traffic signals and signs; do not tailgate, let other drivers merge, and report incidents of road rage.
2. Some of the rules of cycling are always wear a helmet, ride with traffic, watch for cars pulling into traffic, obey the same rules as drivers.

Lesson 4 Read to Learn

1. Some of the supplies to put into an emergency survival kit include water and food; phone, radio, lighting, and blankets; and other supplies such as medicine and money.
2. Some of the ways to keep safe if an earthquake occurs include stand or crouch in a doorway, stay away from buildings or trees, and use care once the tremor stops.

CHAPTER 28

Lesson 1 Read to Learn

1. First aid is the immediate, temporary care given to an ill or injured person until professional medical care can be provided.
2. The first three steps to an emergency are check, call, and care:
   1) Check the scene and the victim.
   2) Call for help.
   3) Provide care for the victim.
3. The four types of open wounds are as follows:
   - Abrasion
   - Laceration
   - Puncture
   - Avulsion
4. The steps to control bleeding are as follows:
   - Cover the wound with a sterile cloth and press firmly.
   - Elevate the wound above the heart if possible.
   - Cover the cloth with a sterile bandage.
   - Cover it with a pressure bandage if needed. Use a pressure point to control bleeding.
   - Call for help or have someone else call for help.
5. The three types of burns and how you treat them are as follows:
   1) First-degree burns—treat them with cold running water for 10 minutes, pat dry, and cover with a clean cloth.
   2) Second-degree burns—treat them with cold water, elevate the burned area, and wrap loosely in sterile dressing. Get medical help.
   3) Third-degree burns—get medical help right away. Treat with large amounts of cold water. Cover with sterile cloth.

Lesson 2 Read to Learn

1. The chain of survival is a sequence of actions that maximize the victim's chances of survival.
2. CPR is cardiopulmonary resuscitation. It is a life-saving first-aid procedure that combines rescue breaths with chest compressions, supplying oxygen to the body until normal functions can resume.

3. The ABCs of adult CPR are:
   - Airway
   - Breathing
   - Circulation
4. The steps of first aid for shock are as follows:
   - Phone 911.
   - Control any external bleeding.
   - Elevate legs about 12 inches.
   - Never give the person anything to eat or drink.
   - Let the person know help is on the way.
5. The steps of an abdominal thrust for adults:
   1) Stand behind the person and place your arms around him or her.
   2) Make a fist with one hand and grasp it with your other hand.
   3) Pull inward and upward just under the ribcage.

Lesson 3 Read to Learn

1. The steps of the R.I.C.E. method:
   - Rest
   - Ice
   - Compression
   - Elevation
2. Fainting and concussion are the two types of unconsciousness. The recovery position is on the side with the head on a pillow.
3. The steps of first aid for a dog bite are as follows:
   - Wash the bite area with a mild soap and warm water.
   - Use direct pressure to stop any bleeding.
   - Apply ice for 10 minutes.
   - Cover the wound with a clean bandage.
4. The steps to follow when a person has a nosebleed are as follows:
   - Keep the person quiet.
   - Have the person sit forward.
   - Press on the bleeding nostril.
   - Maintain the pressure for 15 minutes.
   - Repeat this if the nose is still bleeding after 15 minutes.
   - Call for help if the nose continues to bleed.
5. You can help a person who has something in his or her eye by telling the person to blink, washing your hands and gently pulling down the lid to try to find the object, lightly touching the object with a cotton swab if you find it, flushing the person's eye with water if you still cannot find it, and seeking medical help if the object is still in the eye.

Lesson 4 Read to Learn

1. Some of the types of poisoning are swallowed poisons, inhaled poisons, poison on the skin, and poison in the eye. A poison can be a chemical, pesticide, or insect bite. It can come from a poisonous plant or food, or when a person breathes poisonous fumes.
2. The steps of first aid for a snakebite are:
   - Move to a safe area. Scrape the stinger off.
   - Wash the area with mild soap and water. Apply a cold compress.
   - Call 911 right away if the person begins to have trouble breathing.
3. If someone has had contact with a poisonous plant, remove contaminated clothes, flush the area with water, use calamine lotion, and seek medical help for severe discomfort.

CHAPTER 29

Lesson 1 Read to Learn

1. The five main air pollutants are ozone; particulate matter; carbon monoxide; sulfur dioxide; and nitrogen oxides.
2. Some of the ways that you can reduce air pollution are by reducing car use, conserving energy, and using air friendly machinery.
3. You can deal with indoor air pollution by making sure your house has enough ventilation and fresh air coming in, making sure that heaters and furnaces have vents, making sure there are detectors for carbon monoxide and radon, and getting help to remove asbestos or lead.
4. You can reduce noise pollution by: keeping the volume down on your stereo and radio; avoiding use of the car horn; and by using manual tools instead of power tools when you can.

Lesson 2 Read to Learn

1. A landfill is an area that is safeguarded to prevent disposed wastes from contaminating groundwater.
2. Deforestation and urban sprawl are two of the ways that population growth can affect the land.

3. Some of the sources of water pollution are illegal dumping, runoff, wastewater, sediment, and oil.
4. You and your family can help keep water clean by recycling materials to reduce the waste that goes into landfills, throwing away all materials in the right place, following directions carefully when using cleaning products and fertilizers, and reducing your use of water.

Lesson 3 Read to Learn

1. You and your family can help conserve natural resources by sealing leaks around windows and doors; keeping doors and windows shut, closing fireplace vents, wearing an extra layer in the winter, washing clothes in warm or cold water, doing a full load when you wash clothes or dishes, replacing regular light bulbs with fluorescent bulbs, and switching off lights when you leave a room.
2. Precycling is reducing waste before you generate it. Some of the benefits of recycling are conserving resources, reducing the use of landfills, and protecting the environmental health.
3. You can protect your family and your environment by becoming an informed consumer, contacting organizations that promote conservation of resources, and taking action against local polluters.